DRAWN &
QUARTERLY
SHOWCASE
Nº4

An anthology of new illustrated fiction.

Drawn & Quarterly Showcase; book four. Entire contents © copyright 2006 by
Gabrielle Bell, Martin Cendreda, and Dan Zettwoch. All rights reserved. No part of this
book (except small portions for review purposes) may be reproduced in any form without
written permission from the respective cartoonists or Drawn & Quarterly.

Publisher: Chris Oliveros.
Editing and Production: Tom Devlin, Chris Oliveros, Jamie Quail, and Rebecca Rosen.
Publicity: Peggy Burns and Jamie Quail.

Drawn & Quarterly
Post Office Box 48056
Montreal, Quebec
Canada H2V 4S8
www.drawnandquarterly.com

The first three volumes of DRAWN & QUARTERLY SHOWCASE are available
from many fine book and comic stores or direct from the publisher.

Printed in Singapore in July 2006.

10 9 8 7 6 5 4 3 2 1
National Library of Canada Cataloguing in Publication
    Drawn & Quarterly Showcase : book 4 : an anthology of new illustrated
fiction / Gabrielle Bell, Martin Cendreda, and Dan Zettwoch.
ISBN 1-896597-98-X
    1. Comic books, strips, etc. I. Bell, Gabrielle II. Cendreda, Martin III. Zettwoch, Dan
IV. Title: Drawn & Quarterly Showcase.

Distributed in the USA by:
Farrar, Straus & Giroux
19 Union Square West
New York, NY 10003
888.330.8477

Distributed in Canada by:
Raincoast Books
9050 Shaughnessy Street
Vancouver, BC V6P 6E5
800.663.5714

COVERS:

DAN ZETTWOCH

ENDPAPERS:

DAN ZETTWOCH

PAGES 5 TO 40:

GABRIELLE BELL

PAGES 43 TO 68:

MARTIN CENDREDA

PAGES 71 TO 102:

DAN ZETTWOCH

Gabrielle Bell

Born in London, England in 1976, Gabrielle Bell grew up in the mountains of Northern California, spending a lot of time reading and drawing. She eschewed a formal education in favor of creating mini-comics and reading novels, citing narrative skill in film and literature as her greatest sources of inspiration. Compelled by adept storytelling, she states, "It's not as satisfying anymore just to draw. It's much more satisfying to draw in comics form... What I want is to draw a story that people are interested in and they want to know what's going to happen next."

In 2002 Alternative Comics collected Bell's mini-comics in the book *When I'm Old and Other Stories*. The following year she won an Ignatz award for Most Outstanding Mini-Comic for the third issue of her series *Lucky*. A French edition of her work, *Quand Je Serai Vieille et Autres Histories*, was published by Editions de l'An 2 in 2005. Gabrielle Bell lives in Brooklyn, New York and is a contributor to the quarterly comics anthology *Mome*.

For this story, Gabrielle would like to thank Karen Sneider for the Honey Bran Flakes jingle, and Tony Groutsis for photo reference assistance.

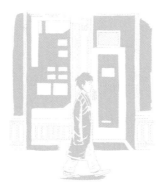

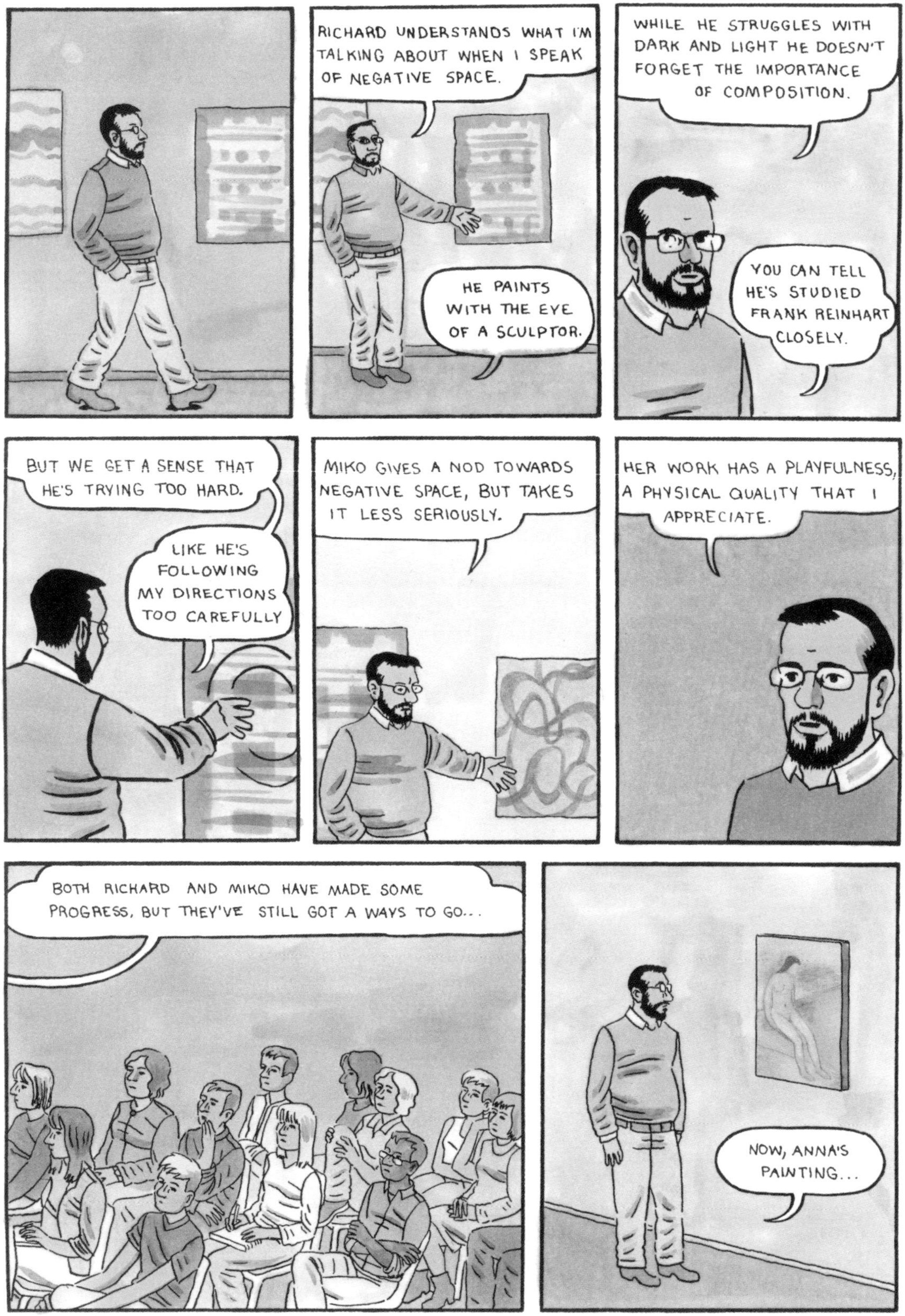
RICHARD UNDERSTANDS WHAT I'M TALKING ABOUT WHEN I SPEAK OF NEGATIVE SPACE.
HE PAINTS WITH THE EYE OF A SCULPTOR.
WHILE HE STRUGGLES WITH DARK AND LIGHT HE DOESN'T FORGET THE IMPORTANCE OF COMPOSITION.
YOU CAN TELL HE'S STUDIED FRANK REINHART CLOSELY.
BUT WE GET A SENSE THAT HE'S TRYING TOO HARD.
LIKE HE'S FOLLOWING MY DIRECTIONS TOO CAREFULLY
MIKO GIVES A NOD TOWARDS NEGATIVE SPACE, BUT TAKES IT LESS SERIOUSLY.
HER WORK HAS A PLAYFULNESS, A PHYSICAL QUALITY THAT I APPRECIATE.
BOTH RICHARD AND MIKO HAVE MADE SOME PROGRESS, BUT THEY'VE STILL GOT A WAYS TO GO...
NOW, ANNA'S PAINTING...

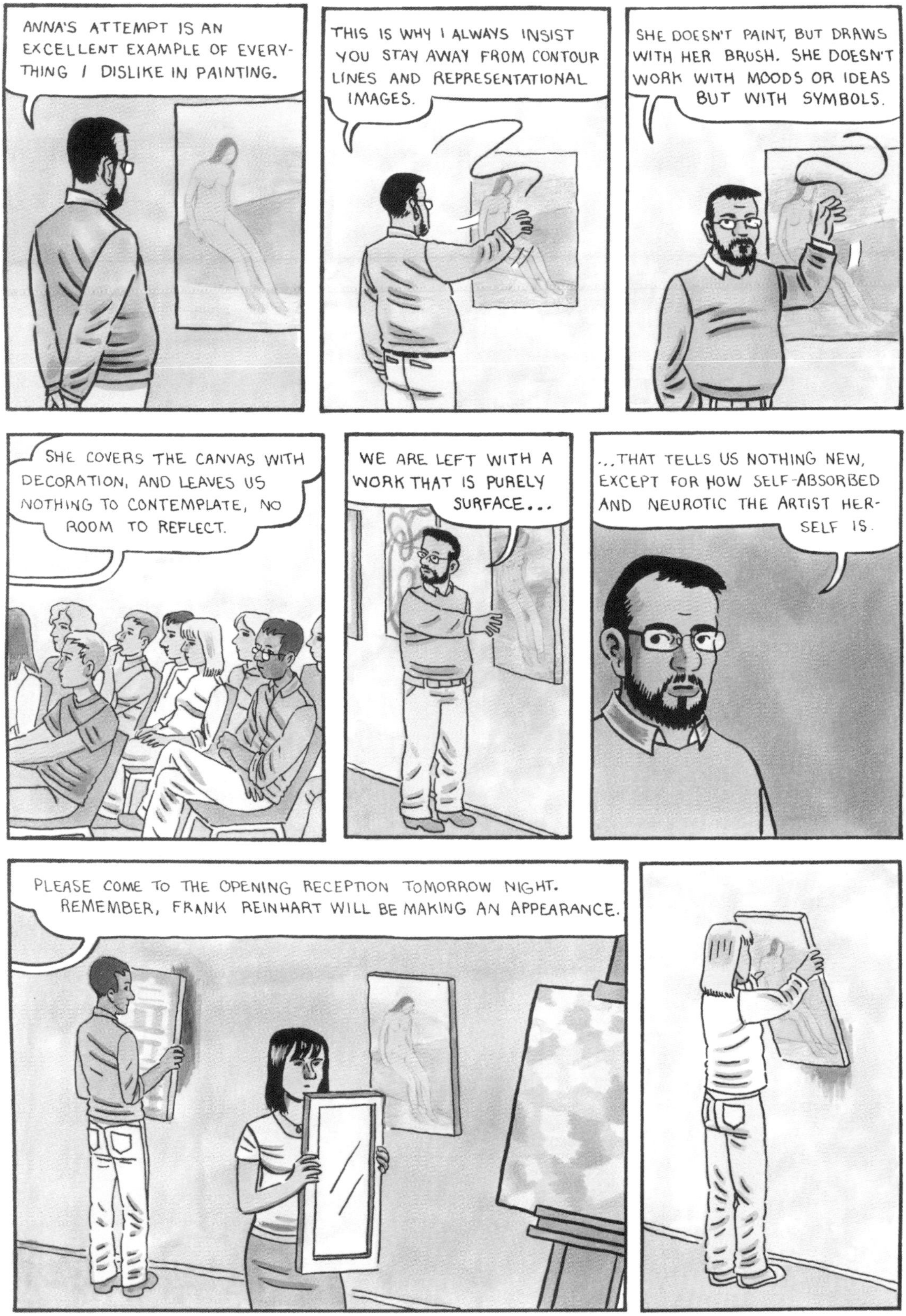
ANNA'S ATTEMPT IS AN EXCELLENT EXAMPLE OF EVERYTHING I DISLIKE IN PAINTING.
THIS IS WHY I ALWAYS INSIST YOU STAY AWAY FROM CONTOUR LINES AND REPRESENTATIONAL IMAGES.
SHE DOESN'T PAINT, BUT DRAWS WITH HER BRUSH. SHE DOESN'T WORK WITH MOODS OR IDEAS BUT WITH SYMBOLS.
SHE COVERS THE CANVAS WITH DECORATION, AND LEAVES US NOTHING TO CONTEMPLATE, NO ROOM TO REFLECT.
WE ARE LEFT WITH A WORK THAT IS PURELY SURFACE...
...THAT TELLS US NOTHING NEW, EXCEPT FOR HOW SELF-ABSORBED AND NEUROTIC THE ARTIST HERSELF IS.
PLEASE COME TO THE OPENING RECEPTION TOMORROW NIGHT. REMEMBER, FRANK REINHART WILL BE MAKING AN APPEARANCE.

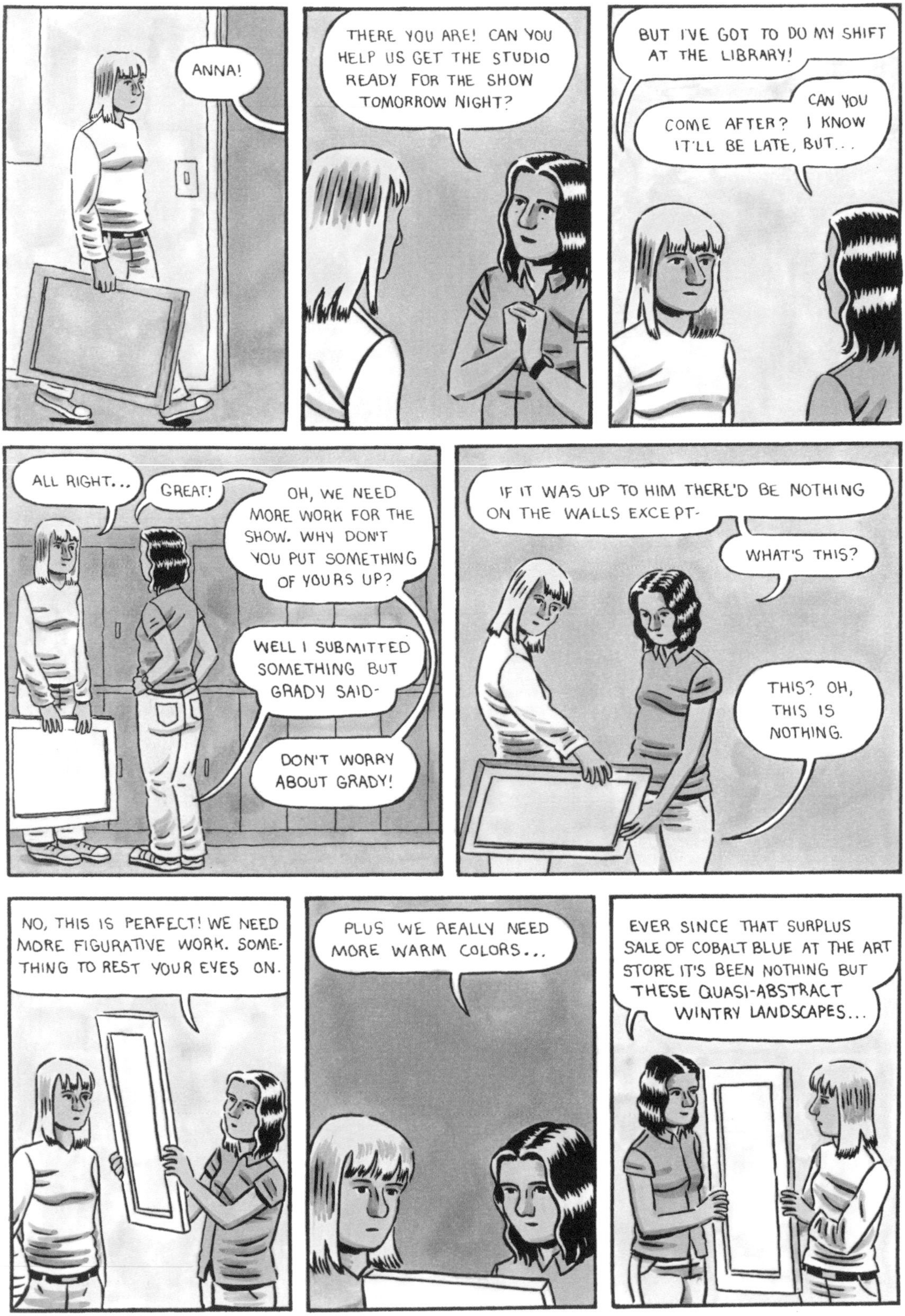
ANNA!
THERE YOU ARE! CAN YOU HELP US GET THE STUDIO READY FOR THE SHOW TOMORROW NIGHT?
BUT I'VE GOT TO DO MY SHIFT AT THE LIBRARY!
CAN YOU COME AFTER? I KNOW IT'LL BE LATE, BUT...
ALL RIGHT...
GREAT!
OH, WE NEED MORE WORK FOR THE SHOW. WHY DON'T YOU PUT SOMETHING OF YOURS UP?
WELL I SUBMITTED SOMETHING BUT GRADY SAID-
DON'T WORRY ABOUT GRADY!
IF IT WAS UP TO HIM THERE'D BE NOTHING ON THE WALLS EXCEPT-
WHAT'S THIS?
THIS? OH, THIS IS NOTHING.
NO, THIS IS PERFECT! WE NEED MORE FIGURATIVE WORK. SOMETHING TO REST YOUR EYES ON.
PLUS WE REALLY NEED MORE WARM COLORS...
EVER SINCE THAT SURPLUS SALE OF COBALT BLUE AT THE ART STORE IT'S BEEN NOTHING BUT THESE QUASI-ABSTRACT WINTRY LANDSCAPES...

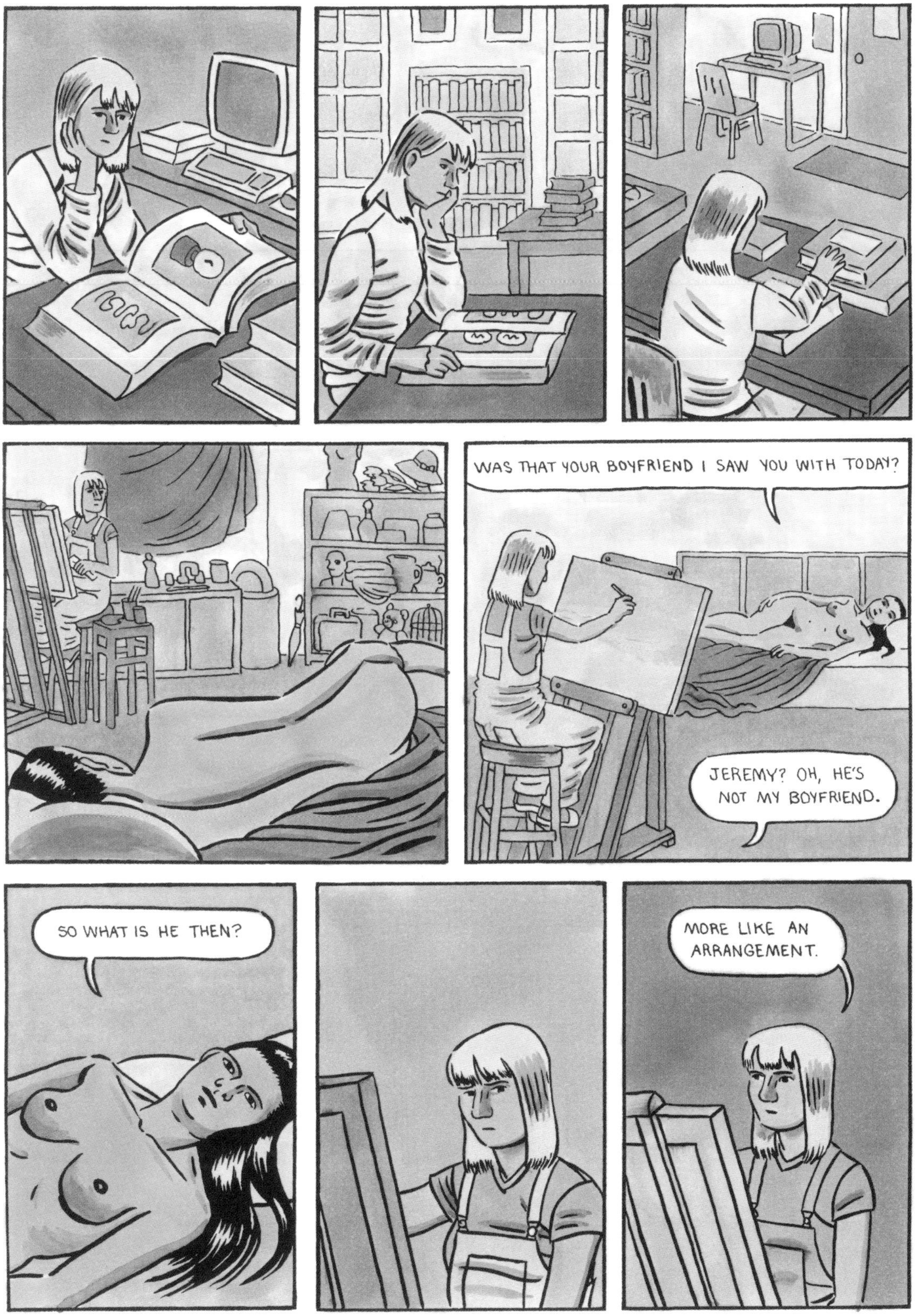
WAS THAT YOUR BOYFRIEND I SAW YOU WITH TODAY?
JEREMY? OH, HE'S NOT MY BOYFRIEND.
SO WHAT IS HE THEN?
MORE LIKE AN ARRANGEMENT.

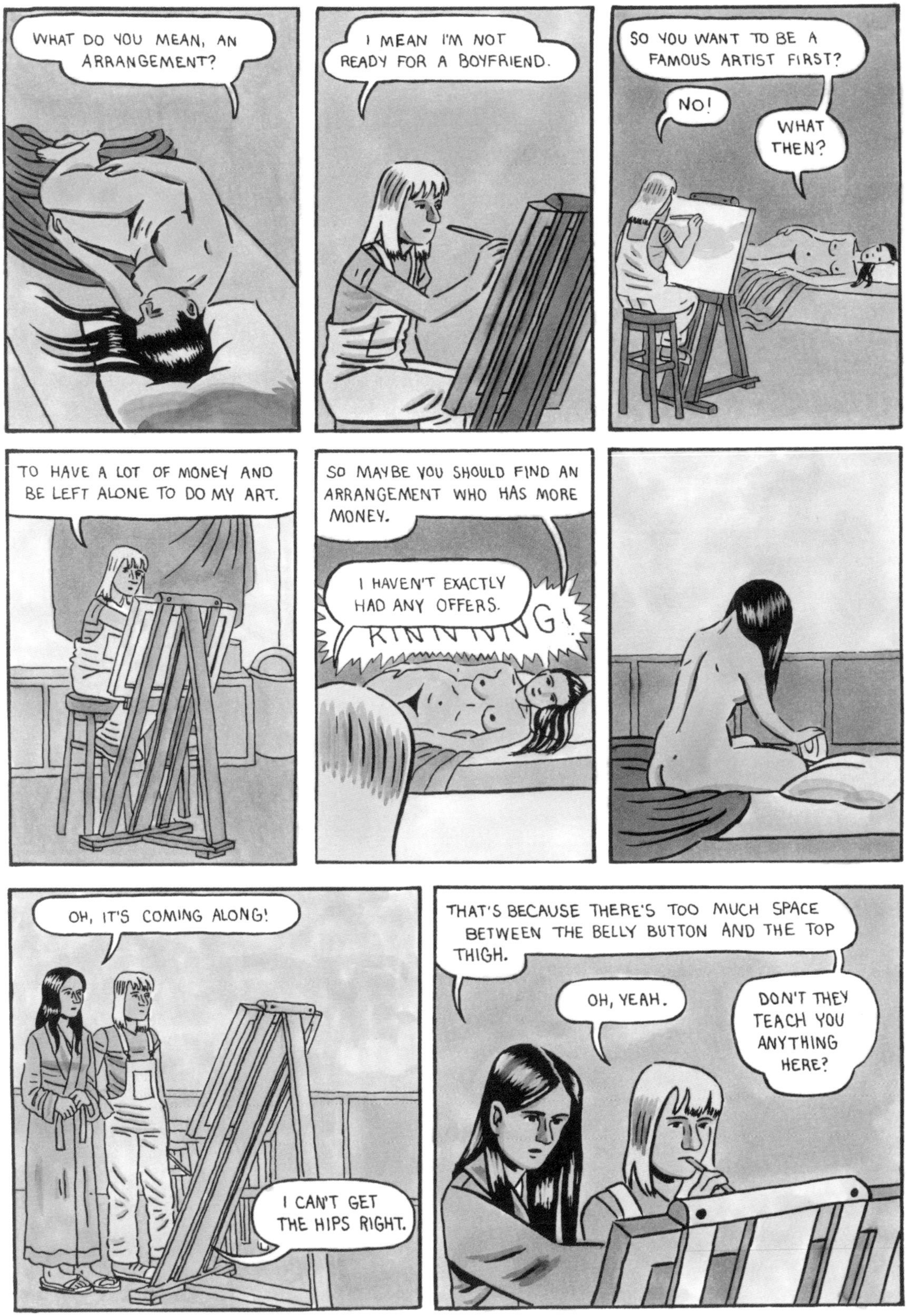
WHAT DO YOU MEAN, AN ARRANGEMENT?
I MEAN I'M NOT READY FOR A BOYFRIEND.
SO YOU WANT TO BE A FAMOUS ARTIST FIRST?
NO!
WHAT THEN?
TO HAVE A LOT OF MONEY AND BE LEFT ALONE TO DO MY ART.
SO MAYBE YOU SHOULD FIND AN ARRANGEMENT WHO HAS MORE MONEY.
I HAVEN'T EXACTLY HAD ANY OFFERS.
OH, IT'S COMING ALONG!
I CAN'T GET THE HIPS RIGHT.
THAT'S BECAUSE THERE'S TOO MUCH SPACE BETWEEN THE BELLY BUTTON AND THE TOP THIGH.
OH, YEAH.
DON'T THEY TEACH YOU ANYTHING HERE?

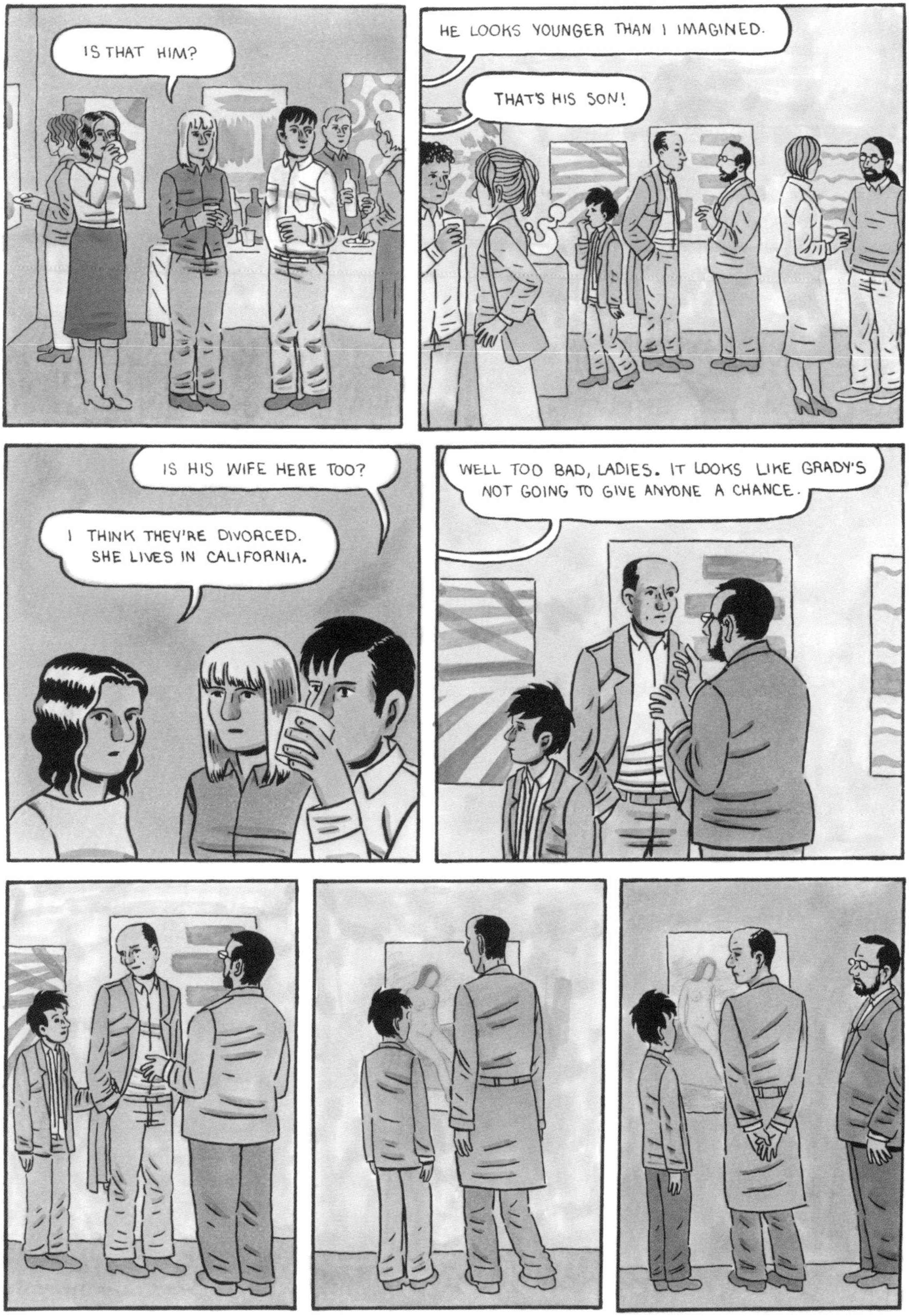
IS THAT HIM?
HE LOOKS YOUNGER THAN I IMAGINED.
THAT'S HIS SON!
IS HIS WIFE HERE TOO?
I THINK THEY'RE DIVORCED. SHE LIVES IN CALIFORNIA.
WELL TOO BAD, LADIES. IT LOOKS LIKE GRADY'S NOT GOING TO GIVE ANYONE A CHANCE.

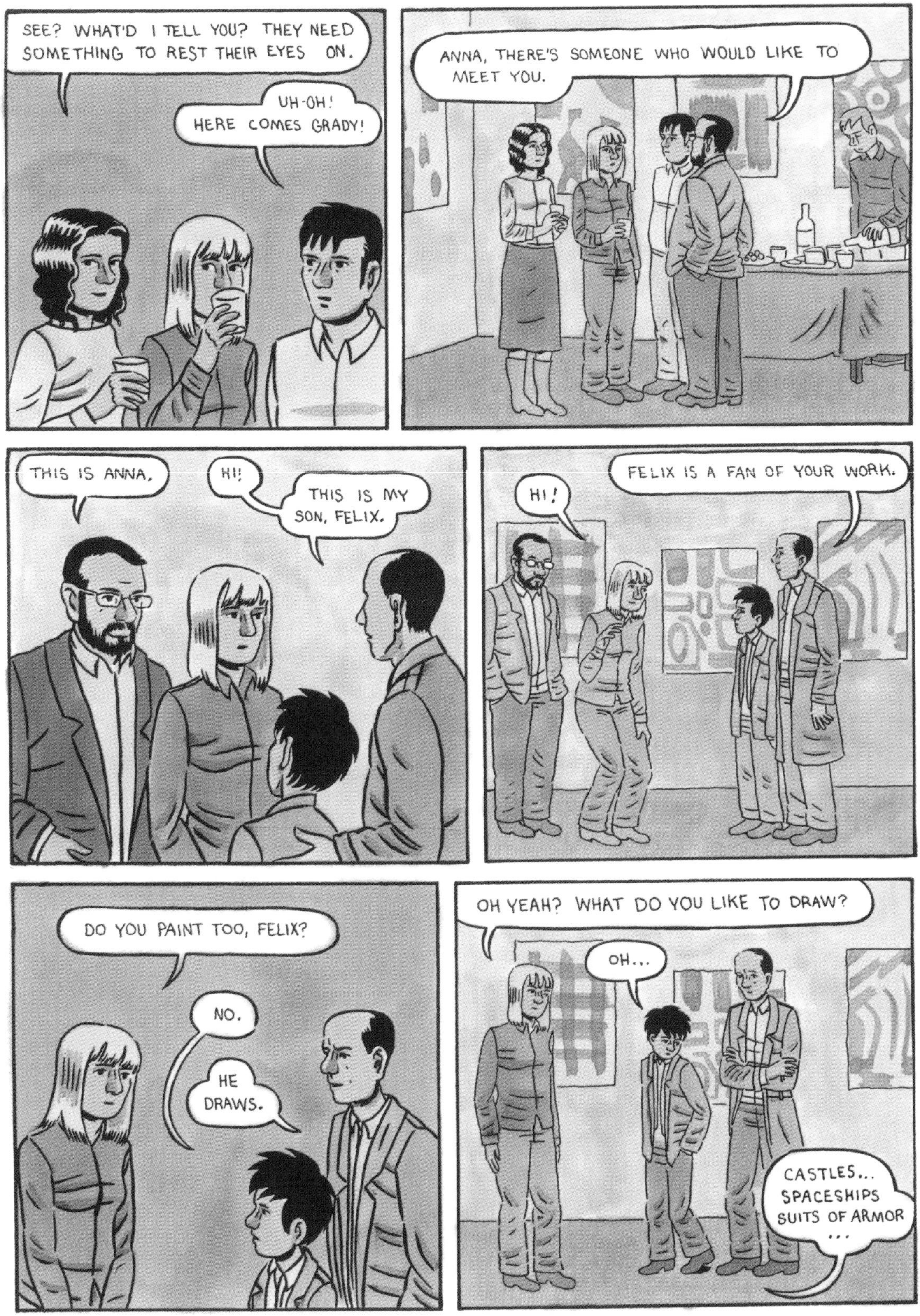
SEE? WHAT'D I TELL YOU? THEY NEED SOMETHING TO REST THEIR EYES ON.
UH-OH! HERE COMES GRADY!
ANNA, THERE'S SOMEONE WHO WOULD LIKE TO MEET YOU.
THIS IS ANNA.
HI!
THIS IS MY SON, FELIX.
HI!
FELIX IS A FAN OF YOUR WORK.
DO YOU PAINT TOO, FELIX?
NO.
HE DRAWS.
OH YEAH? WHAT DO YOU LIKE TO DRAW?
OH...
CASTLES... SPACESHIPS SUITS OF ARMOR ...

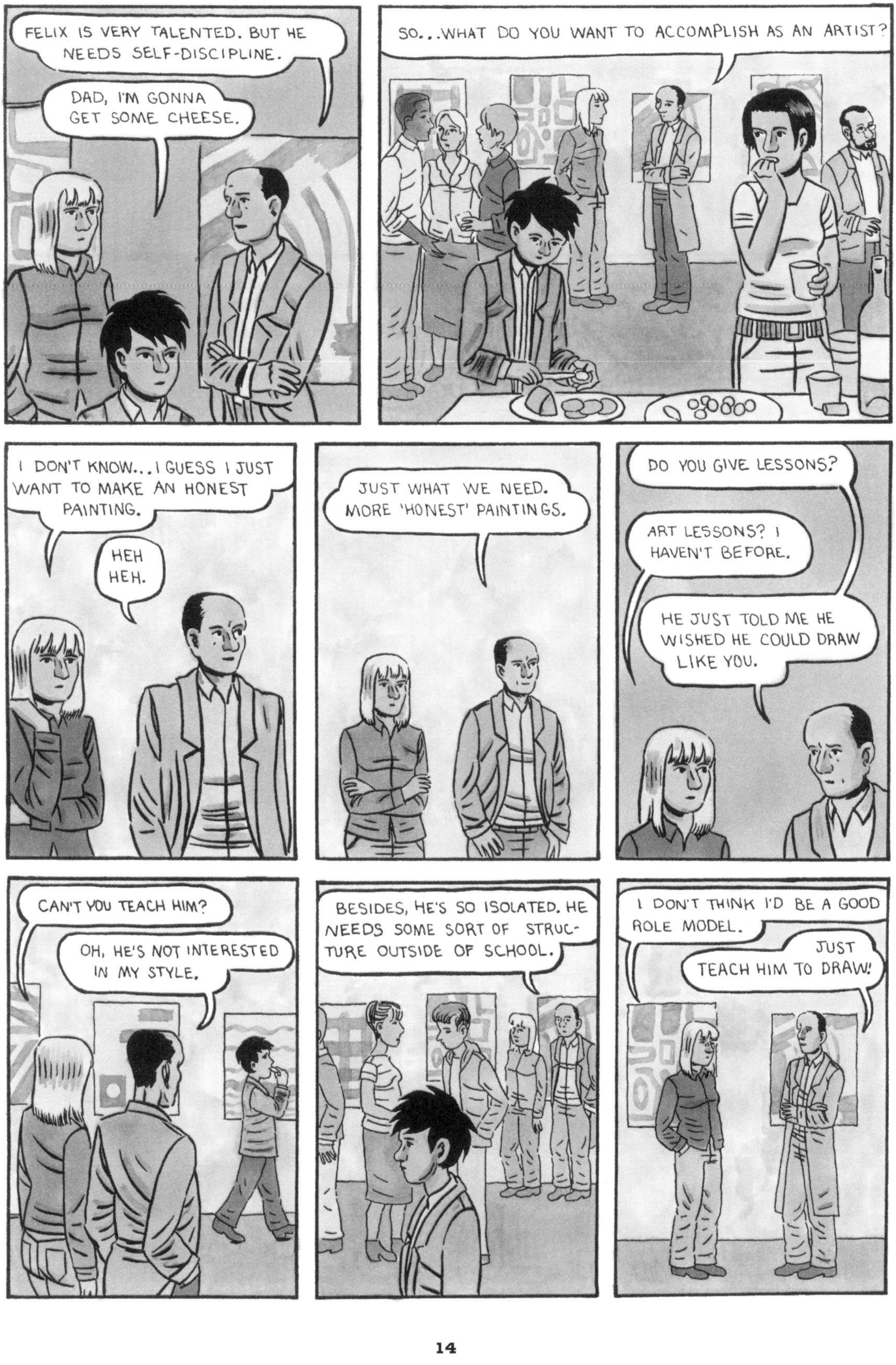
FELIX IS VERY TALENTED. BUT HE NEEDS SELF-DISCIPLINE.
DAD, I'M GONNA GET SOME CHEESE.
SO...WHAT DO YOU WANT TO ACCOMPLISH AS AN ARTIST?
I DON'T KNOW...I GUESS I JUST WANT TO MAKE AN HONEST PAINTING.
HEH HEH.
JUST WHAT WE NEED. MORE 'HONEST' PAINTINGS.
DO YOU GIVE LESSONS?
ART LESSONS? I HAVEN'T BEFORE.
HE JUST TOLD ME HE WISHED HE COULD DRAW LIKE YOU.
CAN'T YOU TEACH HIM?
OH, HE'S NOT INTERESTED IN MY STYLE.
BESIDES, HE'S SO ISOLATED. HE NEEDS SOME SORT OF STRUCTURE OUTSIDE OF SCHOOL.
I DON'T THINK I'D BE A GOOD ROLE MODEL.
JUST TEACH HIM TO DRAW!

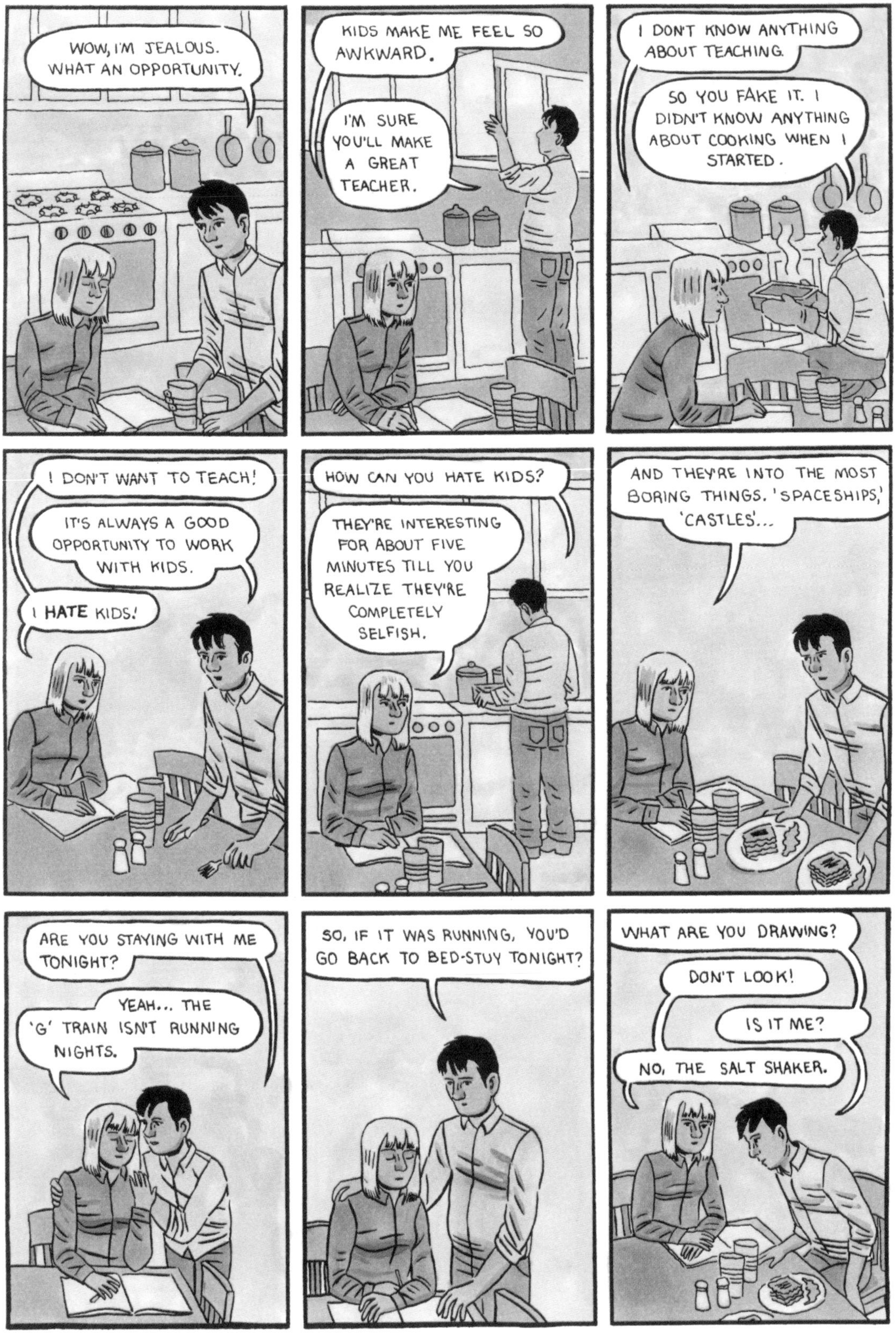
WOW, I'M JEALOUS. WHAT AN OPPORTUNITY.
KIDS MAKE ME FEEL SO AWKWARD.
I'M SURE YOU'LL MAKE A GREAT TEACHER.
I DON'T KNOW ANYTHING ABOUT TEACHING.
SO YOU FAKE IT. I DIDN'T KNOW ANYTHING ABOUT COOKING WHEN I STARTED.
I DON'T WANT TO TEACH!
IT'S ALWAYS A GOOD OPPORTUNITY TO WORK WITH KIDS.
I **HATE** KIDS!
HOW CAN YOU HATE KIDS?
THEY'RE INTERESTING FOR ABOUT FIVE MINUTES TILL YOU REALIZE THEY'RE COMPLETELY SELFISH.
AND THEY'RE INTO THE MOST BORING THINGS. 'SPACESHIPS,' 'CASTLES'...
ARE YOU STAYING WITH ME TONIGHT?
YEAH... THE 'G' TRAIN ISN'T RUNNING NIGHTS.
SO, IF IT WAS RUNNING, YOU'D GO BACK TO BED-STUY TONIGHT?
WHAT ARE YOU DRAWING?
DON'T LOOK!
IS IT ME?
NO, THE SALT SHAKER.

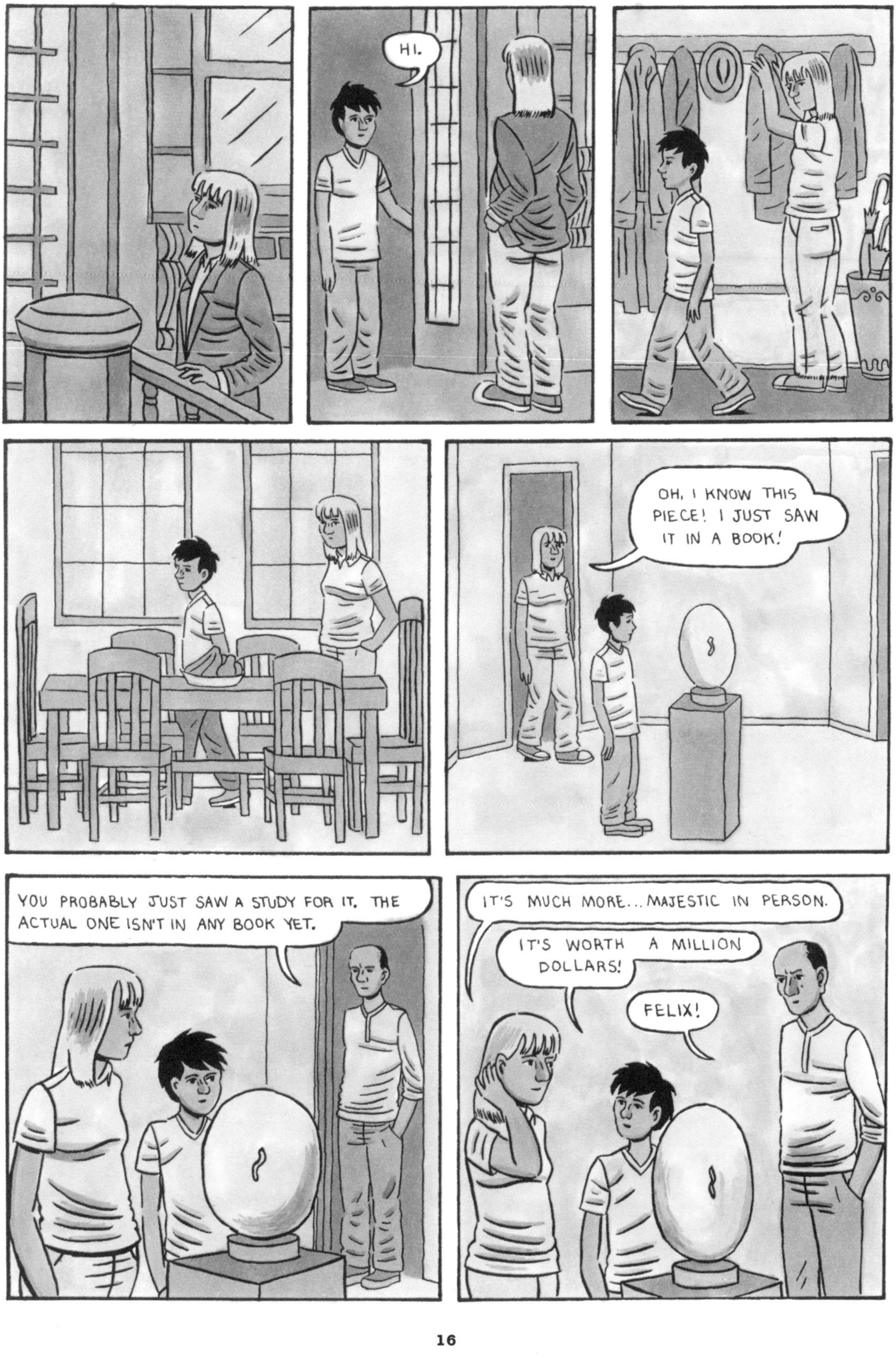
HI.
OH, I KNOW THIS PIECE! I JUST SAW IT IN A BOOK!
YOU PROBABLY JUST SAW A STUDY FOR IT. THE ACTUAL ONE ISN'T IN ANY BOOK YET.
IT'S MUCH MORE... MAJESTIC IN PERSON.
IT'S WORTH A MILLION DOLLARS!
FELIX!

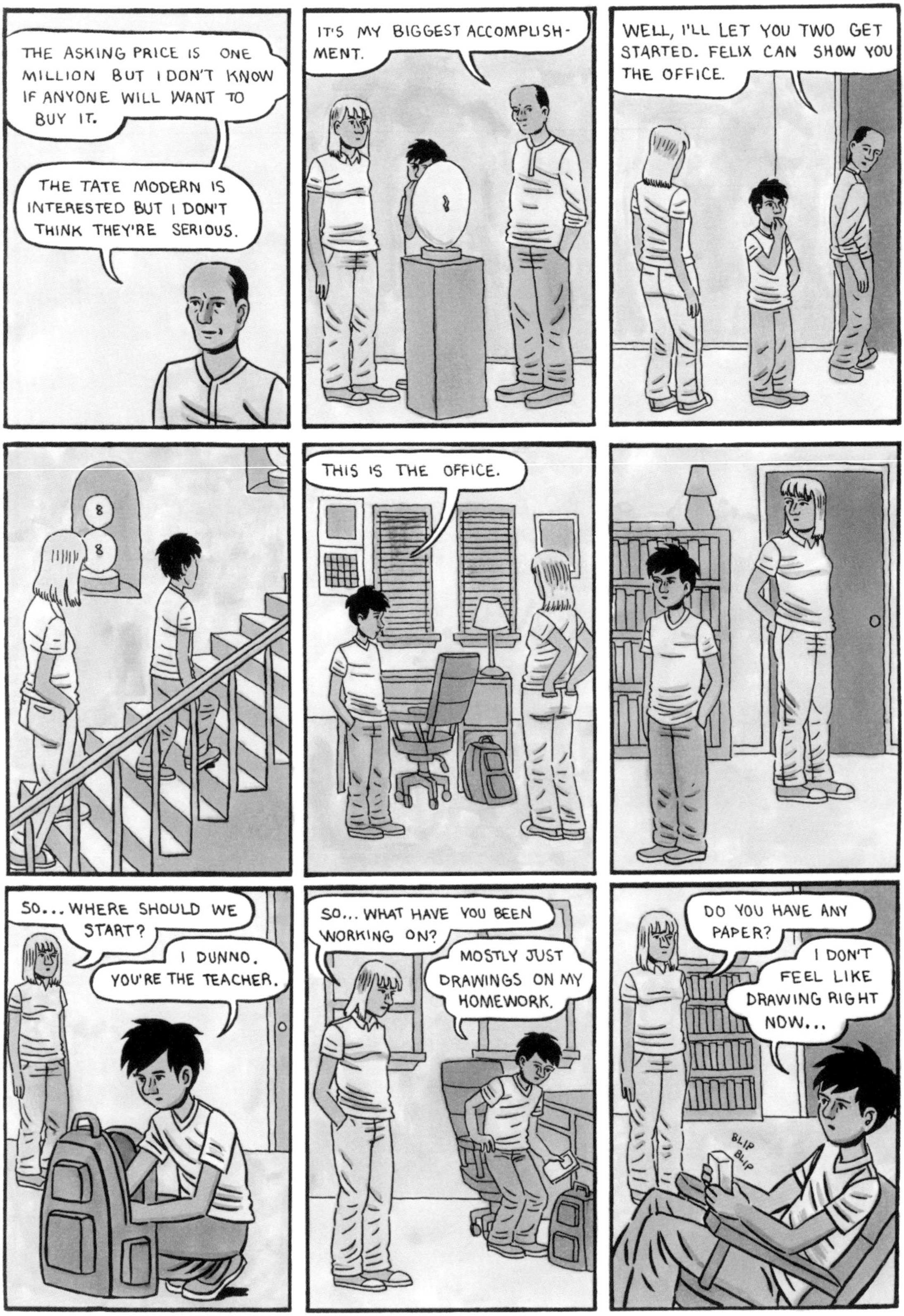
THE ASKING PRICE IS ONE MILLION BUT I DON'T KNOW IF ANYONE WILL WANT TO BUY IT.
THE TATE MODERN IS INTERESTED BUT I DON'T THINK THEY'RE SERIOUS.
IT'S MY BIGGEST ACCOMPLISH-MENT.
WELL, I'LL LET YOU TWO GET STARTED. FELIX CAN SHOW YOU THE OFFICE.
8
8
THIS IS THE OFFICE.
SO... WHERE SHOULD WE START?
I DUNNO. YOU'RE THE TEACHER.
SO... WHAT HAVE YOU BEEN WORKING ON?
MOSTLY JUST DRAWINGS ON MY HOMEWORK.
DO YOU HAVE ANY PAPER?
I DON'T FEEL LIKE DRAWING RIGHT NOW...
BLIP BLIP

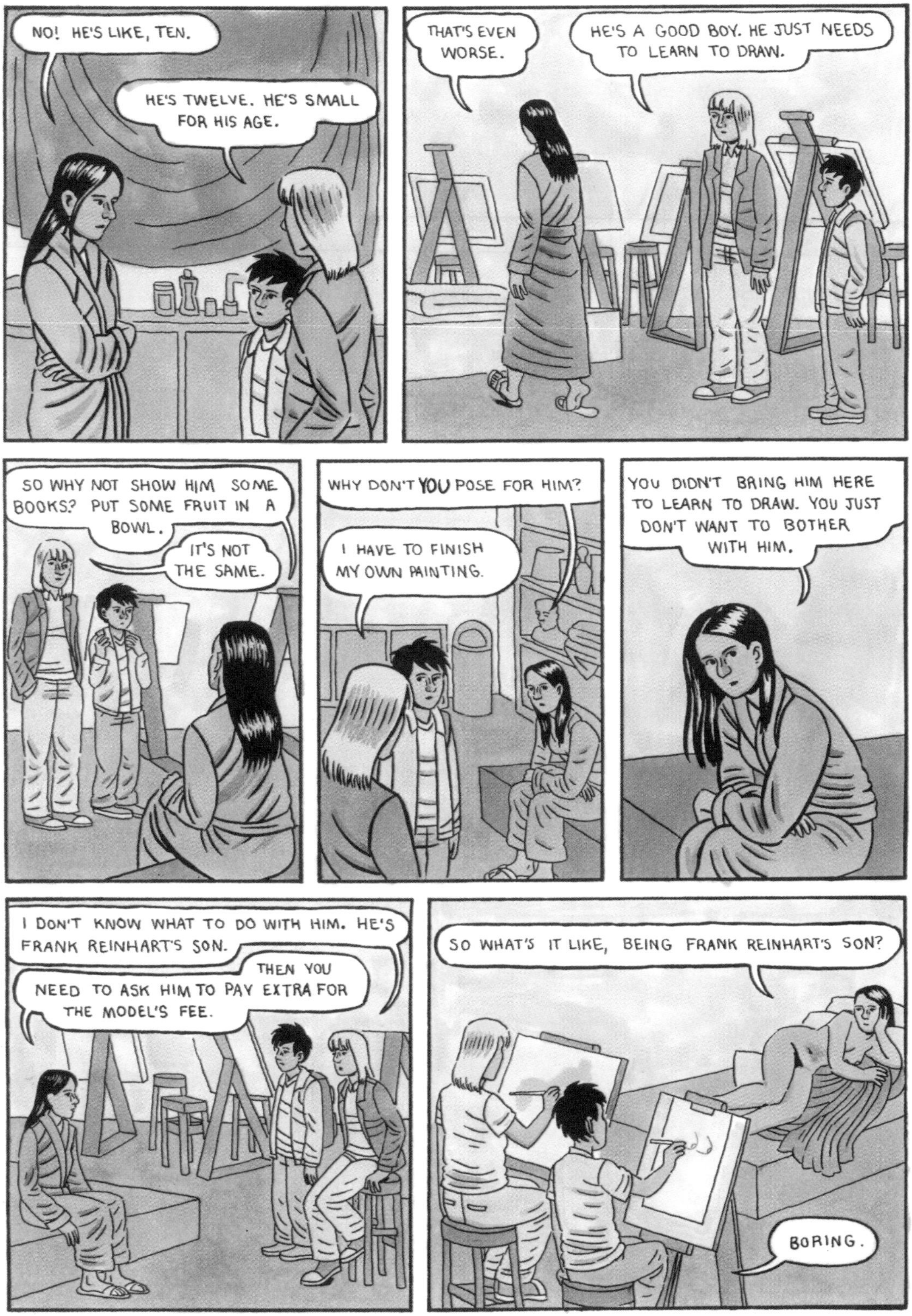
NO! HE'S LIKE, TEN.
HE'S TWELVE. HE'S SMALL FOR HIS AGE.
THAT'S EVEN WORSE.
HE'S A GOOD BOY. HE JUST NEEDS TO LEARN TO DRAW.
SO WHY NOT SHOW HIM SOME BOOKS? PUT SOME FRUIT IN A BOWL.
IT'S NOT THE SAME.
WHY DON'T YOU POSE FOR HIM?
I HAVE TO FINISH MY OWN PAINTING.
YOU DIDN'T BRING HIM HERE TO LEARN TO DRAW. YOU JUST DON'T WANT TO BOTHER WITH HIM.
I DON'T KNOW WHAT TO DO WITH HIM. HE'S FRANK REINHART'S SON.
THEN YOU NEED TO ASK HIM TO PAY EXTRA FOR THE MODEL'S FEE.
SO WHAT'S IT LIKE, BEING FRANK REINHART'S SON?
BORING.

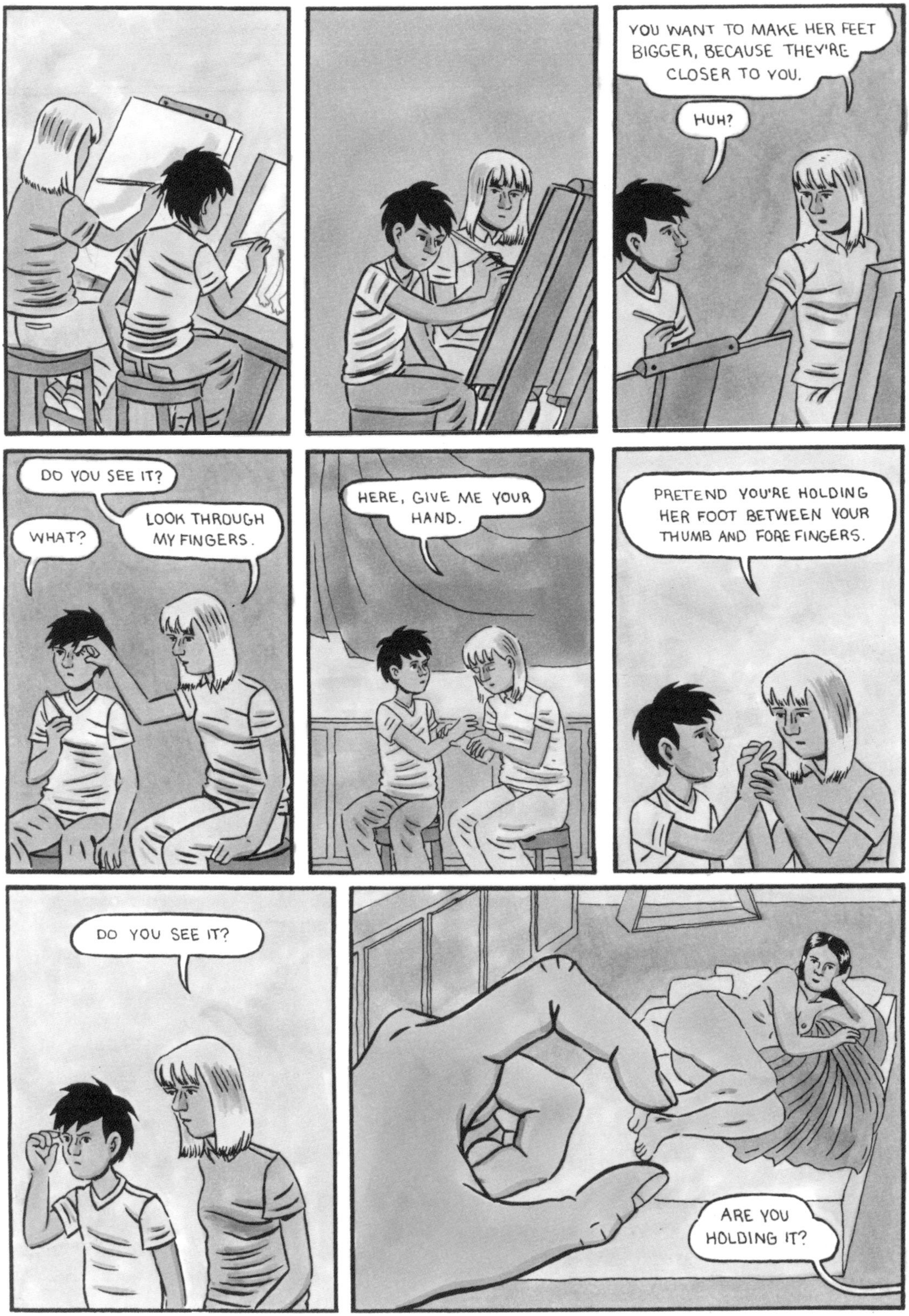
YOU WANT TO MAKE HER FEET BIGGER, BECAUSE THEY'RE CLOSER TO YOU.
HUH?
DO YOU SEE IT?
WHAT?
LOOK THROUGH MY FINGERS.
HERE, GIVE ME YOUR HAND.
PRETEND YOU'RE HOLDING HER FOOT BETWEEN YOUR THUMB AND FORE FINGERS.
DO YOU SEE IT?
ARE YOU HOLDING IT?

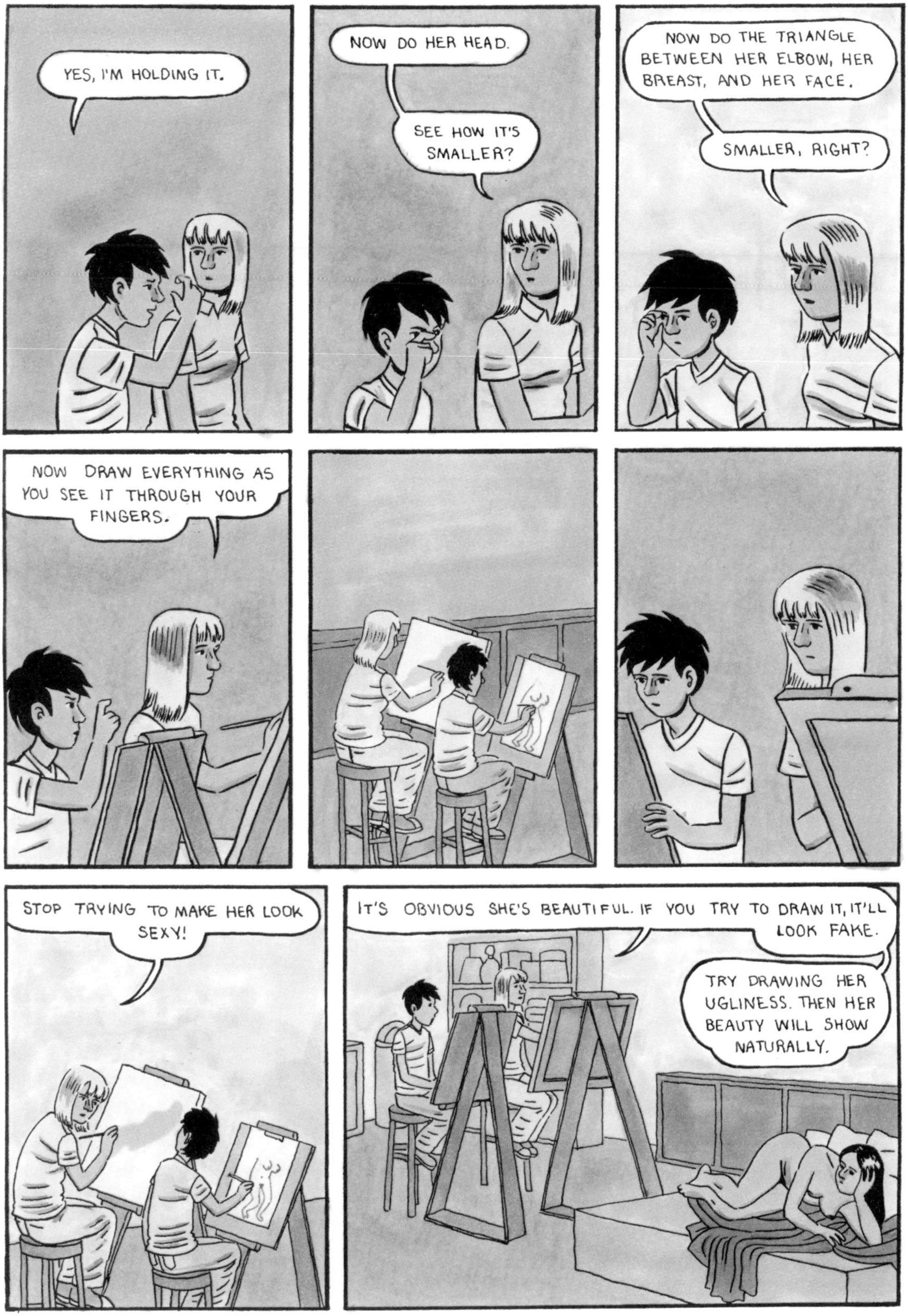
YES, I'M HOLDING IT.
NOW DO HER HEAD.
SEE HOW IT'S SMALLER?
NOW DO THE TRIANGLE BETWEEN HER ELBOW, HER BREAST, AND HER FACE.
SMALLER, RIGHT?
NOW DRAW EVERYTHING AS YOU SEE IT THROUGH YOUR FINGERS.
STOP TRYING TO MAKE HER LOOK SEXY!
IT'S OBVIOUS SHE'S BEAUTIFUL. IF YOU TRY TO DRAW IT, IT'LL LOOK FAKE.
TRY DRAWING HER UGLINESS. THEN HER BEAUTY WILL SHOW NATURALLY.

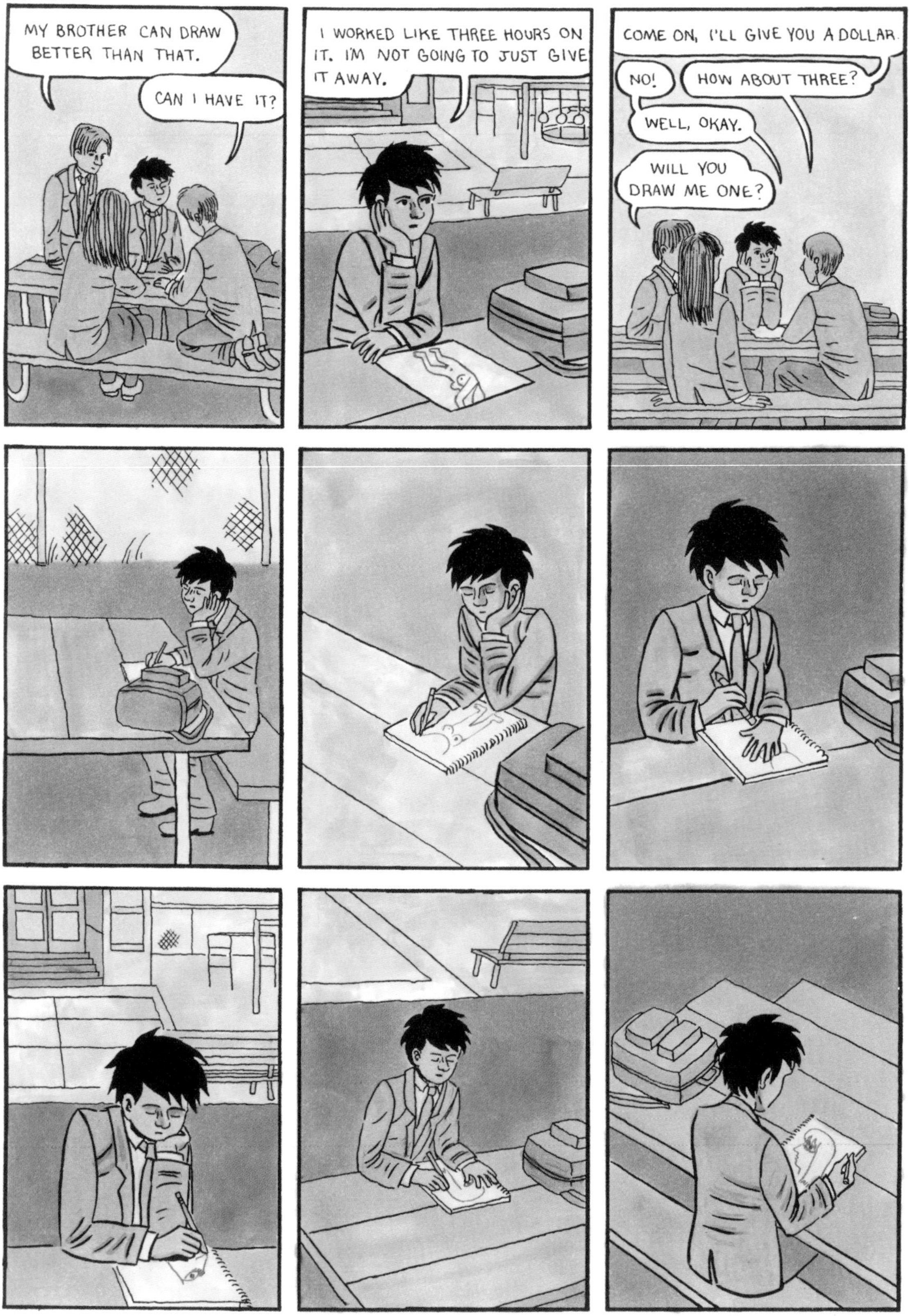
MY BROTHER CAN DRAW BETTER THAN THAT.
CAN I HAVE IT?
I WORKED LIKE THREE HOURS ON IT. I'M NOT GOING TO JUST GIVE IT AWAY.
COME ON, I'LL GIVE YOU A DOLLAR.
NO!
HOW ABOUT THREE?
WELL, OKAY.
WILL YOU DRAW ME ONE?

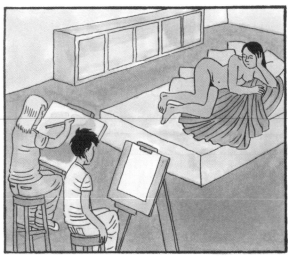

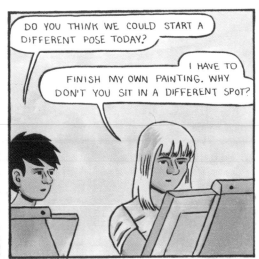

DO YOU THINK WE COULD START A DIFFERENT POSE TODAY?

I HAVE TO FINISH MY OWN PAINTING. WHY DON'T YOU SIT IN A DIFFERENT SPOT?

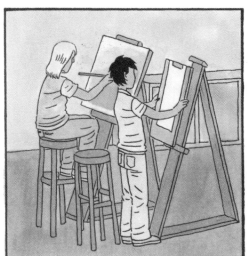

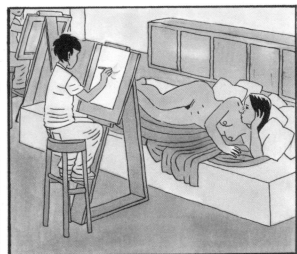

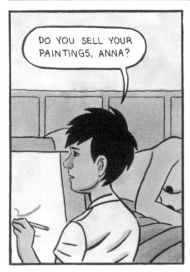

DO YOU SELL YOUR PAINTINGS, ANNA?

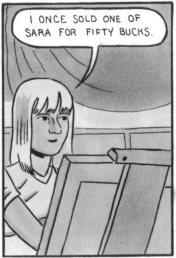

I ONCE SOLD ONE OF SARA FOR FIFTY BUCKS.

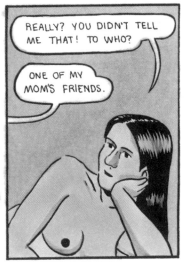

REALLY? YOU DIDN'T TELL ME THAT! TO WHO?

ONE OF MY MOM'S FRIENDS.

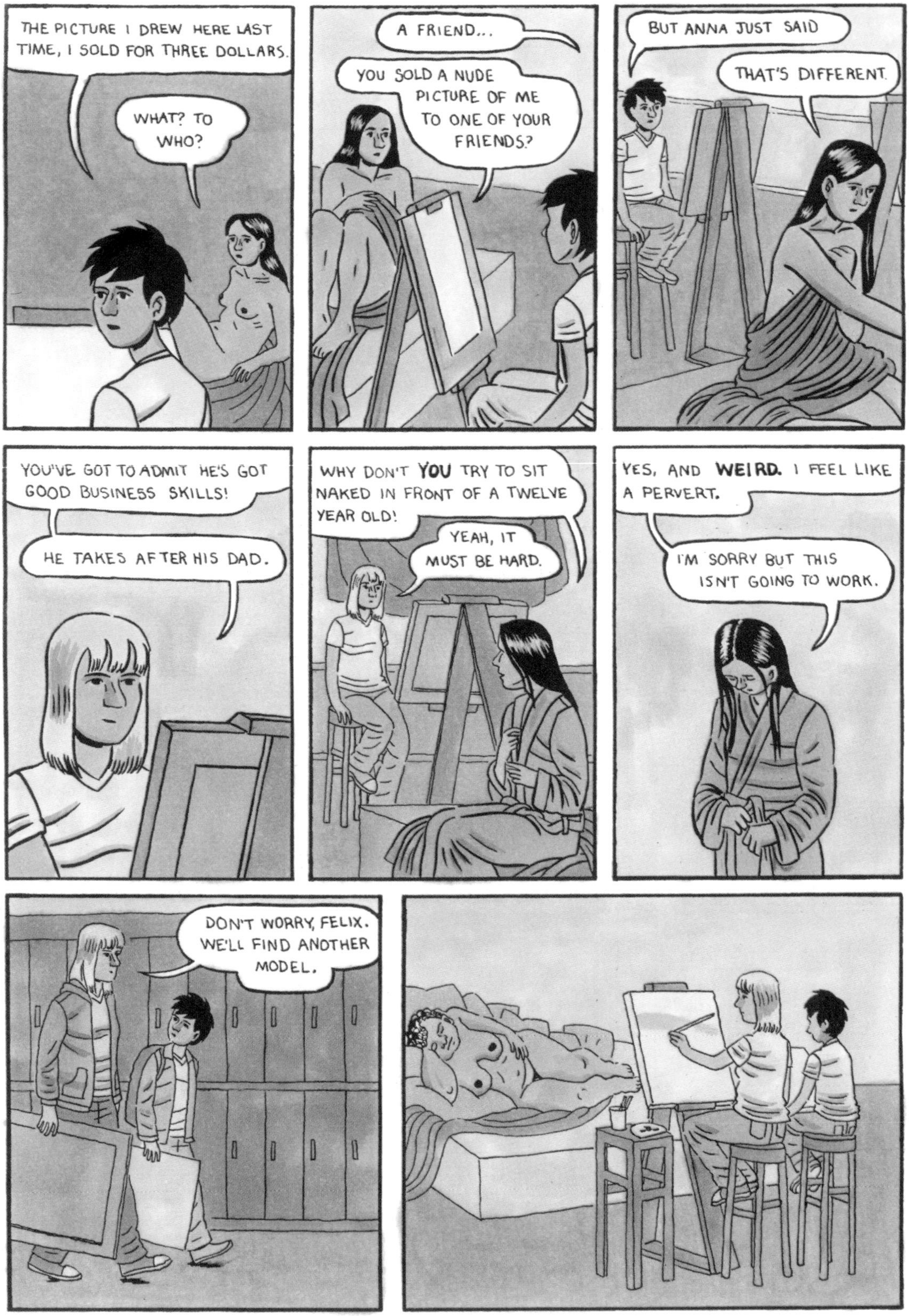
THE PICTURE I DREW HERE LAST TIME, I SOLD FOR THREE DOLLARS.
WHAT? TO WHO?
A FRIEND...
YOU SOLD A NUDE PICTURE OF ME TO ONE OF YOUR FRIENDS?
BUT ANNA JUST SAID
THAT'S DIFFERENT.
YOU'VE GOT TO ADMIT HE'S GOT GOOD BUSINESS SKILLS!
HE TAKES AFTER HIS DAD.
WHY DON'T YOU TRY TO SIT NAKED IN FRONT OF A TWELVE YEAR OLD!
YEAH, IT MUST BE HARD.
YES, AND WEIRD. I FEEL LIKE A PERVERT.
I'M SORRY BUT THIS ISN'T GOING TO WORK.
DON'T WORRY, FELIX. WE'LL FIND ANOTHER MODEL.

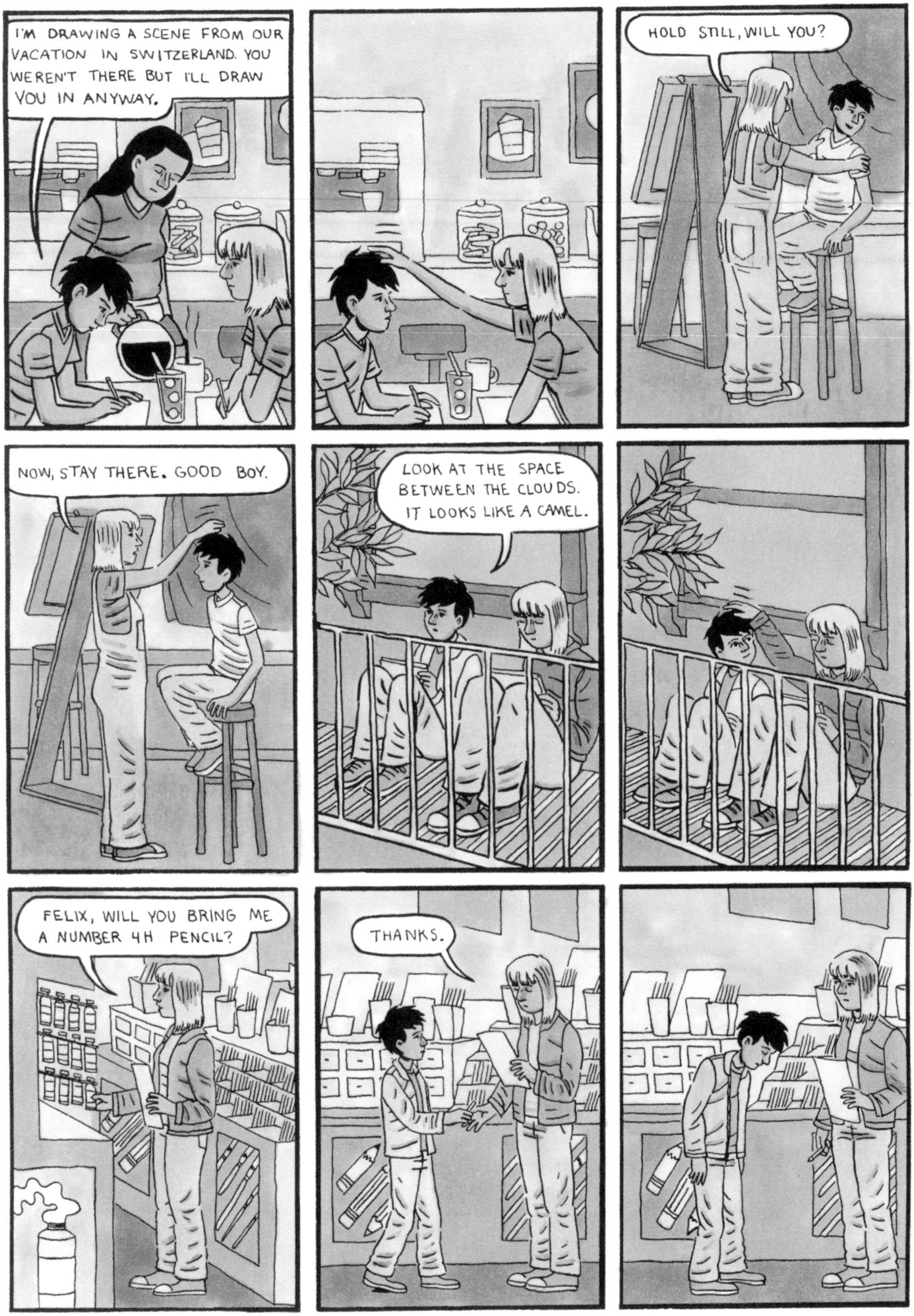
I'M DRAWING A SCENE FROM OUR VACATION IN SWITZERLAND. YOU WEREN'T THERE BUT I'LL DRAW YOU IN ANYWAY.
HOLD STILL, WILL YOU?
NOW, STAY THERE. GOOD BOY.
LOOK AT THE SPACE BETWEEN THE CLOUDS. IT LOOKS LIKE A CAMEL.
FELIX, WILL YOU BRING ME A NUMBER 4H PENCIL?
THANKS.

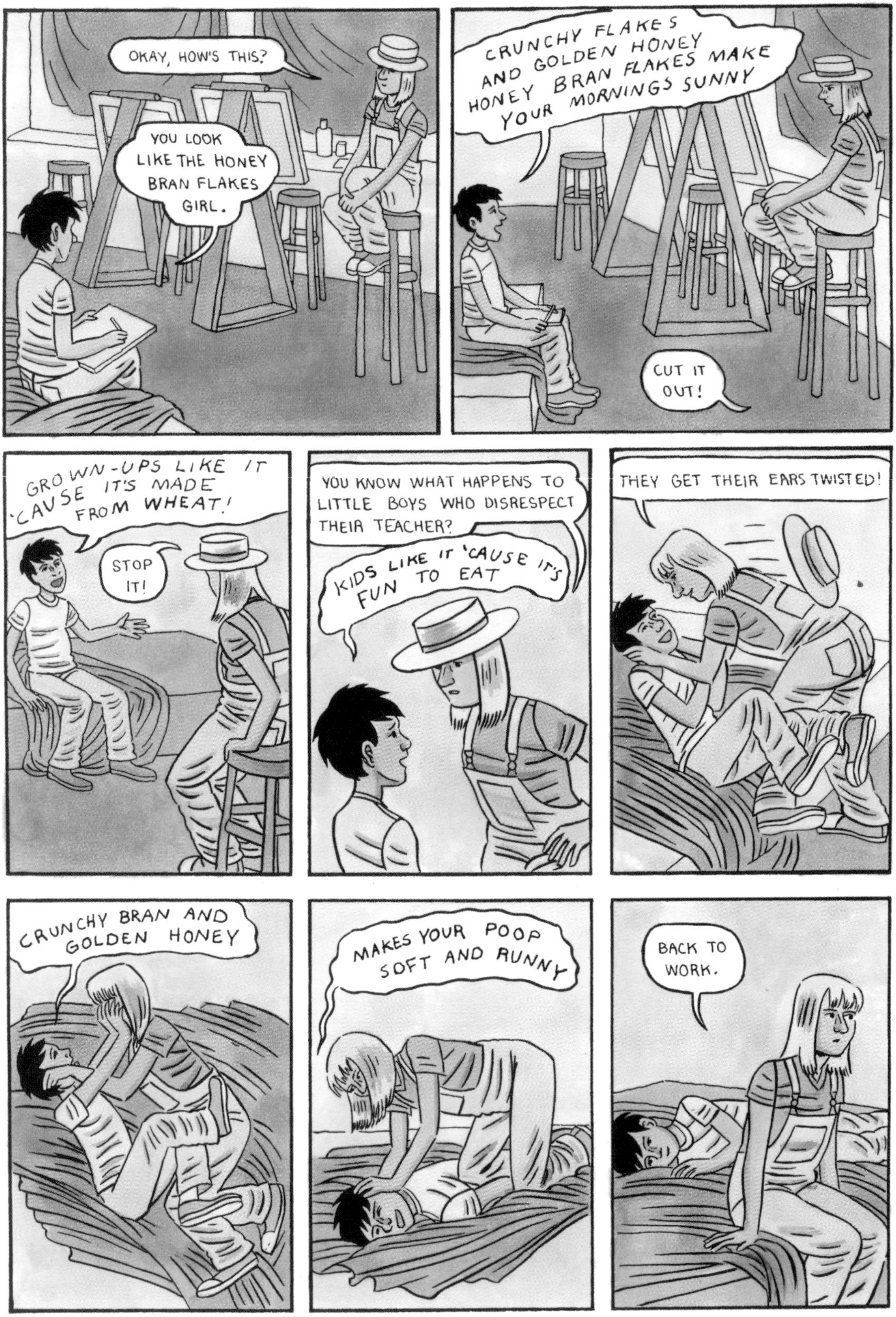

OKAY, HOW'S THIS?
YOU LOOK LIKE THE HONEY BRAN FLAKES GIRL.
CRUNCHY FLAKES AND GOLDEN HONEY HONEY BRAN FLAKES MAKE YOUR MORNINGS SUNNY
CUT IT OUT!
GROWN-UPS LIKE IT 'CAUSE IT'S MADE FROM WHEAT!
STOP IT!
YOU KNOW WHAT HAPPENS TO LITTLE BOYS WHO DISRESPECT THEIR TEACHER?
KIDS LIKE IT 'CAUSE IT'S FUN TO EAT
THEY GET THEIR EARS TWISTED!
CRUNCHY BRAN AND GOLDEN HONEY
MAKES YOUR POOP SOFT AND RUNNY
BACK TO WORK.

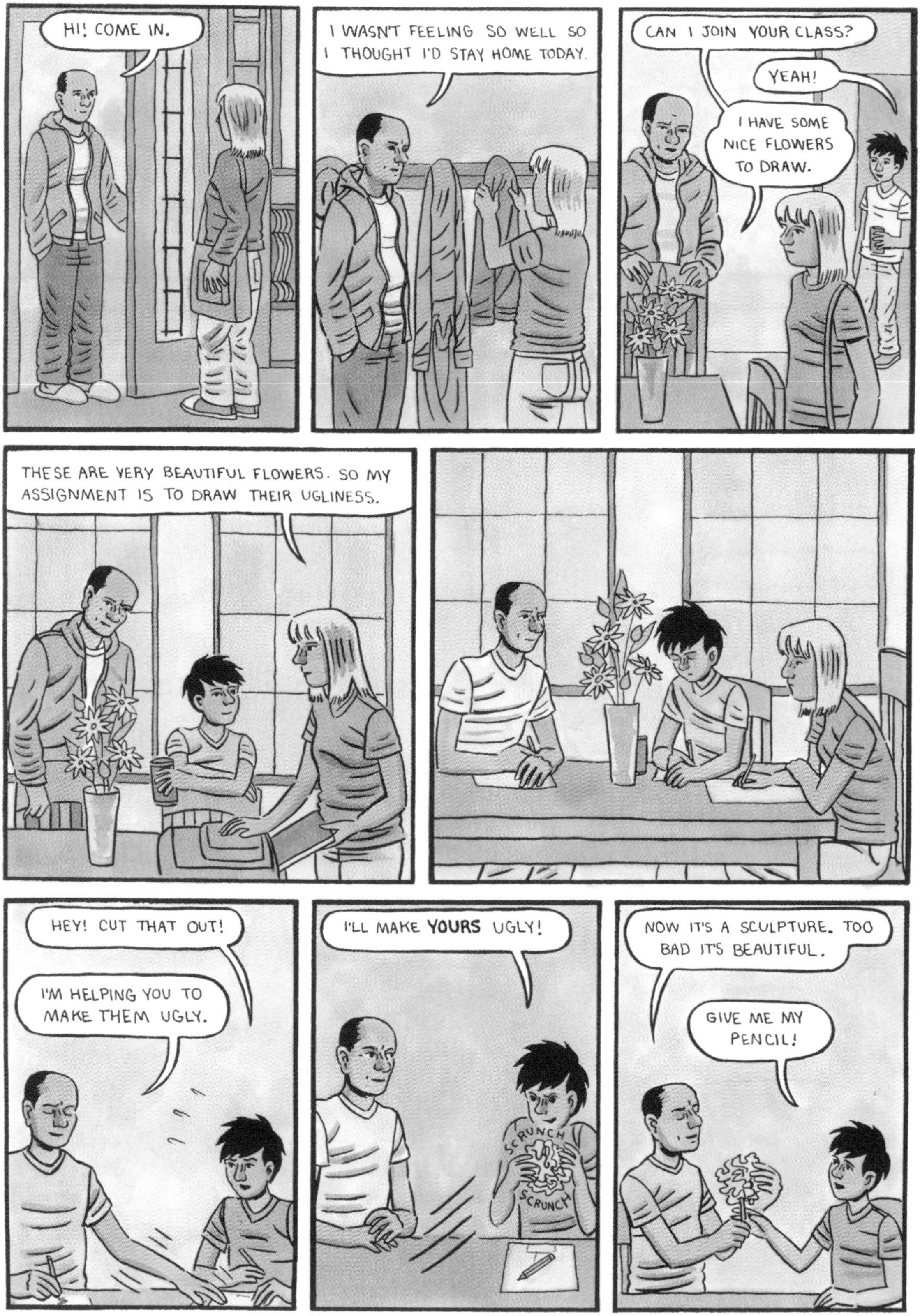
HI! COME IN.
I WASN'T FEELING SO WELL SO I THOUGHT I'D STAY HOME TODAY.
CAN I JOIN YOUR CLASS?
YEAH!
I HAVE SOME NICE FLOWERS TO DRAW.
THESE ARE VERY BEAUTIFUL FLOWERS. SO MY ASSIGNMENT IS TO DRAW THEIR UGLINESS.
HEY! CUT THAT OUT!
I'M HELPING YOU TO MAKE THEM UGLY.
I'LL MAKE **YOURS** UGLY!
SCRUNCH
SCRUNCH
NOW IT'S A SCULPTURE. TOO BAD IT'S BEAUTIFUL.
GIVE ME MY PENCIL!

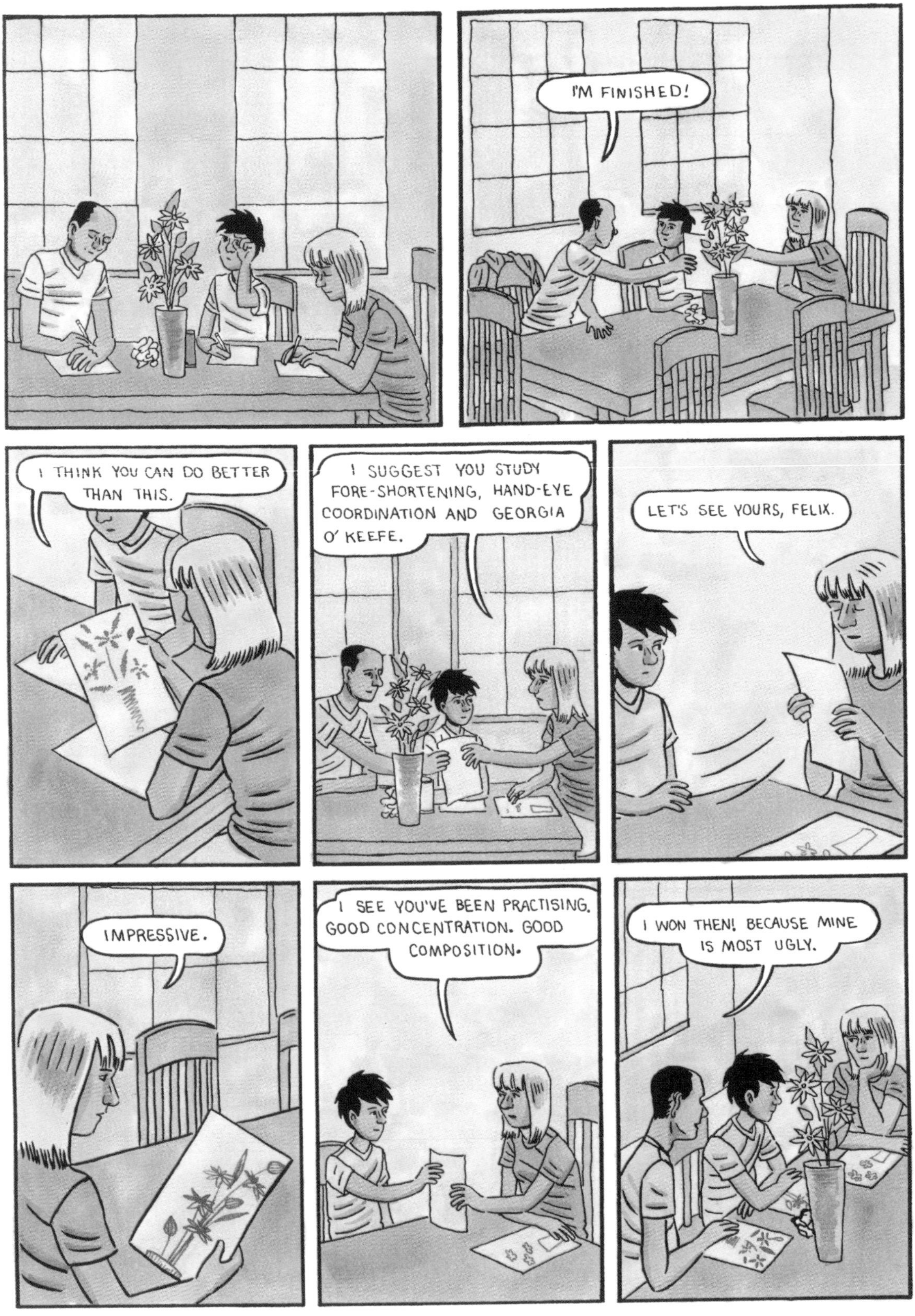
I'M FINISHED!
I THINK YOU CAN DO BETTER THAN THIS.
I SUGGEST YOU STUDY FORE-SHORTENING, HAND-EYE COORDINATION AND GEORGIA O' KEEFE.
LET'S SEE YOURS, FELIX.
IMPRESSIVE.
I SEE YOU'VE BEEN PRACTISING. GOOD CONCENTRATION. GOOD COMPOSITION.
I WON THEN! BECAUSE MINE IS MOST UGLY.

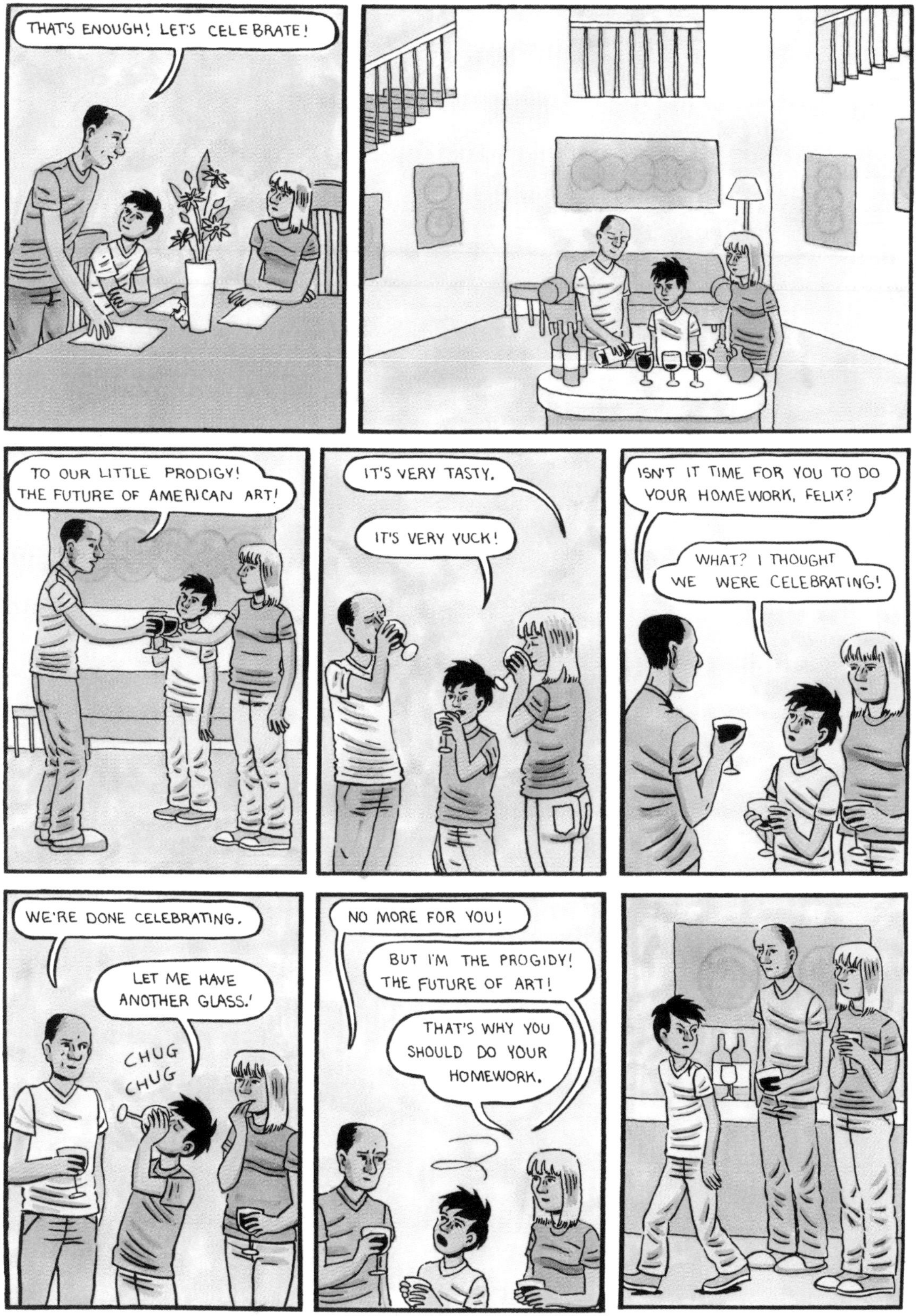
THAT'S ENOUGH! LET'S CELEBRATE!
TO OUR LITTLE PRODIGY! THE FUTURE OF AMERICAN ART!
IT'S VERY TASTY.
IT'S VERY YUCK!
ISN'T IT TIME FOR YOU TO DO YOUR HOMEWORK, FELIX?
WHAT? I THOUGHT WE WERE CELEBRATING!
WE'RE DONE CELEBRATING.
LET ME HAVE ANOTHER GLASS!
CHUG CHUG
NO MORE FOR YOU!
BUT I'M THE PROGIDY! THE FUTURE OF ART!
THAT'S WHY YOU SHOULD DO YOUR HOMEWORK.

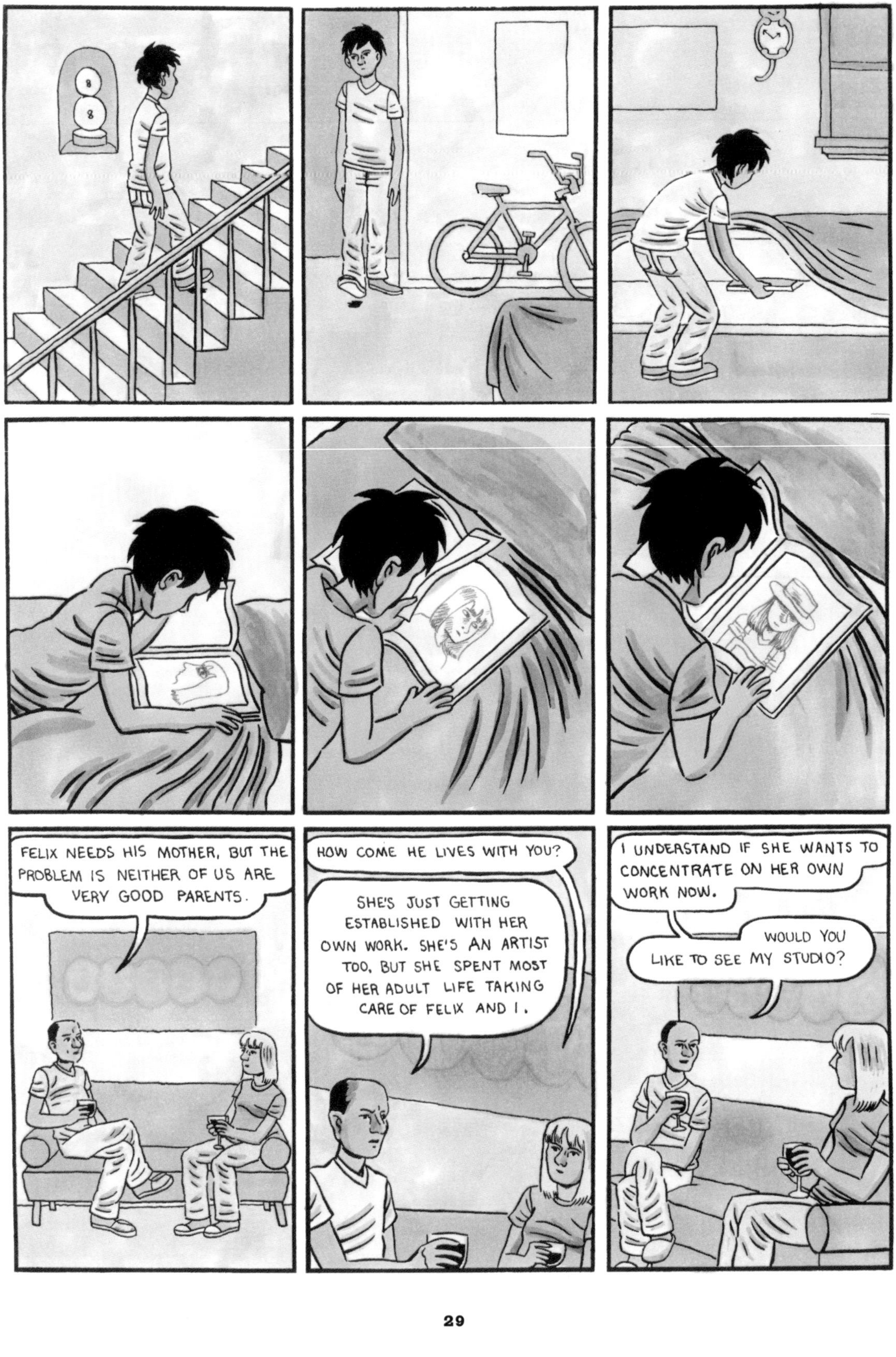
FELIX NEEDS HIS MOTHER, BUT THE PROBLEM IS NEITHER OF US ARE VERY GOOD PARENTS.
HOW COME HE LIVES WITH YOU?
SHE'S JUST GETTING ESTABLISHED WITH HER OWN WORK. SHE'S AN ARTIST TOO, BUT SHE SPENT MOST OF HER ADULT LIFE TAKING CARE OF FELIX AND I.
I UNDERSTAND IF SHE WANTS TO CONCENTRATE ON HER OWN WORK NOW.
WOULD YOU LIKE TO SEE MY STUDIO?

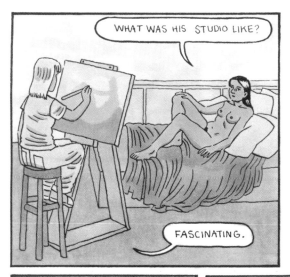

WHAT WAS HIS STUDIO LIKE?

FASCINATING.

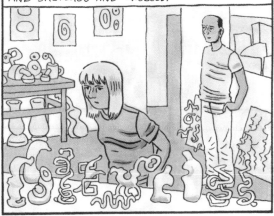

IT WASN'T WHERE THE ACTUAL STRUCTURES WERE MADE BUT IT WAS FULL OF LITTLE DIAGRAMS AND SKETCHES AND MODELS.

YOU KNOW, I'VE NEVER UNDERSTOOD HIS SCULPTURE BEFORE, BUT SUDDENLY I SAW HOW HIS MIND WORKED.

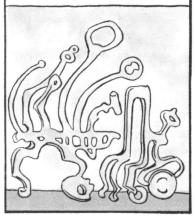

ALL THAT STUFF GRADY SAYS ABOUT NEGATIVE SPACE, I THOUGHT I UNDERSTOOD IT, BUT I HAD NO CLUE!

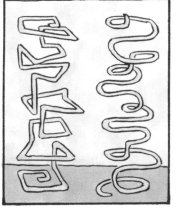

IT WAS LIKE I'D DISCOVERED A WHOLE NEW WAY TO COMMUNICATE, AND WAS INSTINCTIVELY FLUENT IN IT.

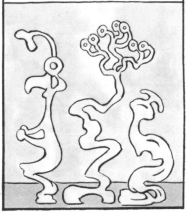

I WAS SO INSPIRED! I LEARNED MORE IN ONE EVENING WHAT THIS SCHOOL HAS BEEN TRYING TO DRUM INTO MY HEAD FOR THE PAST THREE YEARS!

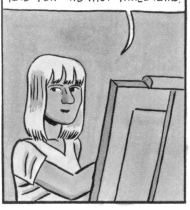

THEN WHAT HAPPENED?

NOTHING.

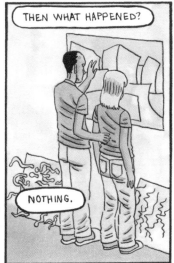

EXCEPT THAT HE'S TAKING ME TO DINNER TOMORROW NIGHT!

OH HO!

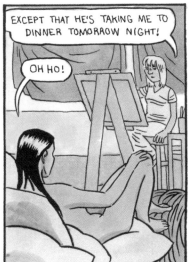

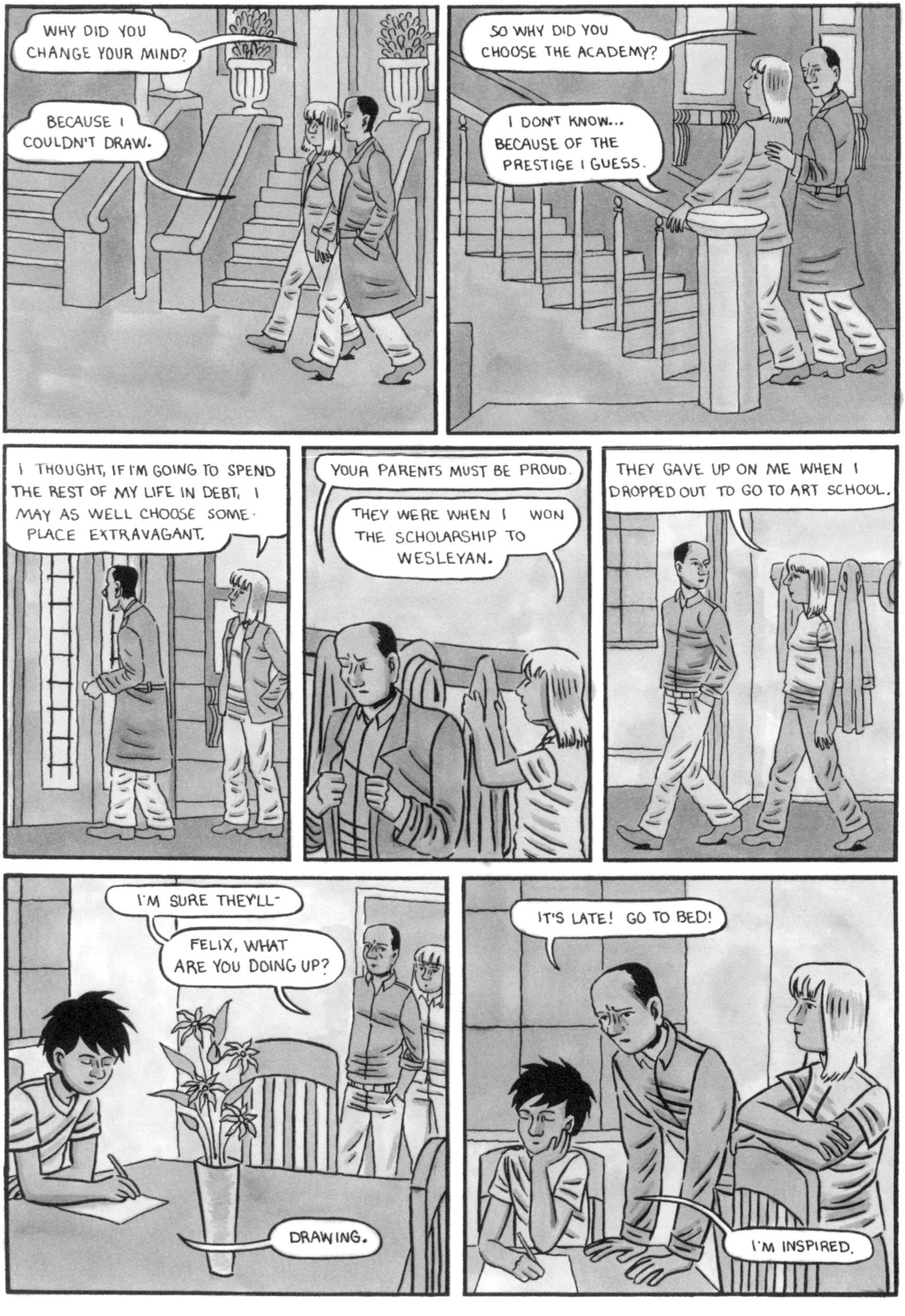
WHY DID YOU CHANGE YOUR MIND?
BECAUSE I COULDN'T DRAW.
SO WHY DID YOU CHOOSE THE ACADEMY?
I DON'T KNOW... BECAUSE OF THE PRESTIGE I GUESS.
I THOUGHT, IF I'M GOING TO SPEND THE REST OF MY LIFE IN DEBT, I MAY AS WELL CHOOSE SOME-PLACE EXTRAVAGANT.
YOUR PARENTS MUST BE PROUD.
THEY WERE WHEN I WON THE SCHOLARSHIP TO WESLEYAN.
THEY GAVE UP ON ME WHEN I DROPPED OUT TO GO TO ART SCHOOL.
I'M SURE THEY'LL-
FELIX, WHAT ARE YOU DOING UP?
DRAWING.
IT'S LATE! GO TO BED!
I'M INSPIRED.

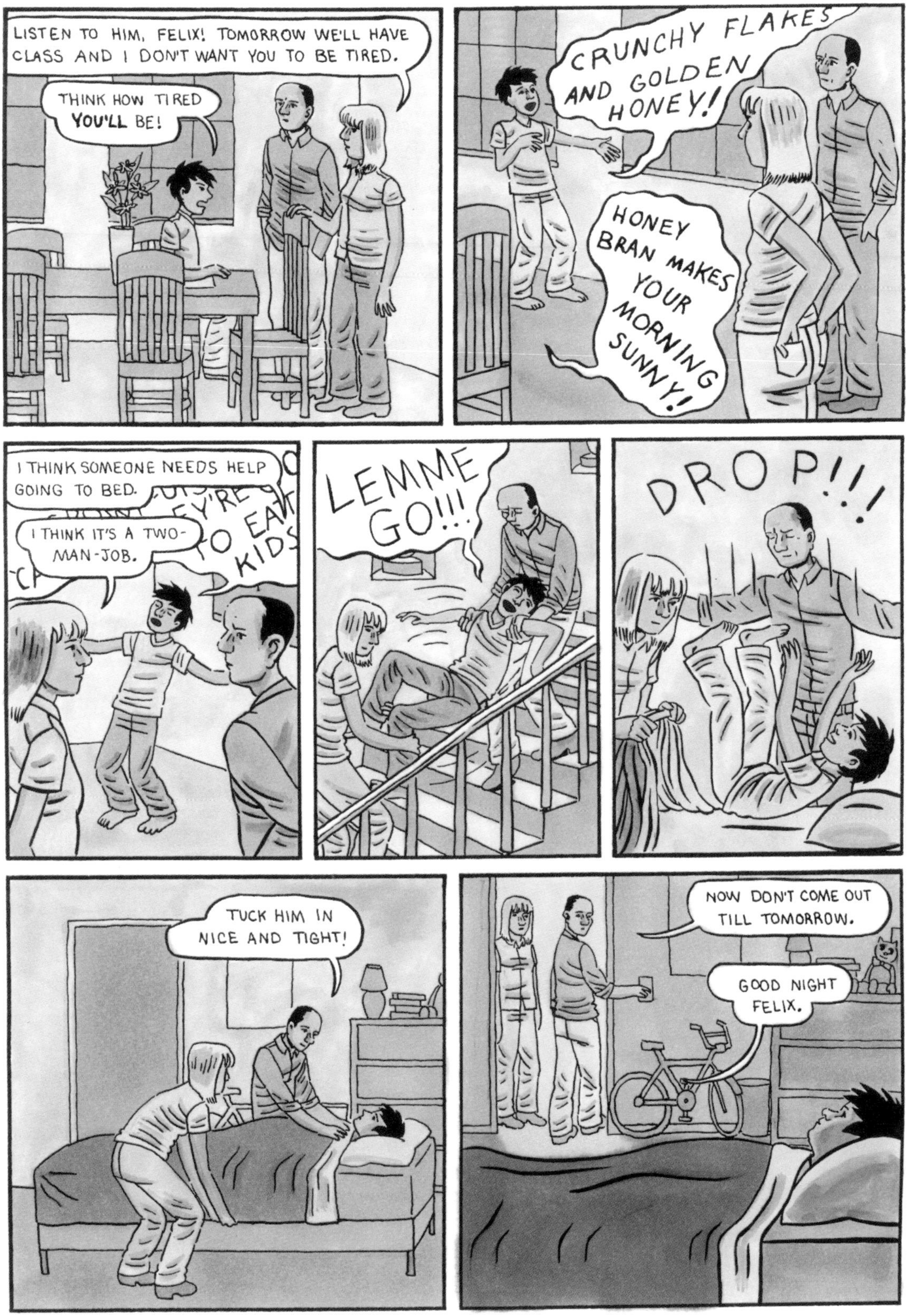
LISTEN TO HIM, FELIX! TOMORROW WE'LL HAVE CLASS AND I DON'T WANT YOU TO BE TIRED.
THINK HOW TIRED **YOU'LL** BE!
CRUNCHY FLAKES AND GOLDEN HONEY!
HONEY BRAN MAKES YOUR MORNING SUNNY!
I THINK SOMEONE NEEDS HELP GOING TO BED.
I THINK IT'S A TWO-MAN-JOB.
LEMME GO!!!
DROP!!!
TUCK HIM IN NICE AND TIGHT!
NOW DON'T COME OUT TILL TOMORROW.
GOOD NIGHT FELIX.

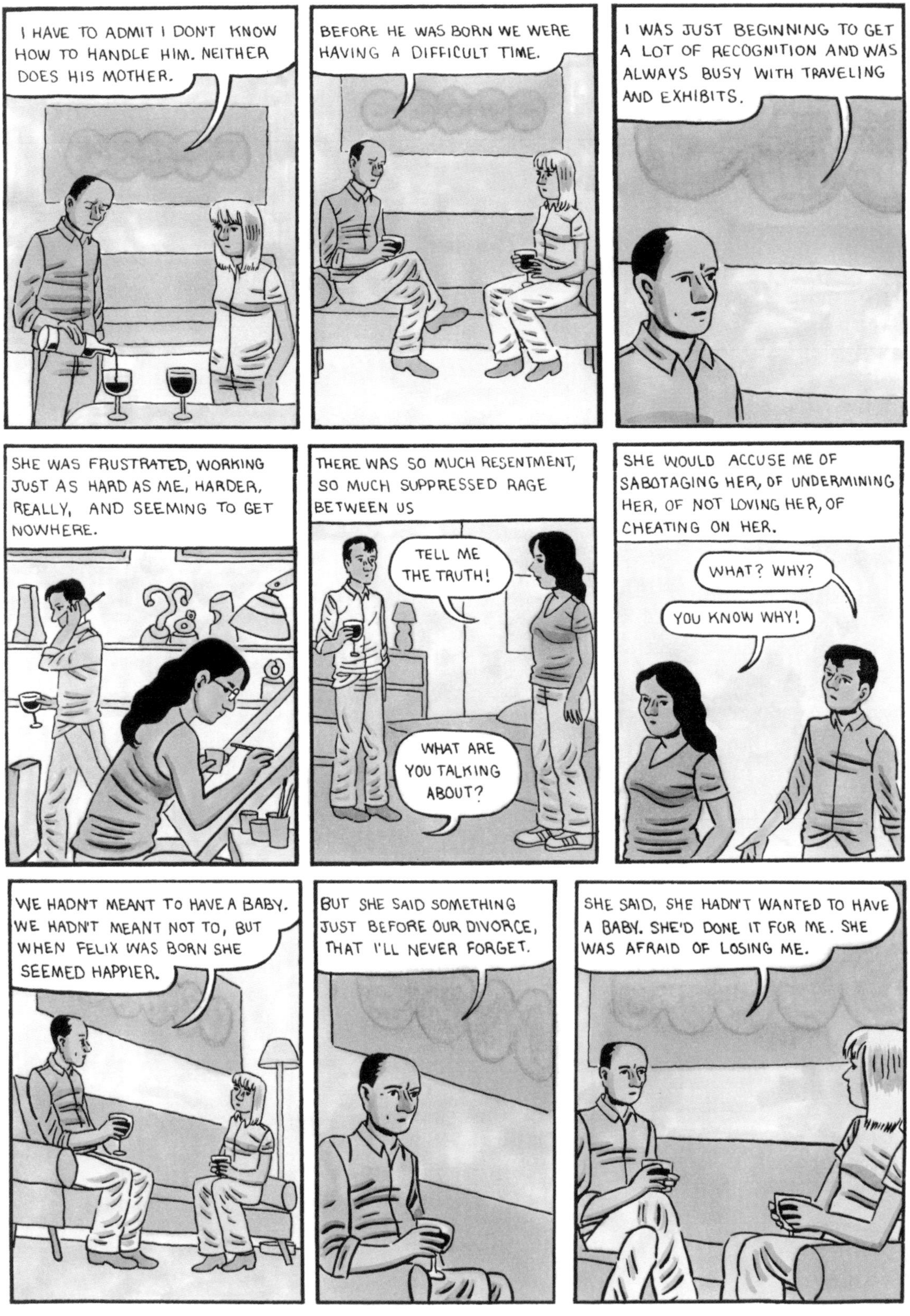
I HAVE TO ADMIT I DON'T KNOW HOW TO HANDLE HIM. NEITHER DOES HIS MOTHER.
BEFORE HE WAS BORN WE WERE HAVING A DIFFICULT TIME.
I WAS JUST BEGINNING TO GET A LOT OF RECOGNITION AND WAS ALWAYS BUSY WITH TRAVELING AND EXHIBITS.
SHE WAS FRUSTRATED, WORKING JUST AS HARD AS ME, HARDER, REALLY, AND SEEMING TO GET NOWHERE.
THERE WAS SO MUCH RESENTMENT, SO MUCH SUPPRESSED RAGE BETWEEN US
TELL ME THE TRUTH!
WHAT ARE YOU TALKING ABOUT?
SHE WOULD ACCUSE ME OF SABOTAGING HER, OF UNDERMINING HER, OF NOT LOVING HER, OF CHEATING ON HER.
WHAT? WHY?
YOU KNOW WHY!
WE HADN'T MEANT TO HAVE A BABY. WE HADN'T MEANT NOT TO, BUT WHEN FELIX WAS BORN SHE SEEMED HAPPIER.
BUT SHE SAID SOMETHING JUST BEFORE OUR DIVORCE, THAT I'LL NEVER FORGET.
SHE SAID, SHE HADN'T WANTED TO HAVE A BABY. SHE'D DONE IT FOR ME. SHE WAS AFRAID OF LOSING ME.

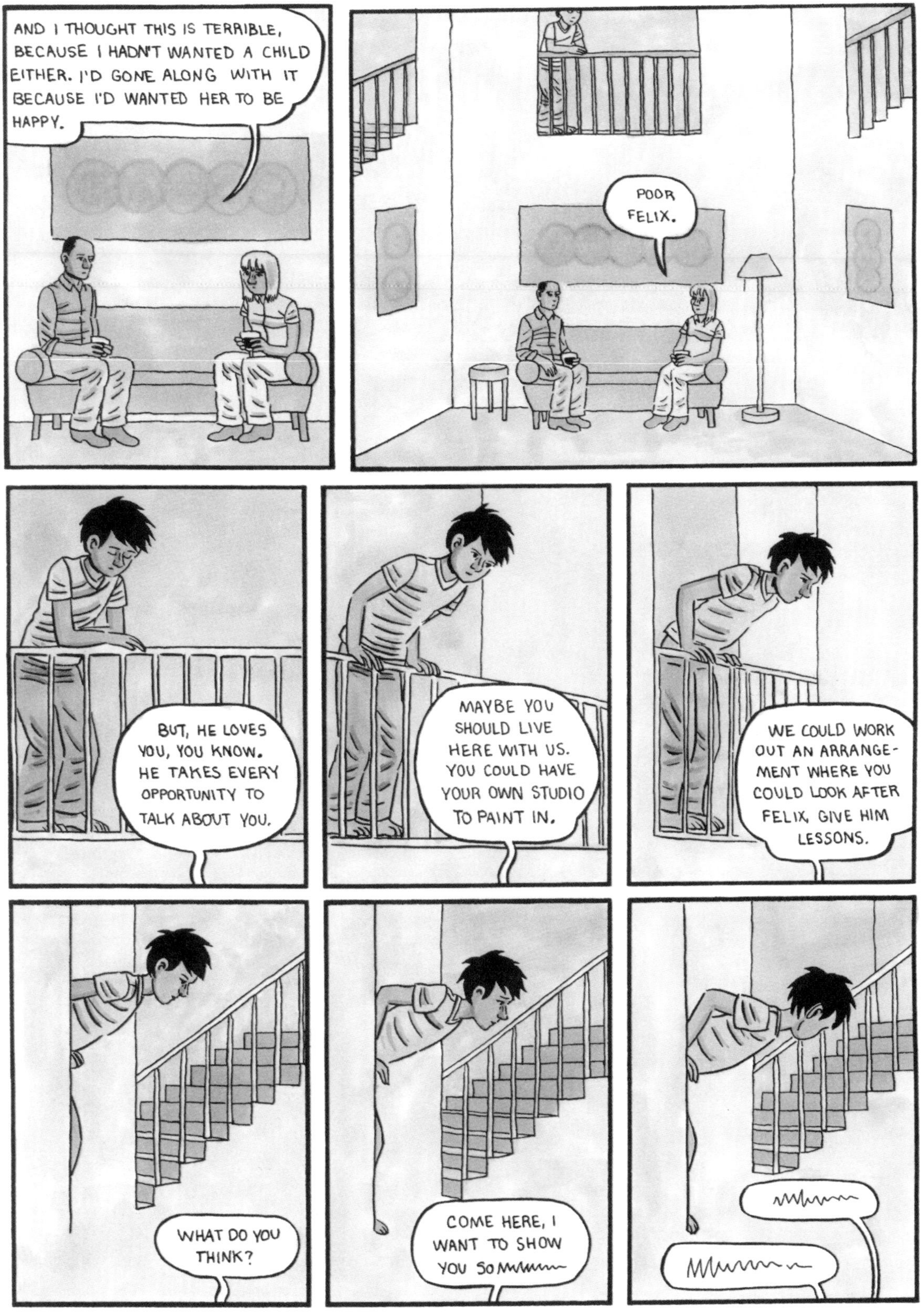
AND I THOUGHT THIS IS TERRIBLE, BECAUSE I HADN'T WANTED A CHILD EITHER. I'D GONE ALONG WITH IT BECAUSE I'D WANTED HER TO BE HAPPY.
POOR FELIX.
BUT, HE LOVES YOU, YOU KNOW. HE TAKES EVERY OPPORTUNITY TO TALK ABOUT YOU.
MAYBE YOU SHOULD LIVE HERE WITH US. YOU COULD HAVE YOUR OWN STUDIO TO PAINT IN.
WE COULD WORK OUT AN ARRANGE-MENT WHERE YOU COULD LOOK AFTER FELIX, GIVE HIM LESSONS.
WHAT DO YOU THINK?
COME HERE, I WANT TO SHOW YOU SO

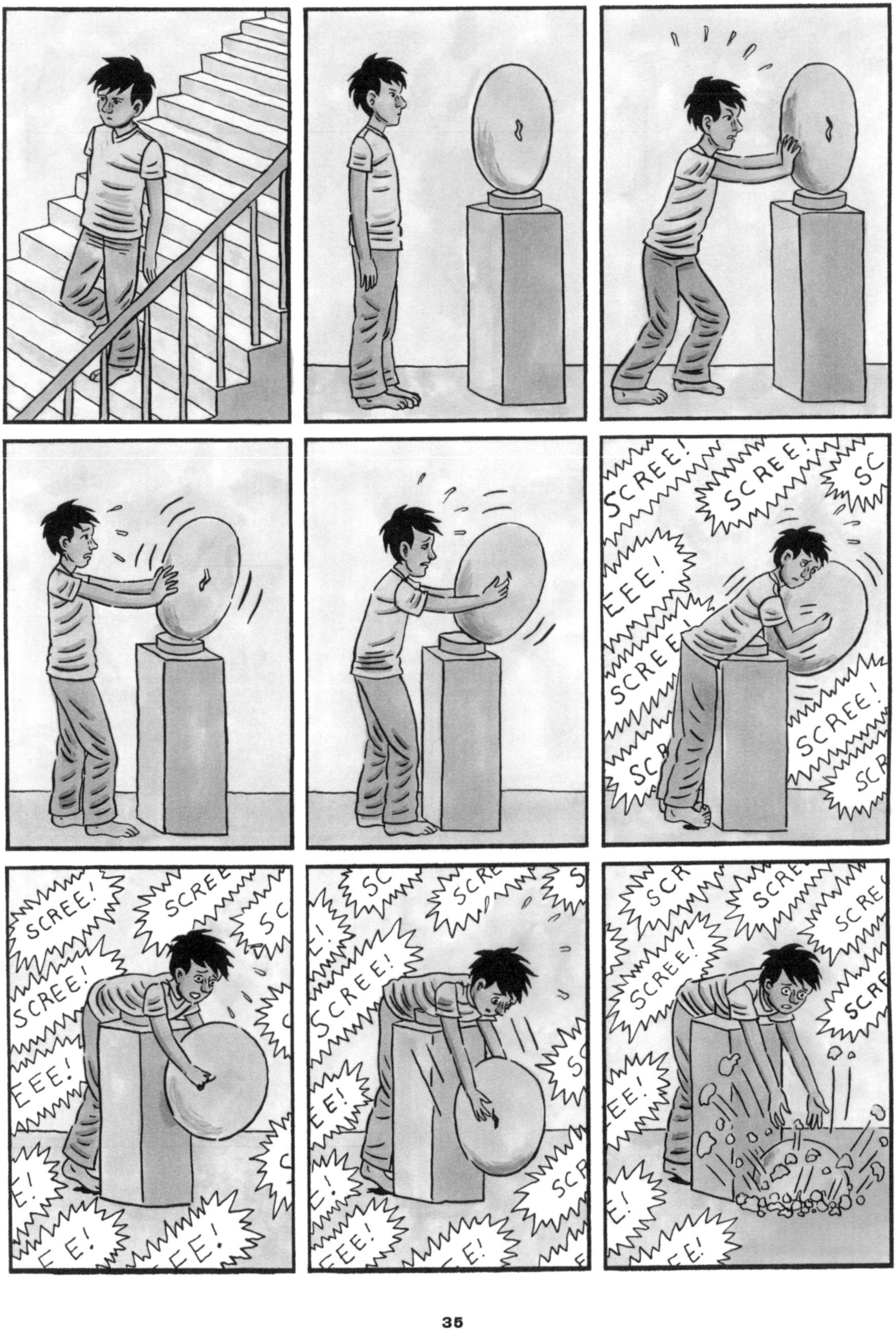
SCREE!
SCREE!
SC
EEE!
SCREE
SCREE!
SCR
SCR
SCREE!
SCREE
SC
SCREE!
EEE!
E!
EE!
EEE!
SC
SCRE
E!
SCREE!
E!
SC
SCR
E!
EEE!
E!
SCR
SCRE
SCRE
SCREE!
SCRE
EE!
E!
EE!

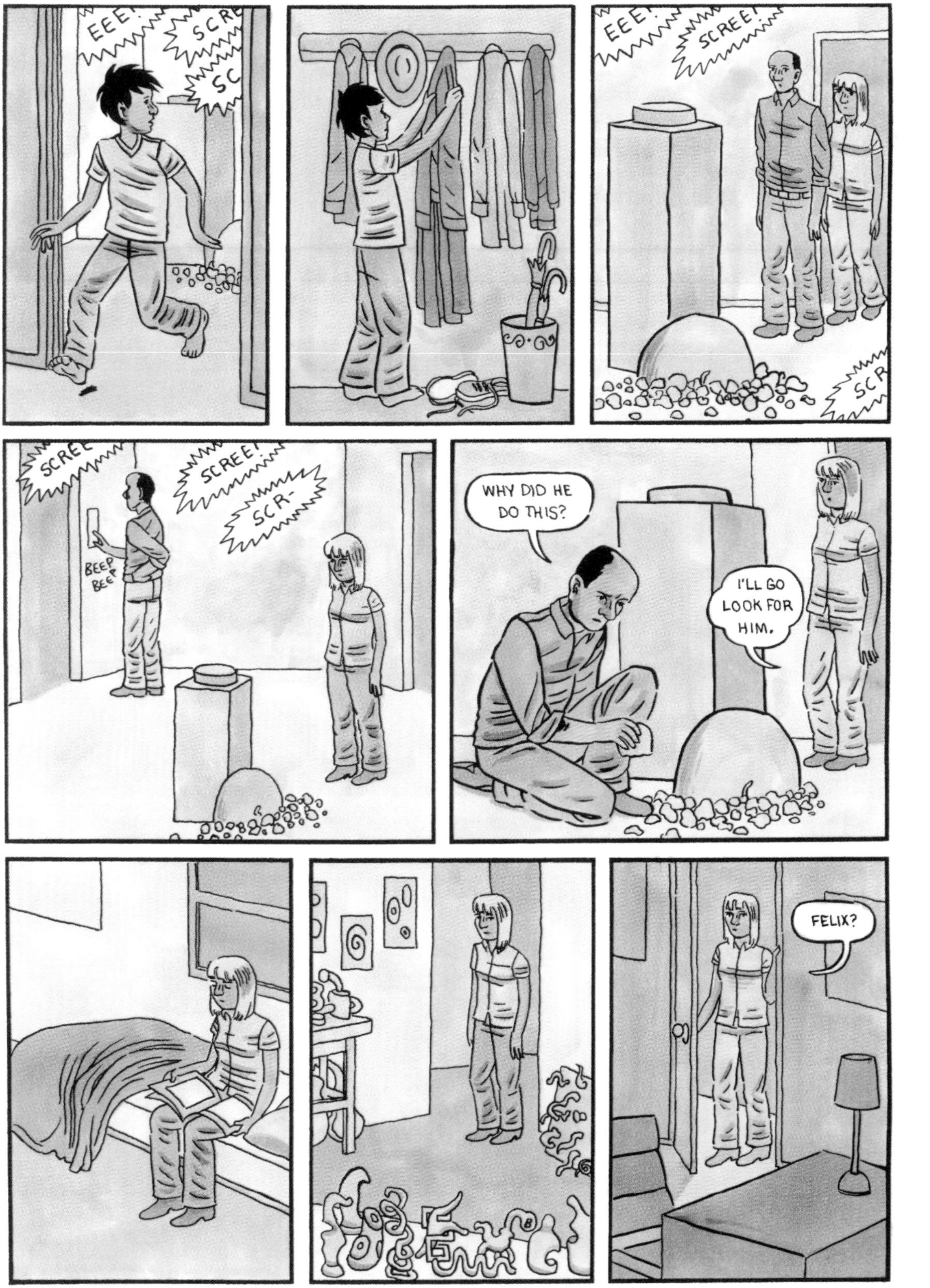
EEEE!
SCRE
SC
EEEE!
SCREE!
SCR
SCREE
SCREE!
SCR-
BEEP BEEP
WHY DID HE DO THIS?
I'LL GO LOOK FOR HIM.
FELIX?

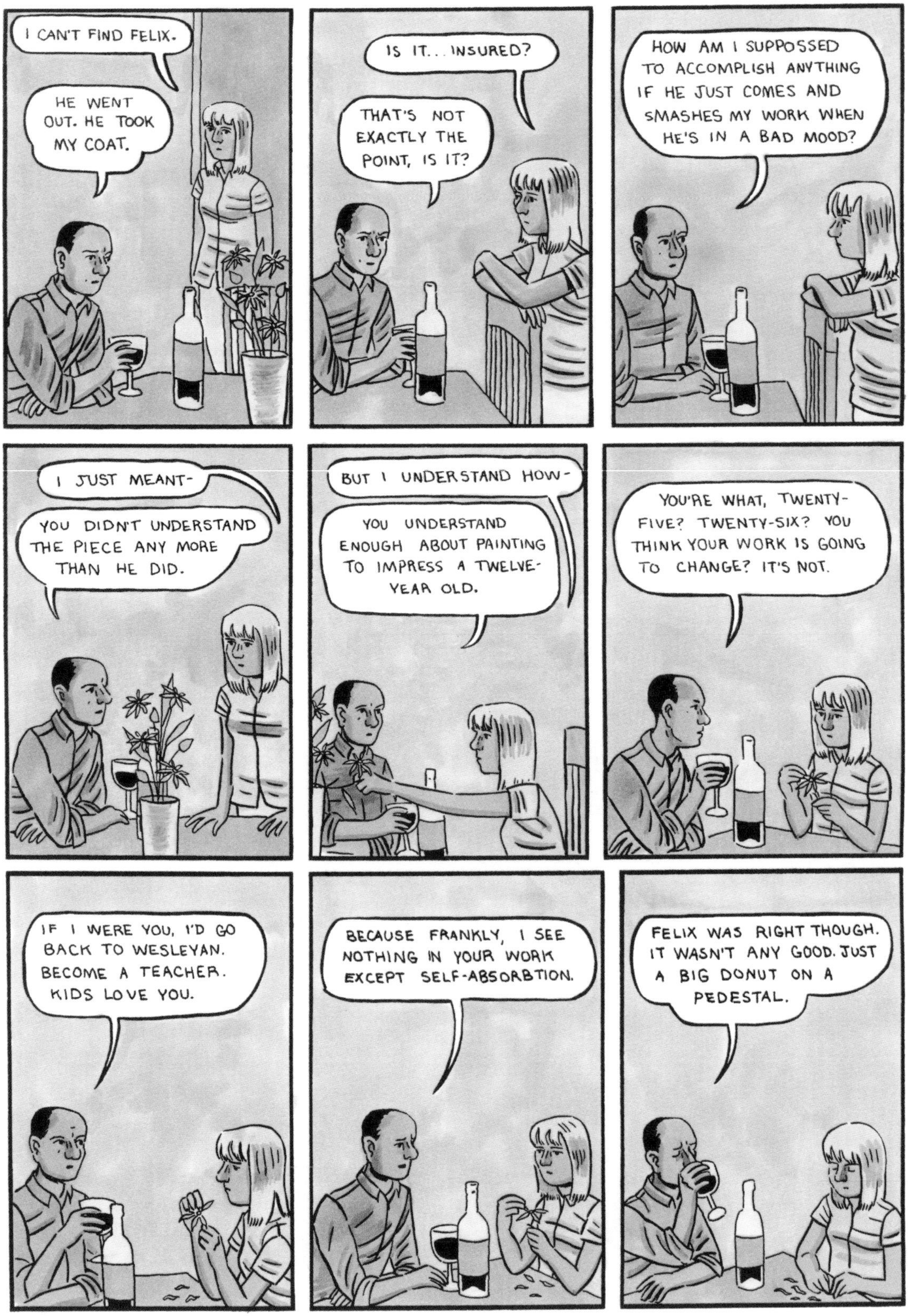
I CAN'T FIND FELIX.
HE WENT OUT. HE TOOK MY COAT.
IS IT... INSURED?
THAT'S NOT EXACTLY THE POINT, IS IT?
HOW AM I SUPPOSSED TO ACCOMPLISH ANYTHING IF HE JUST COMES AND SMASHES MY WORK WHEN HE'S IN A BAD MOOD?
I JUST MEANT-
YOU DIDN'T UNDERSTAND THE PIECE ANY MORE THAN HE DID.
BUT I UNDERSTAND HOW-
YOU UNDERSTAND ENOUGH ABOUT PAINTING TO IMPRESS A TWELVE-YEAR OLD.
YOU'RE WHAT, TWENTY-FIVE? TWENTY-SIX? YOU THINK YOUR WORK IS GOING TO CHANGE? IT'S NOT.
IF I WERE YOU, I'D GO BACK TO WESLEYAN. BECOME A TEACHER. KIDS LOVE YOU.
BECAUSE FRANKLY, I SEE NOTHING IN YOUR WORK EXCEPT SELF-ABSORBTION.
FELIX WAS RIGHT THOUGH. IT WASN'T ANY GOOD. JUST A BIG DONUT ON A PEDESTAL.

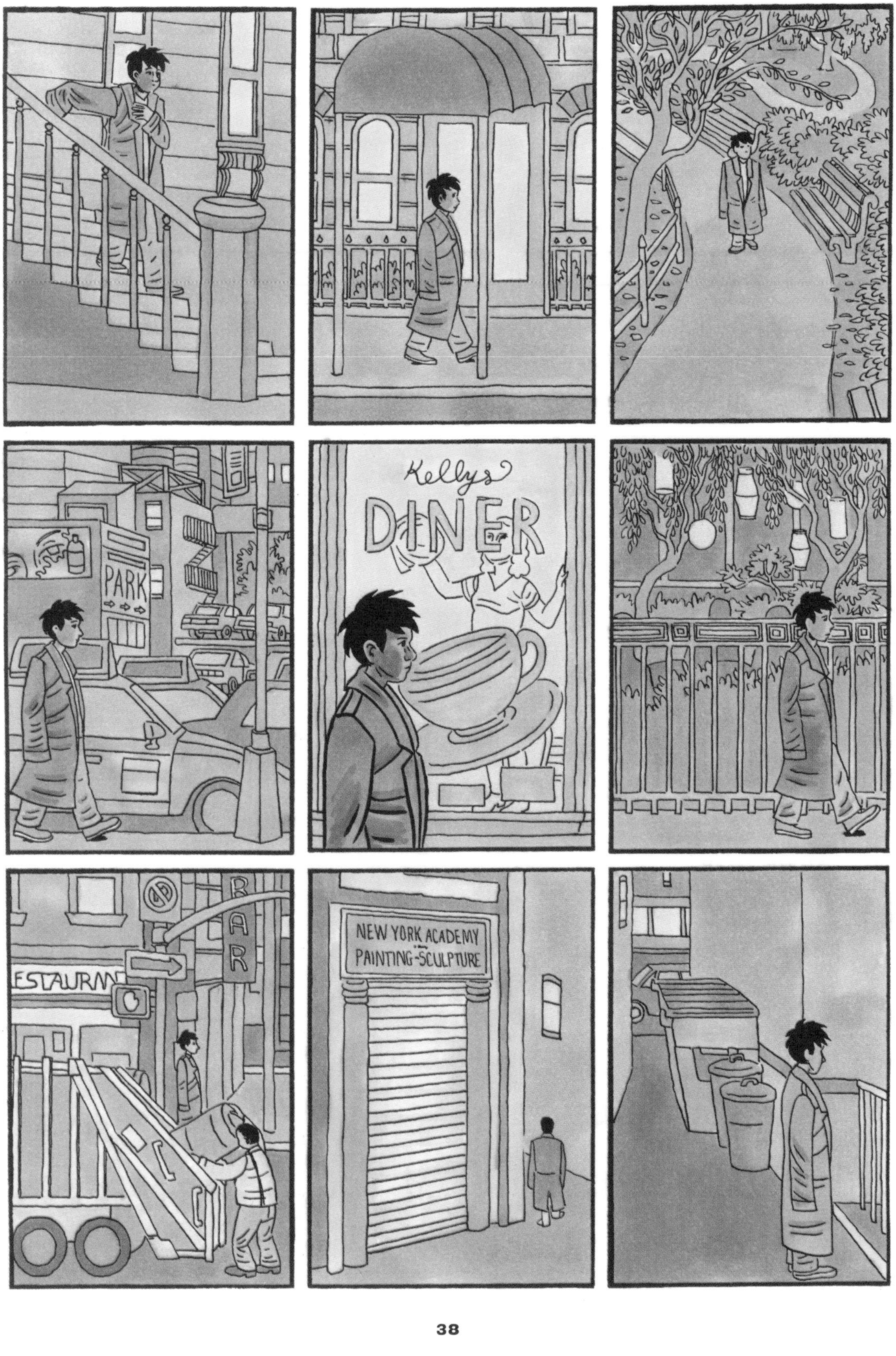
PARK
Kelly's
DINER
ESTAURAN
BAR
NEW YORK ACADEMY
PAINTING-SCULPTURE

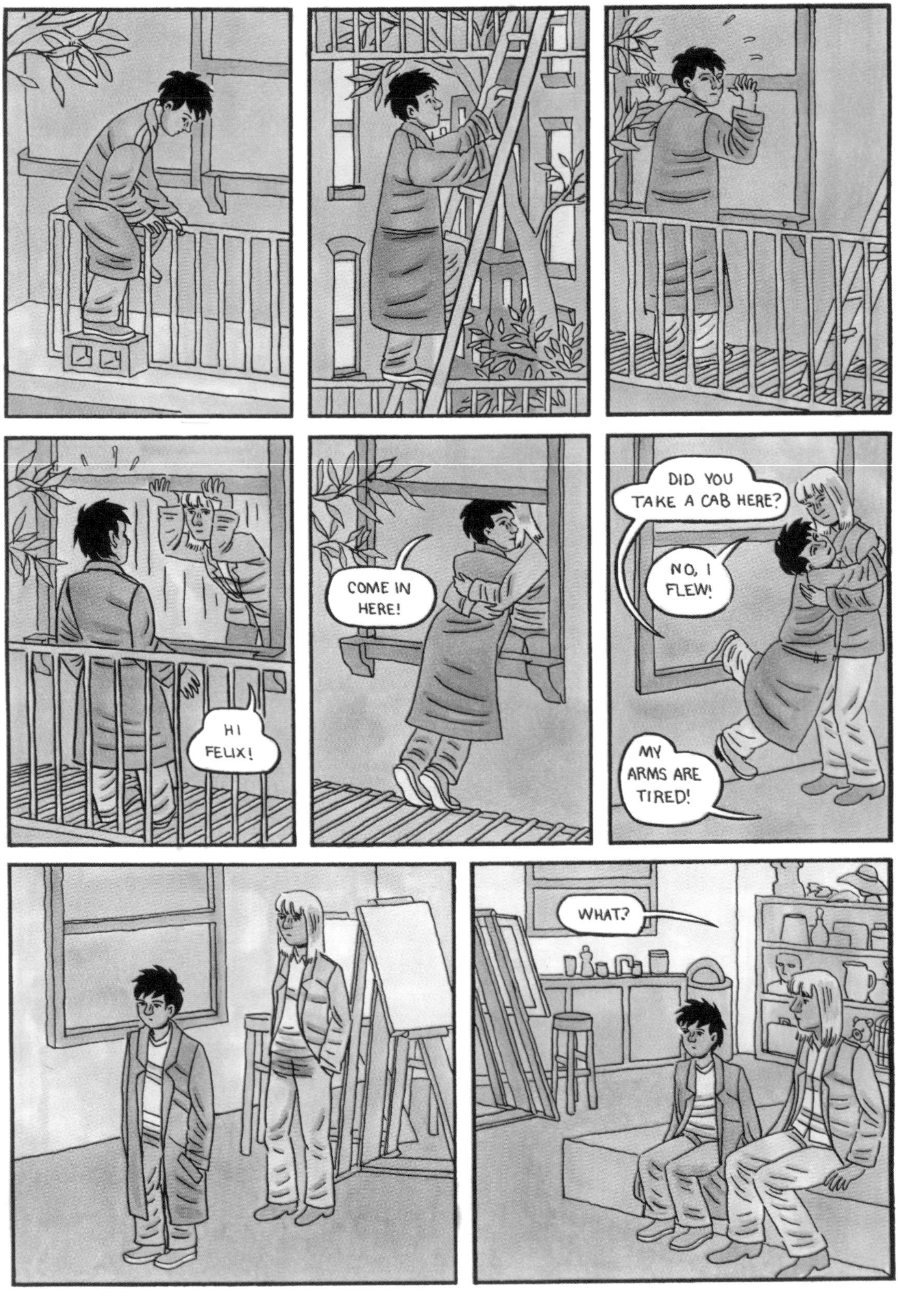
HI FELIX!
COME IN HERE!
DID YOU TAKE A CAB HERE?
NO, I FLEW!
MY ARMS ARE TIRED!
WHAT?

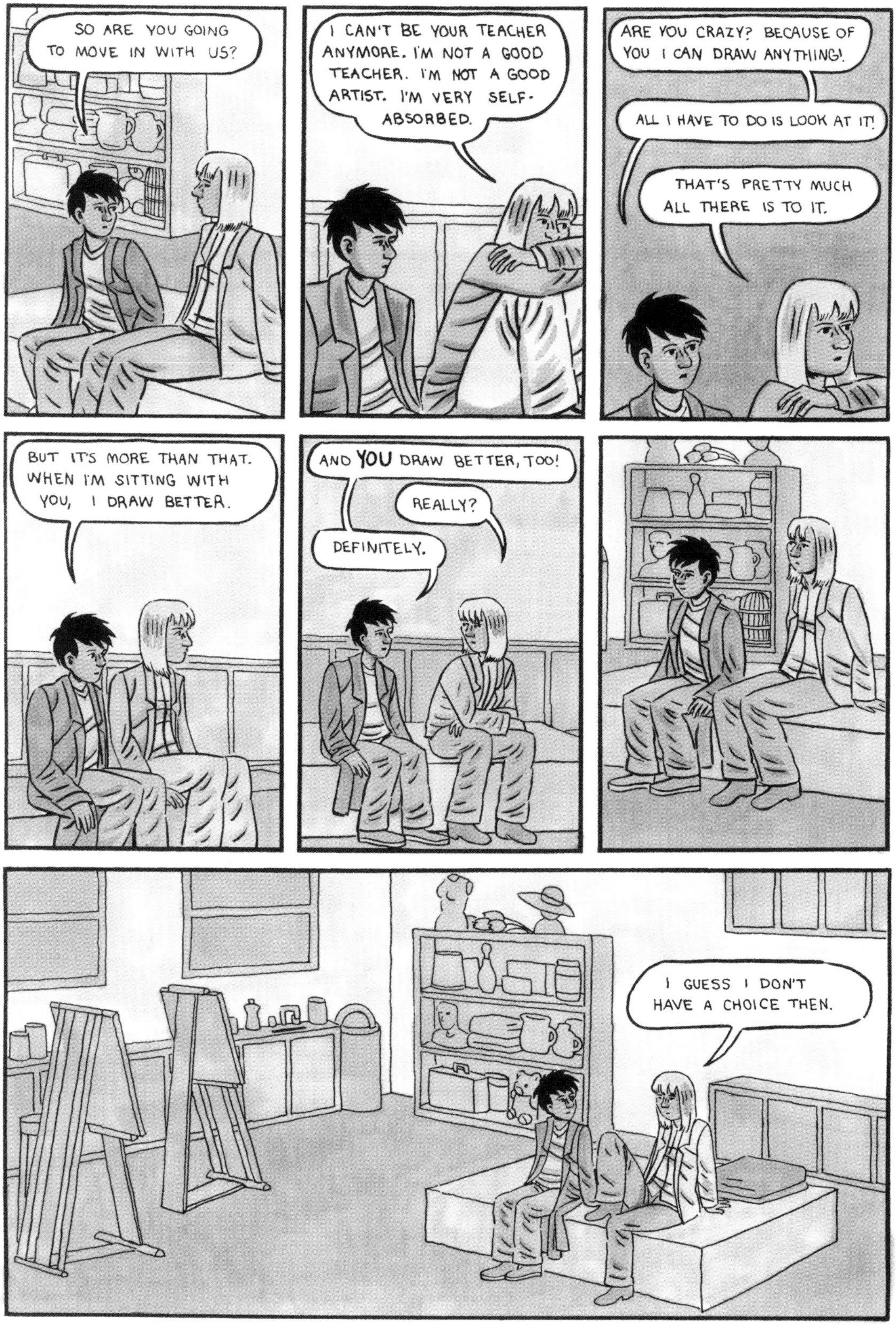
SO ARE YOU GOING TO MOVE IN WITH US?
I CAN'T BE YOUR TEACHER ANYMORE. I'M NOT A GOOD TEACHER. I'M NOT A GOOD ARTIST. I'M VERY SELF-ABSORBED.
ARE YOU CRAZY? BECAUSE OF YOU I CAN DRAW ANYTHING!
ALL I HAVE TO DO IS LOOK AT IT!
THAT'S PRETTY MUCH ALL THERE IS TO IT.
BUT IT'S MORE THAN THAT. WHEN I'M SITTING WITH YOU, I DRAW BETTER.
AND YOU DRAW BETTER, TOO!
REALLY?
DEFINITELY.
I GUESS I DON'T HAVE A CHOICE THEN.

Martin Cendreda

Martin Cendreda was born and raised in the Silverlake area of Los Angeles, California. As a youth, he would spend hours reading through the comics on the spinner racks at the local Safeway, while his Mom shopped for his favorite brand name cereal. As a teen, he would take the bus to the comic book shop, Golden Apple and return home with the latest issues of *X-Men* and *Alpha Flight.* Slightly more emboldened and hungry for adventure, he began frequenting the monthly Sunday comic conventions at the world famous Ambassador Hotel. He would come home with copies of *Weirdo* and R. Crumb comics hidden discreetly between the latest issues of *New Mutants* and *Teenage Mutant Ninja Turtles*, so as not to alarm his mother or grandparents (his roommates at the time). Twenty some-odd years later, the *Alpha Flight* and *Weirdo* comics have a happy home in white long-boxes, but the *Teenage Mutant Ninja Turtle* comics have mysteriously disappeared. To his dismay, demolition of the Ambassador Hotel was completed in 2006.

Cendreda's work has appeared in *Giant Robot, Vice, Dazed and Confused, Peko-Peko, Sturgeon White Moss, Hi-Horse Omnibus, Mome,* and his own series *Dang!* He works part-time in the animation industry, and devotes the rest of his time to comics. He currently lives in Los Angeles, with his wife Jenny, and their two cats. His mother and surviving grandmother live next door.

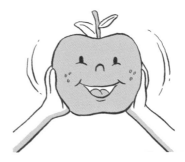

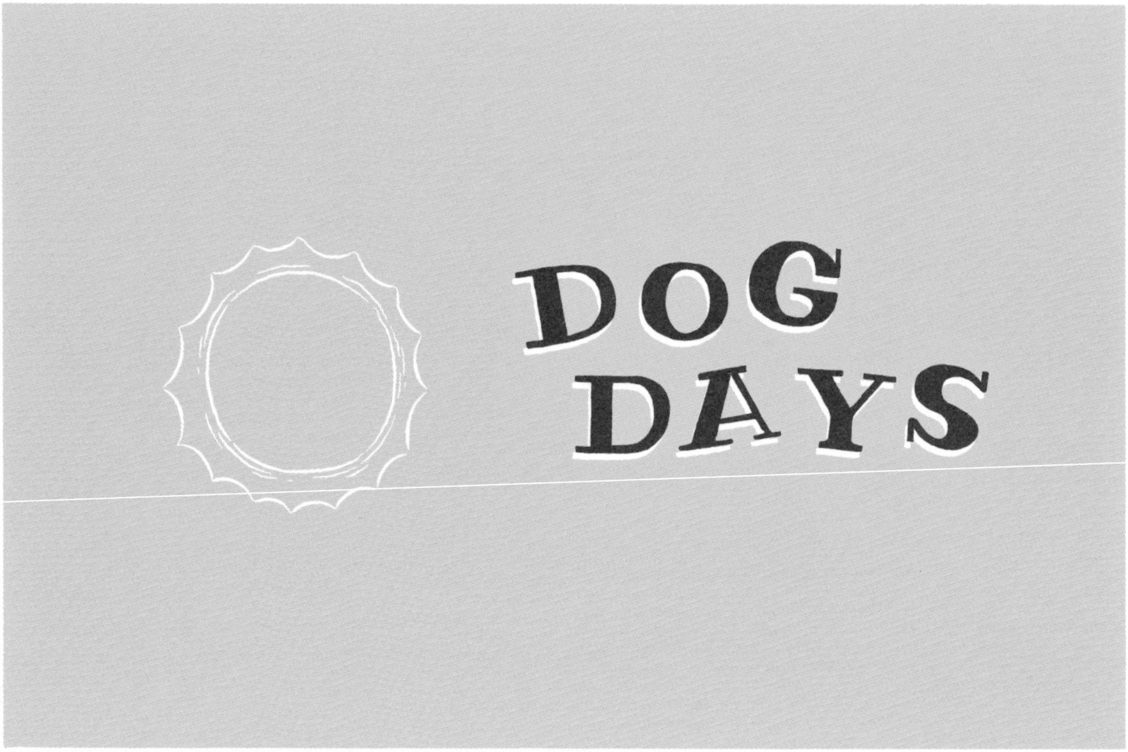
DOG
DAYS

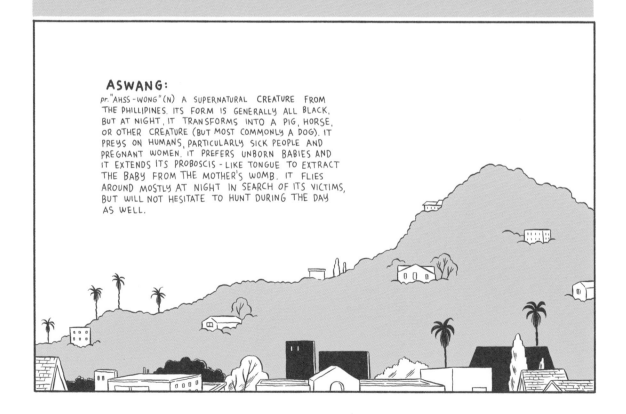

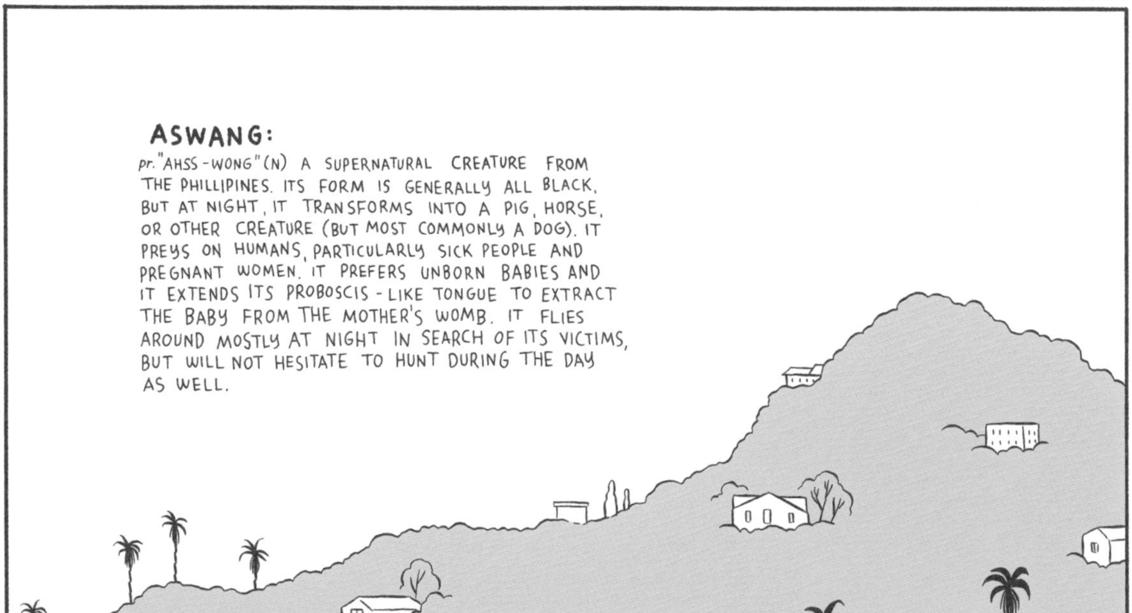
ASWANG:
pr."AHSS-WONG"(N) A SUPERNATURAL CREATURE FROM THE PHILLIPINES. ITS FORM IS GENERALLY ALL BLACK, BUT AT NIGHT, IT TRANSFORMS INTO A PIG, HORSE, OR OTHER CREATURE (BUT MOST COMMONLY A DOG). IT PREYS ON HUMANS, PARTICULARLY SICK PEOPLE AND PREGNANT WOMEN. IT PREFERS UNBORN BABIES AND IT EXTENDS ITS PROBOSCIS-LIKE TONGUE TO EXTRACT THE BABY FROM THE MOTHER'S WOMB. IT FLIES AROUND MOSTLY AT NIGHT IN SEARCH OF ITS VICTIMS, BUT WILL NOT HESITATE TO HUNT DURING THE DAY AS WELL.

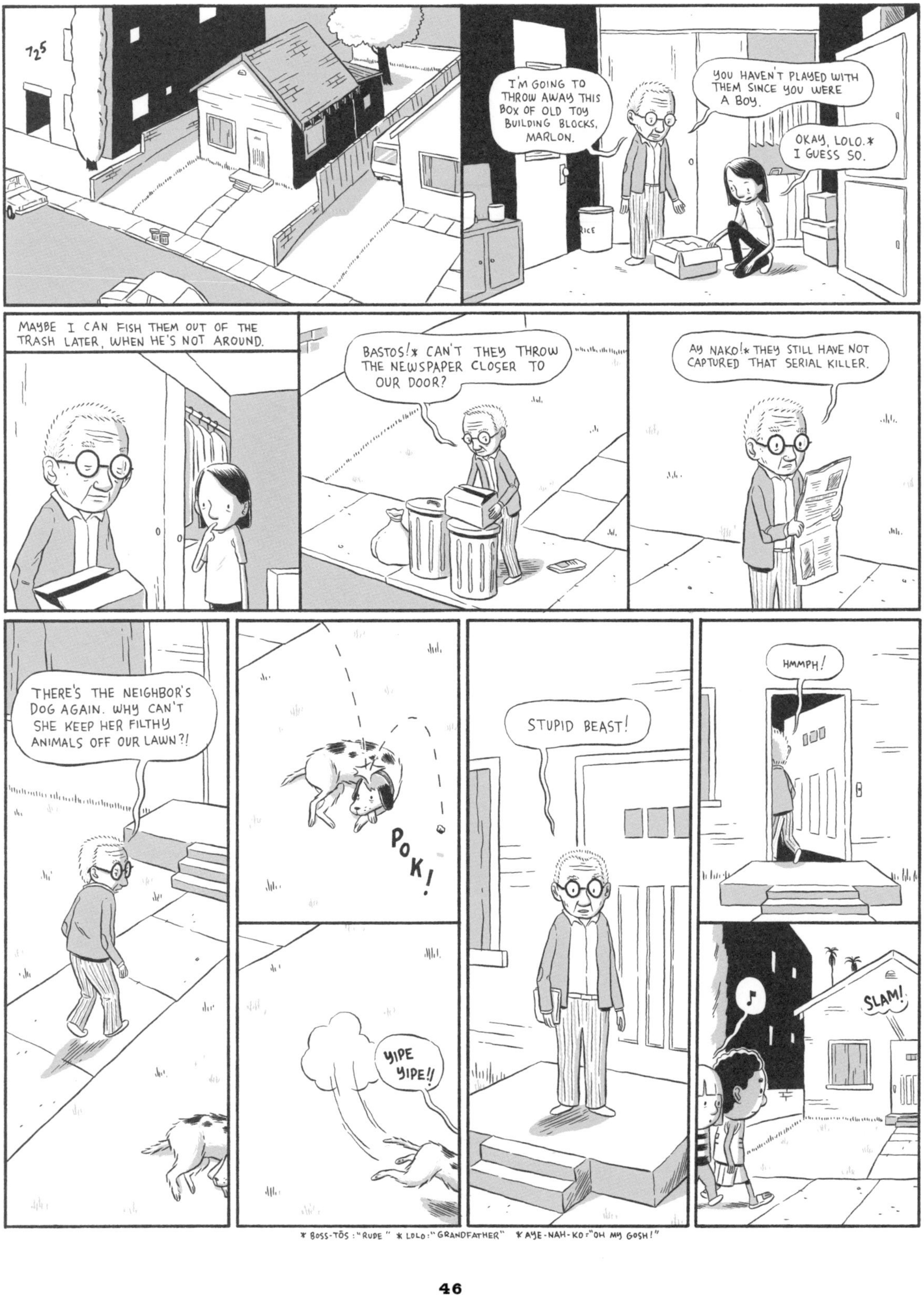
725
I'M GOING TO THROW AWAY THIS BOX OF OLD TOY BUILDING BLOCKS, MARLON.
YOU HAVEN'T PLAYED WITH THEM SINCE YOU WERE A BOY.
OKAY, LOLO.* I GUESS SO.
RICE
MAYBE I CAN FISH THEM OUT OF THE TRASH LATER, WHEN HE'S NOT AROUND.
BASTOS!* CAN'T THEY THROW THE NEWSPAPER CLOSER TO OUR DOOR?
AY NAKO!* THEY STILL HAVE NOT CAPTURED THAT SERIAL KILLER.
THERE'S THE NEIGHBOR'S DOG AGAIN. WHY CAN'T SHE KEEP HER FILTHY ANIMALS OFF OUR LAWN?!
POK!
YIPE YIPE!!
STUPID BEAST!
HMMPH!
♪
SLAM!

* BOSS-TŌS : "RUDE" * LOLO: "GRANDFATHER" * AYE-NAH-KO: "OH MY GOSH!"

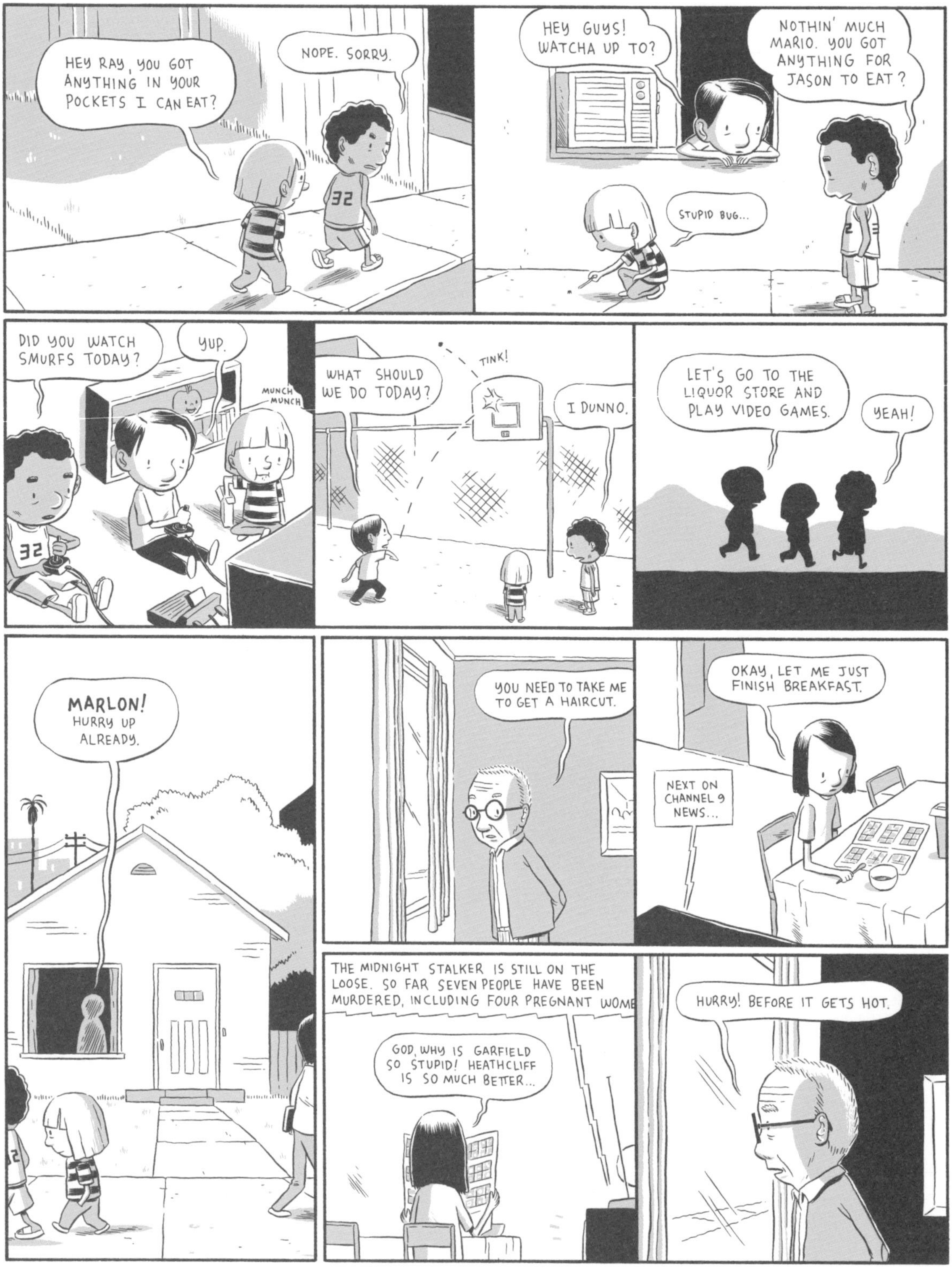
HEY RAY, YOU GOT ANYTHING IN YOUR POCKETS I CAN EAT?
NOPE. SORRY.
HEY GUYS! WATCHA UP TO?
NOTHIN' MUCH MARIO. YOU GOT ANYTHING FOR JASON TO EAT?
STUPID BUG...
DID YOU WATCH SMURFS TODAY?
YUP.
MUNCH MUNCH
TINK!
WHAT SHOULD WE DO TODAY?
I DUNNO.
LET'S GO TO THE LIQUOR STORE AND PLAY VIDEO GAMES.
YEAH!
MARLON! HURRY UP ALREADY.
YOU NEED TO TAKE ME TO GET A HAIRCUT.
OKAY, LET ME JUST FINISH BREAKFAST.
NEXT ON CHANNEL 9 NEWS...
THE MIDNIGHT STALKER IS STILL ON THE LOOSE. SO FAR SEVEN PEOPLE HAVE BEEN MURDERED, INCLUDING FOUR PREGNANT WOME
GOD, WHY IS GARFIELD SO STUPID! HEATHCLIFF IS SO MUCH BETTER...
HURRY! BEFORE IT GETS HOT.

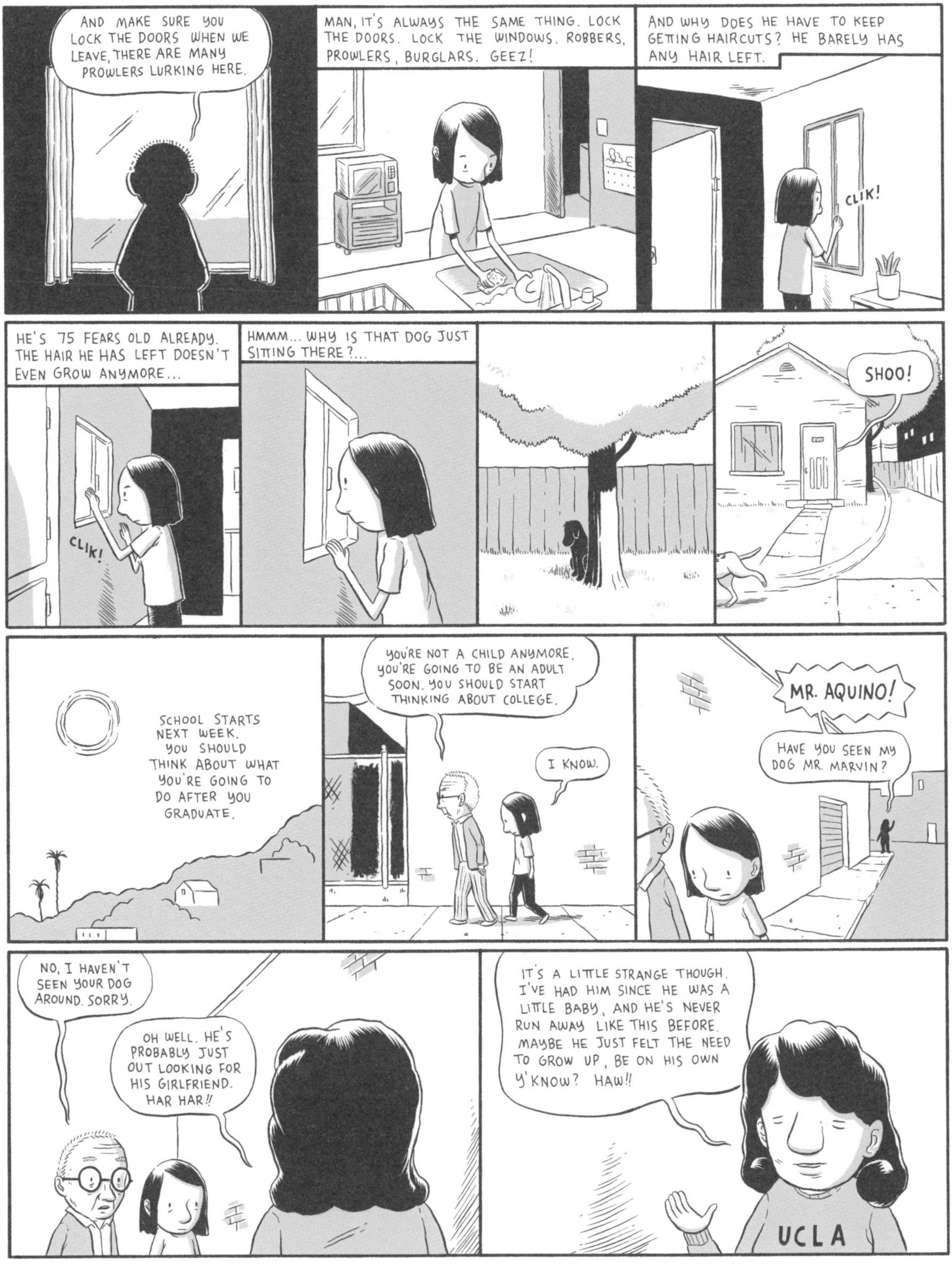
AND MAKE SURE YOU LOCK THE DOORS WHEN WE LEAVE, THERE ARE MANY PROWLERS LURKING HERE.
MAN, IT'S ALWAYS THE SAME THING. LOCK THE DOORS. LOCK THE WINDOWS. ROBBERS, PROWLERS, BURGLARS. GEEZ!
AND WHY DOES HE HAVE TO KEEP GETTING HAIRCUTS? HE BARELY HAS ANY HAIR LEFT.
CLIK!
HE'S 75 FEARS OLD ALREADY. THE HAIR HE HAS LEFT DOESN'T EVEN GROW ANYMORE...
CLIK!
HMMM... WHY IS THAT DOG JUST SITTING THERE?...
SHOO!
SCHOOL STARTS NEXT WEEK. YOU SHOULD THINK ABOUT WHAT YOU'RE GOING TO DO AFTER YOU GRADUATE.
YOU'RE NOT A CHILD ANYMORE. YOU'RE GOING TO BE AN ADULT SOON. YOU SHOULD START THINKING ABOUT COLLEGE.
I KNOW.
MR. AQUINO!
HAVE YOU SEEN MY DOG MR. MARVIN?
NO, I HAVEN'T SEEN YOUR DOG AROUND. SORRY.
OH WELL. HE'S PROBABLY JUST OUT LOOKING FOR HIS GIRLFRIEND. HAR HAR!!
IT'S A LITTLE STRANGE THOUGH. I'VE HAD HIM SINCE HE WAS A LITTLE BABY, AND HE'S NEVER RUN AWAY LIKE THIS BEFORE. MAYBE HE JUST FELT THE NEED TO GROW UP, BE ON HIS OWN Y'KNOW? HAW!!
UCLA

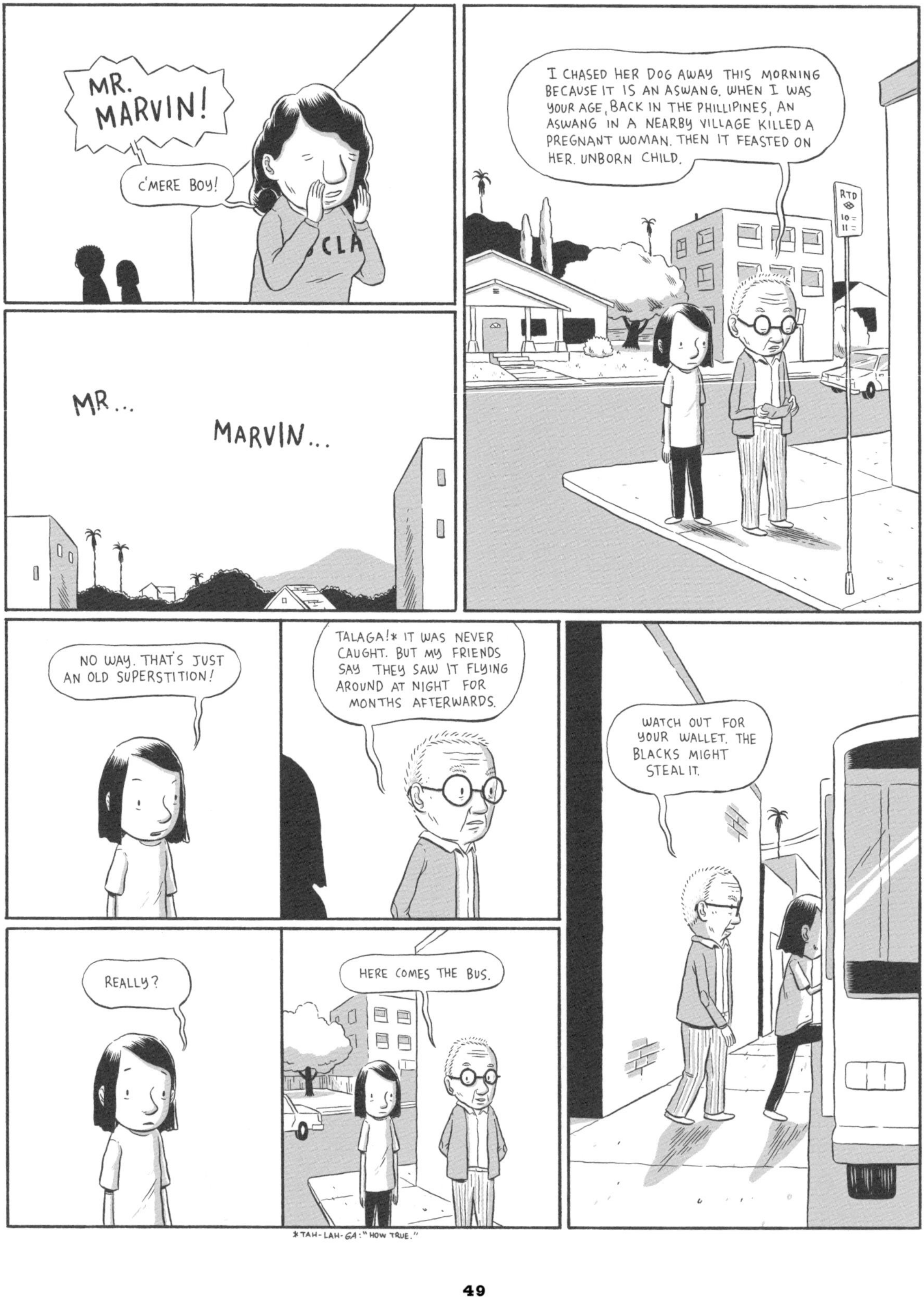
MR. MARVIN!
C'MERE BOY!
UCLA
MR...
MARVIN...
I CHASED HER DOG AWAY THIS MORNING BECAUSE IT IS AN ASWANG. WHEN I WAS YOUR AGE, BACK IN THE PHILLIPINES, AN ASWANG IN A NEARBY VILLAGE KILLED A PREGNANT WOMAN. THEN IT FEASTED ON HER UNBORN CHILD.
RTD
NO WAY. THAT'S JUST AN OLD SUPERSTITION!
TALAGA!* IT WAS NEVER CAUGHT. BUT MY FRIENDS SAY THEY SAW IT FLYING AROUND AT NIGHT FOR MONTHS AFTERWARDS.
WATCH OUT FOR YOUR WALLET. THE BLACKS MIGHT STEAL IT.
REALLY?
HERE COMES THE BUS.

*TAH-LAH-GA: "HOW TRUE."

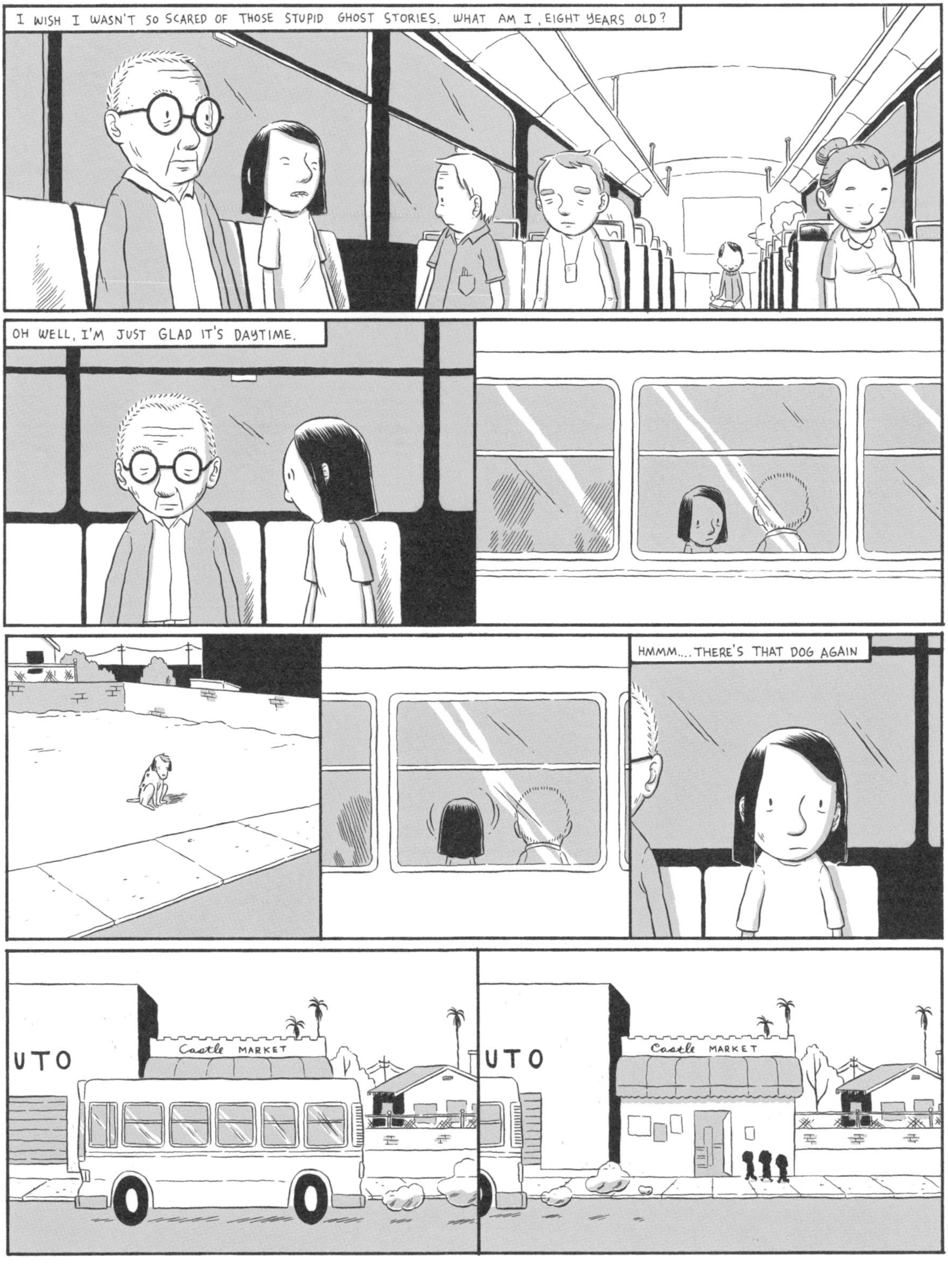
I WISH I WASN'T SO SCARED OF THOSE STUPID GHOST STORIES. WHAT AM I, EIGHT YEARS OLD?
OH WELL, I'M JUST GLAD IT'S DAYTIME.
HMMM.... THERE'S THAT DOG AGAIN
UTO
Castle MARKET
UTO
Castle MARKET

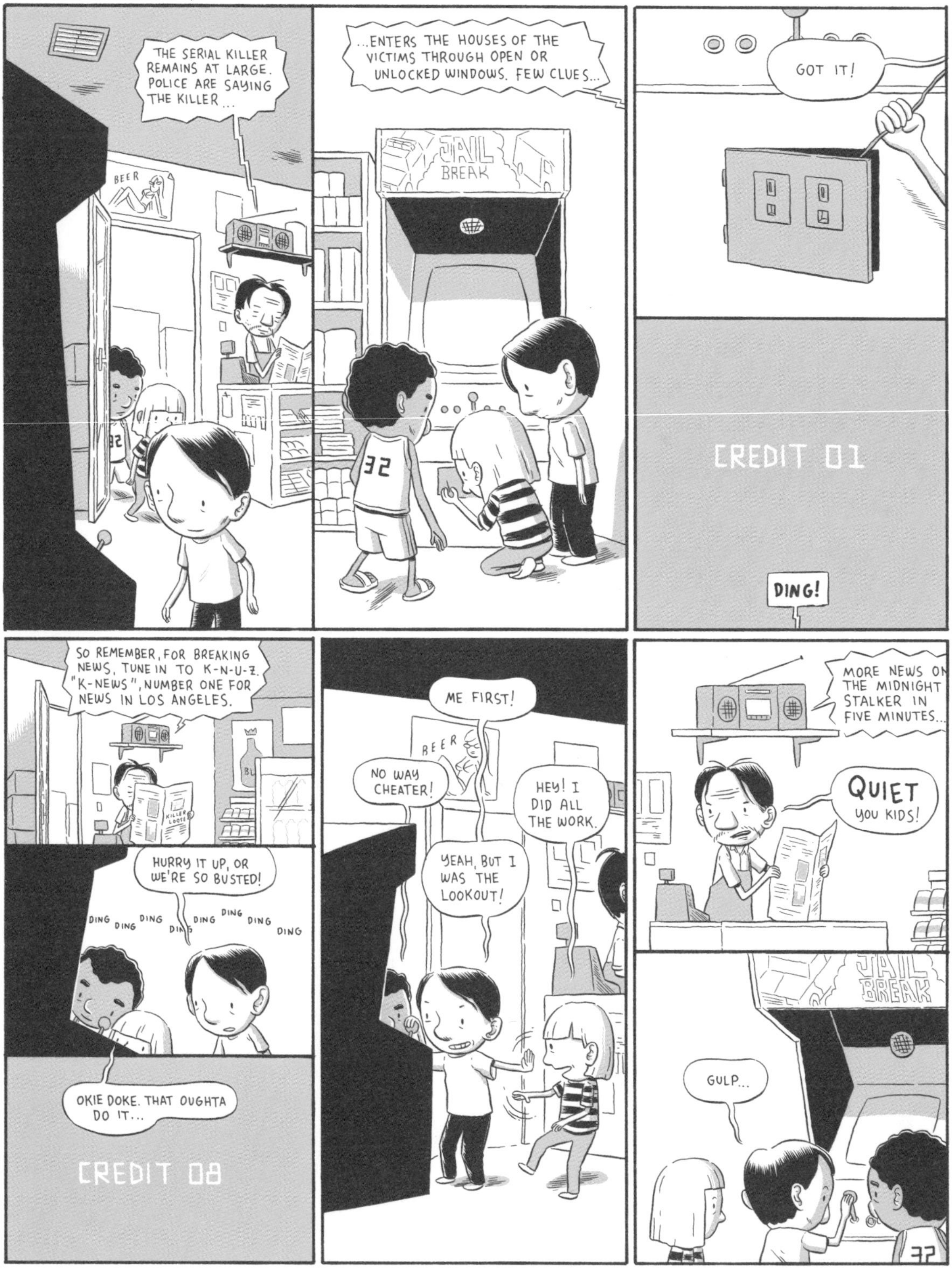

THE SERIAL KILLER REMAINS AT LARGE. POLICE ARE SAYING THE KILLER...
BEER
...ENTERS THE HOUSES OF THE VICTIMS THROUGH OPEN OR UNLOCKED WINDOWS. FEW CLUES...
JAIL BREAK
32
GOT IT!
CREDIT 01
DING!
SO REMEMBER, FOR BREAKING NEWS, TUNE IN TO K-N-U-Z. "K-NEWS", NUMBER ONE FOR NEWS IN LOS ANGELES.
KILLER LOOSE
HURRY IT UP, OR WE'RE SO BUSTED!
DING DING DING DING DING DING DING DING
OKIE DOKE. THAT OUGHTA DO IT...
CREDIT 08
ME FIRST!
NO WAY CHEATER!
HEY! I DID ALL THE WORK.
YEAH, BUT I WAS THE LOOKOUT!
MORE NEWS ON THE MIDNIGHT STALKER IN FIVE MINUTES...
QUIET you KIDS!
JAIL BREAK
GULP...
32

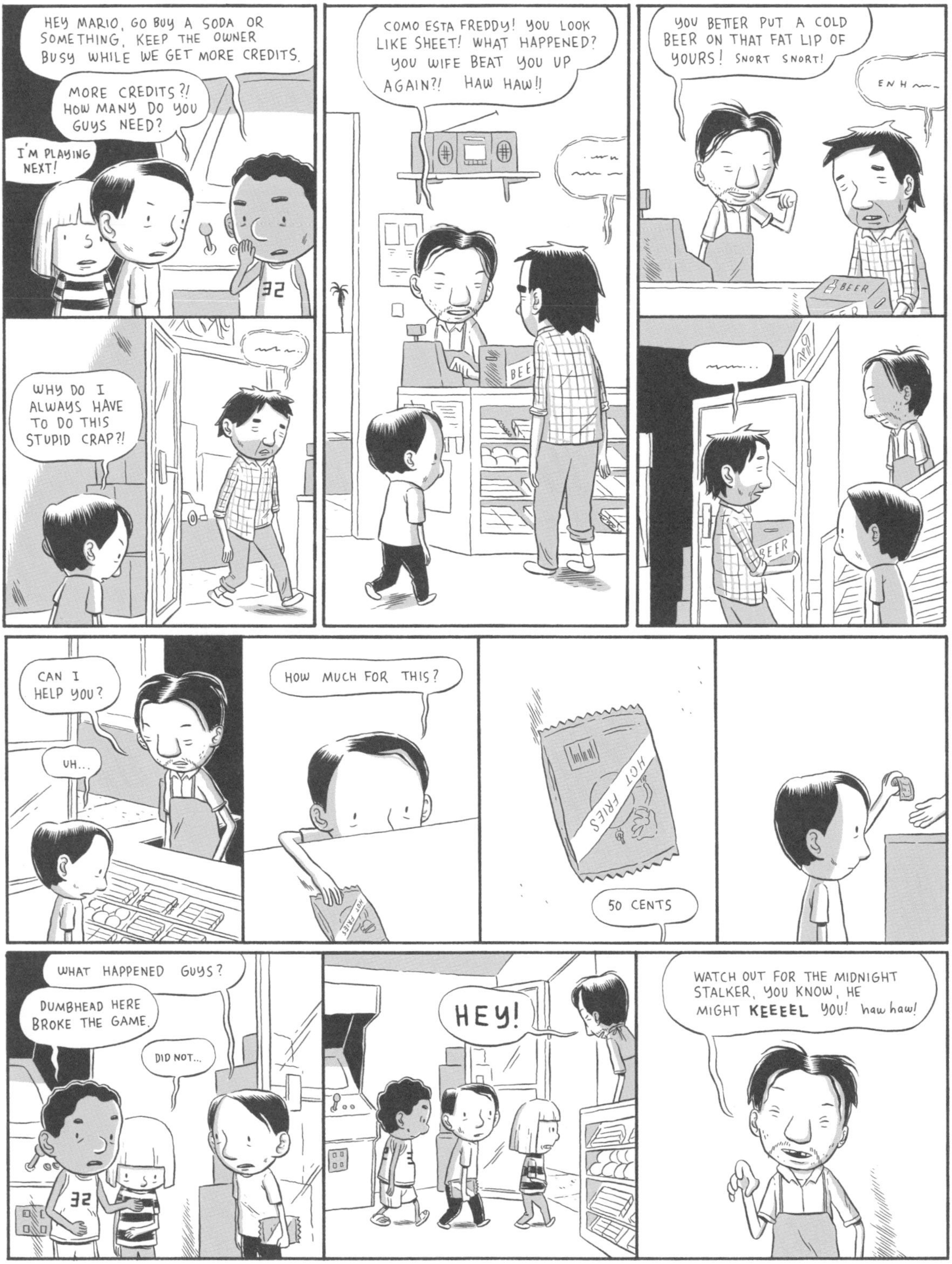
HEY MARIO, GO BUY A SODA OR SOMETHING, KEEP THE OWNER BUSY WHILE WE GET MORE CREDITS.
MORE CREDITS?! HOW MANY DO YOU GUYS NEED?
I'M PLAYING NEXT!
32
COMO ESTA FREDDY! YOU LOOK LIKE SHEET! WHAT HAPPENED? YOU WIFE BEAT YOU UP AGAIN?! HAW HAW!!
BEER
YOU BETTER PUT A COLD BEER ON THAT FAT LIP OF YOURS! SNORT SNORT!
ENH
BEER
WHY DO I ALWAYS HAVE TO DO THIS STUPID CRAP?!
BEER
CAN I HELP YOU?
UH...
HOW MUCH FOR THIS?
HOT FRIES
HOT FRIES
50 CENTS
WHAT HAPPENED GUYS?
DUMBHEAD HERE BROKE THE GAME.
DID NOT...
32
HEY!
WATCH OUT FOR THE MIDNIGHT STALKER, YOU KNOW, HE MIGHT **KEEEEL** YOU! haw haw!

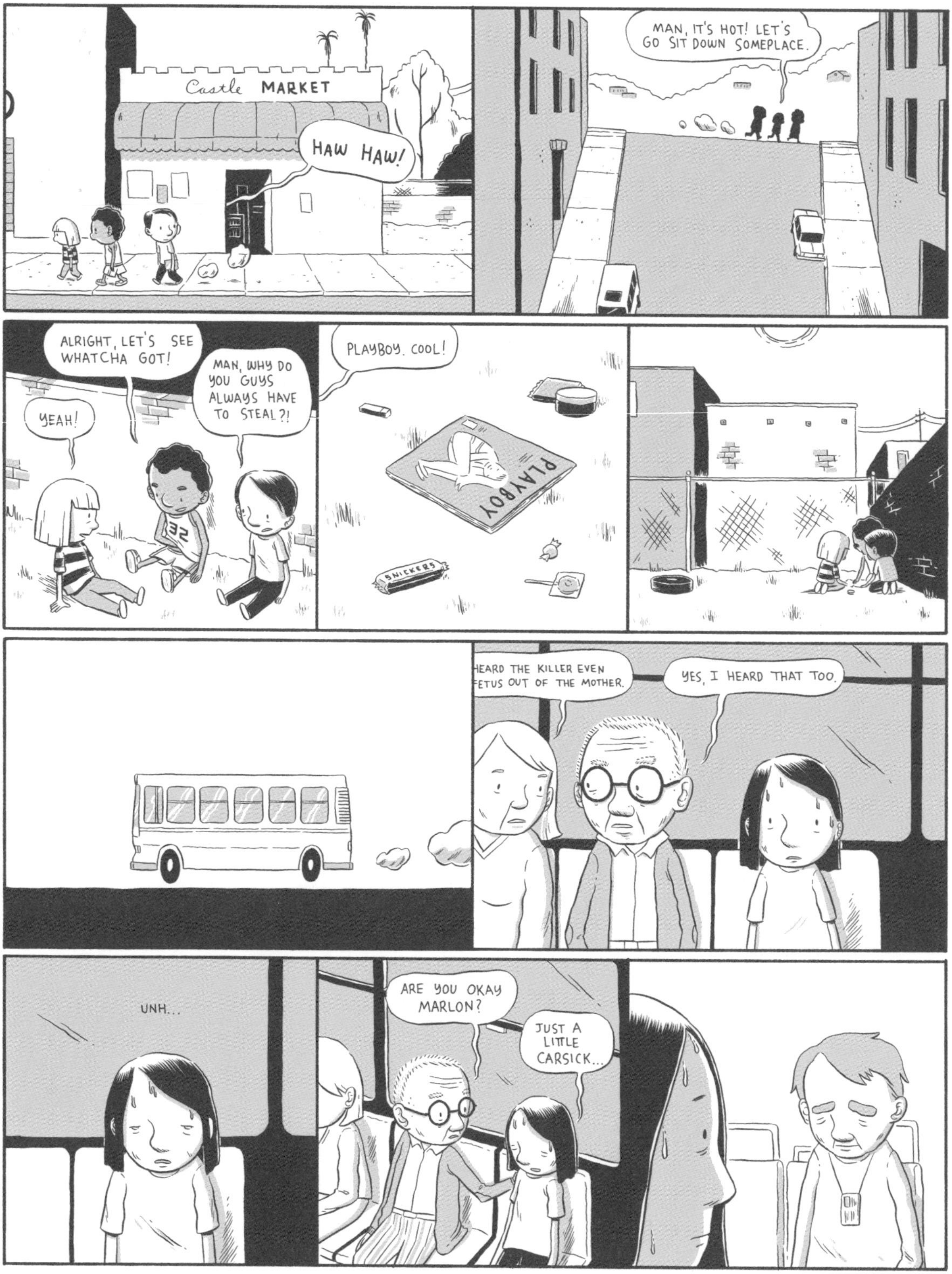

Castle MARKET
HAW HAW!
MAN, IT'S HOT! LET'S GO SIT DOWN SOMEPLACE.
ALRIGHT, LET'S SEE WHATCHA GOT!
YEAH!
MAN, WHY DO YOU GUYS ALWAYS HAVE TO STEAL?!
PLAYBOY. COOL!
PLAYBOY
SNICKERS
HEARD THE KILLER EVEN
FETUS OUT OF THE MOTHER.
YES, I HEARD THAT TOO.
UNH...
ARE YOU OKAY MARLON?
JUST A LITTLE CARSICK...

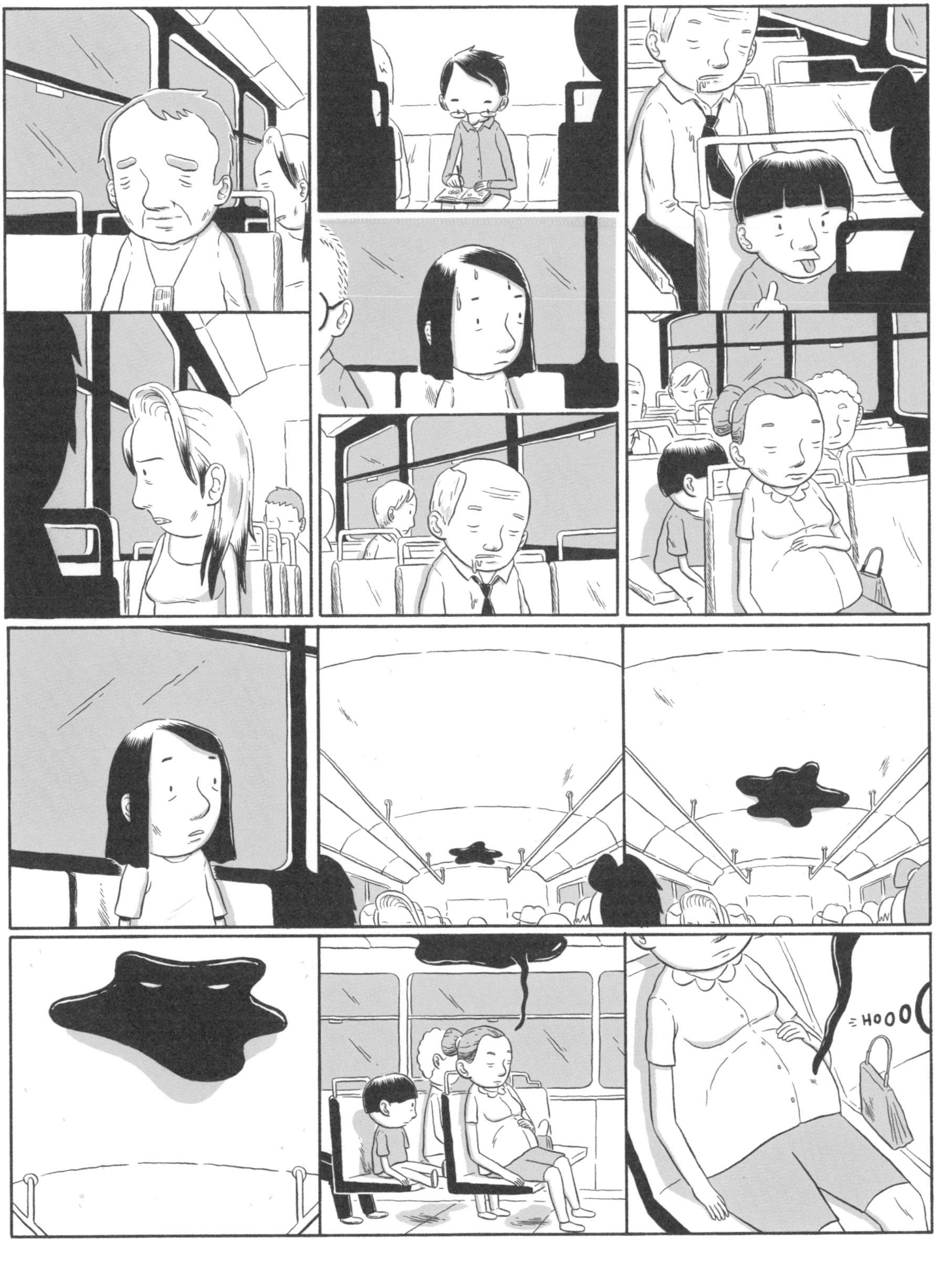
HOOO

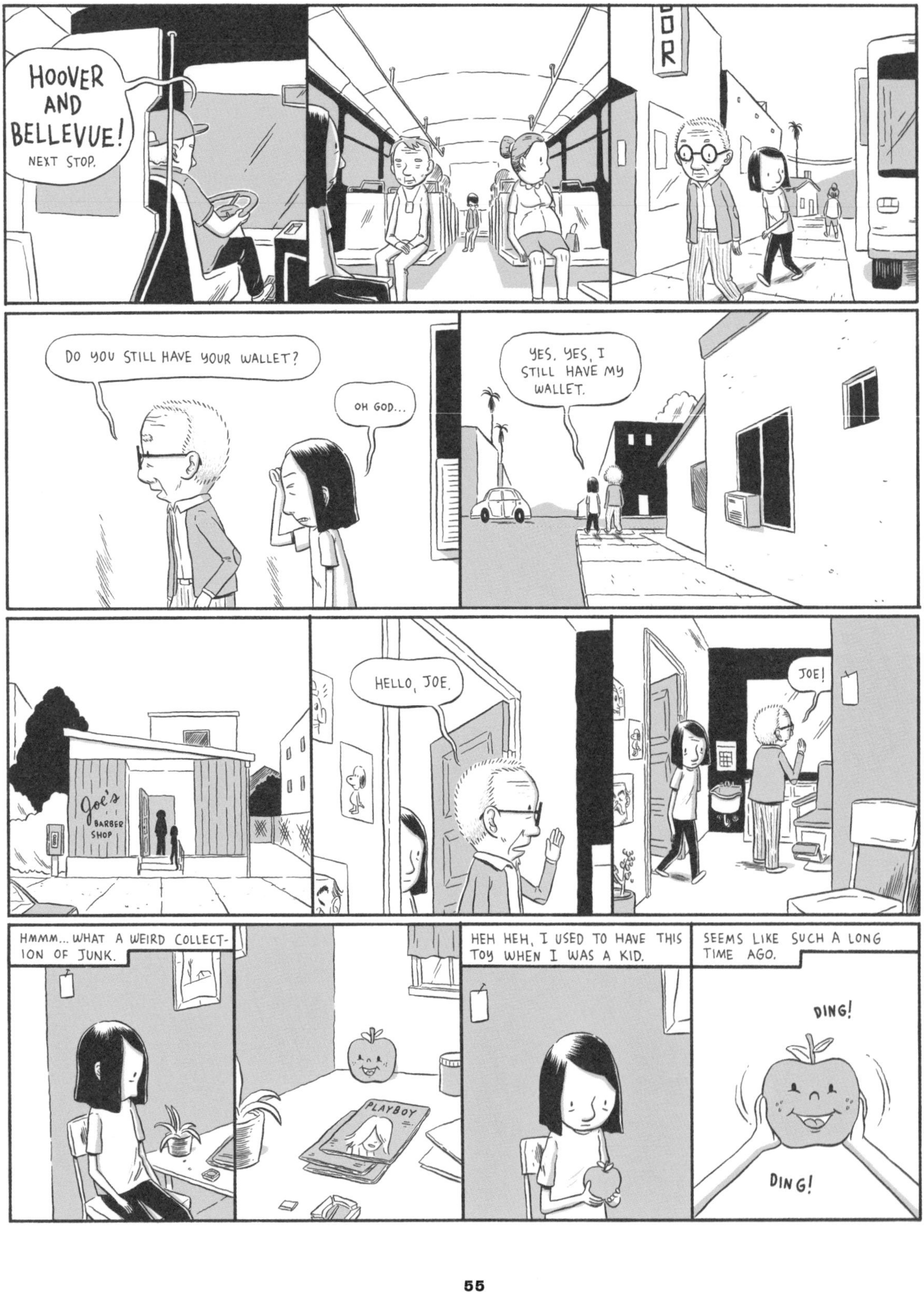
HOOVER AND BELLEVUE! NEXT STOP.
BOOR
DO YOU STILL HAVE YOUR WALLET?
OH GOD...
YES. YES. I STILL HAVE MY WALLET.
Joe's BARBER SHOP
HELLO, JOE.
JOE!
HMMM... WHAT A WEIRD COLLECT-ION OF JUNK.
PLAYBOY
HEH HEH, I USED TO HAVE THIS TOY WHEN I WAS A KID.
SEEMS LIKE SUCH A LONG TIME AGO.
DING!
DING!

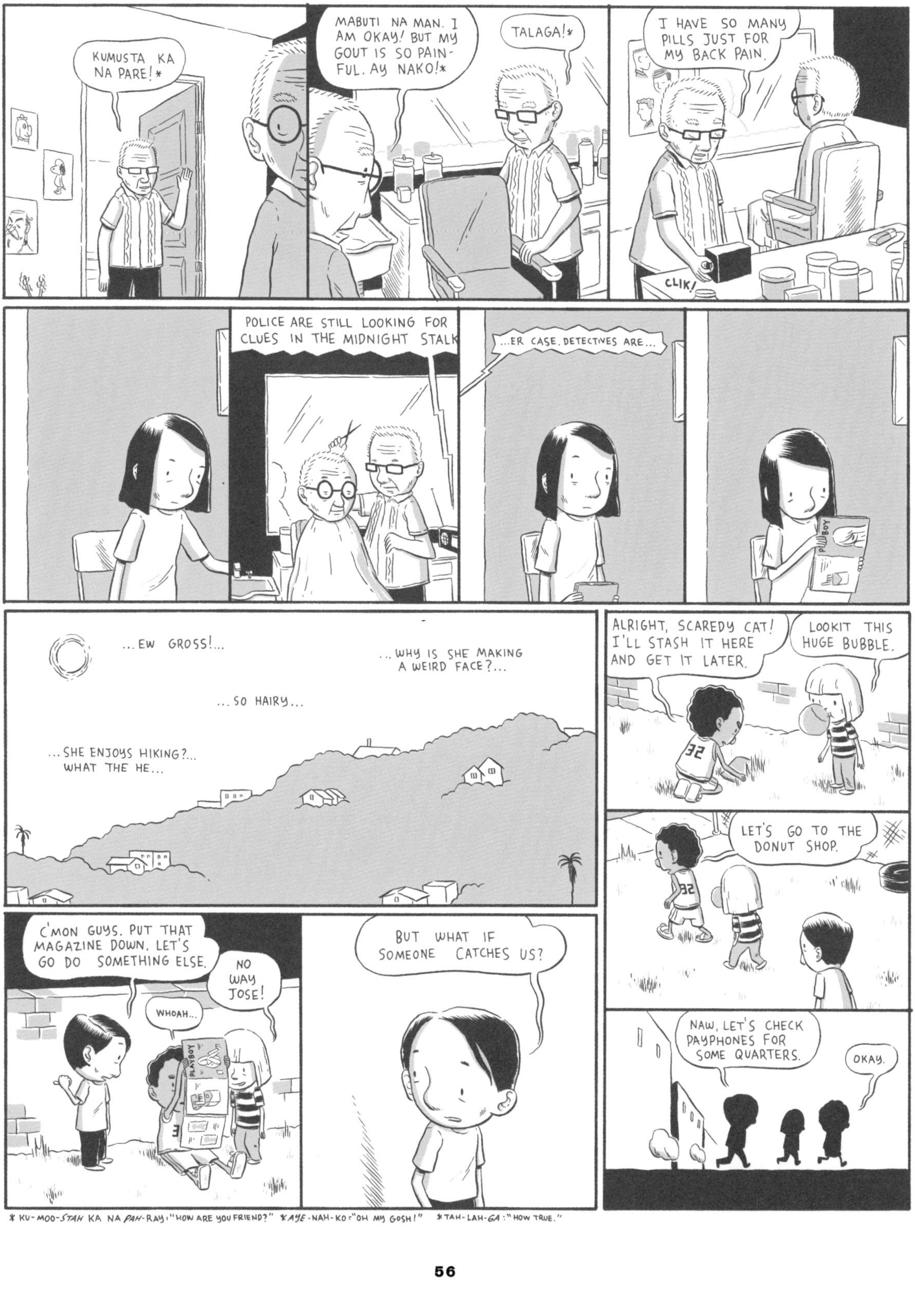
KUMUSTA KA NA PARE!*
MABUTI NA MAN. I AM OKAY! BUT MY GOUT IS SO PAINFUL. AY NAKO!*
TALAGA!*
I HAVE SO MANY PILLS JUST FOR MY BACK PAIN.
CLIK!
POLICE ARE STILL LOOKING FOR CLUES IN THE MIDNIGHT STALK
...ER CASE. DETECTIVES ARE...
PLAYBOY
...EW GROSS!...
...WHY IS SHE MAKING A WEIRD FACE?...
...SO HAIRY...
...SHE ENJOYS HIKING?... WHAT THE HE...
ALRIGHT, SCAREDY CAT! I'LL STASH IT HERE AND GET IT LATER.
LOOKIT THIS HUGE BUBBLE.
32
LET'S GO TO THE DONUT SHOP.
32
C'MON GUYS. PUT THAT MAGAZINE DOWN. LET'S GO DO SOMETHING ELSE.
NO WAY JOSE!
WHOAH...
PLAYBOY
BUT WHAT IF SOMEONE CATCHES US?
NAW, LET'S CHECK PAYPHONES FOR SOME QUARTERS.
OKAY.

* KU-MOO-*STAH* KA NA *PAH*-RAY: "HOW ARE YOU FRIEND?" *AYE*-NAH-KO: "OH MY GOSH!" * TAH-LAH-*GA*: "HOW TRUE."

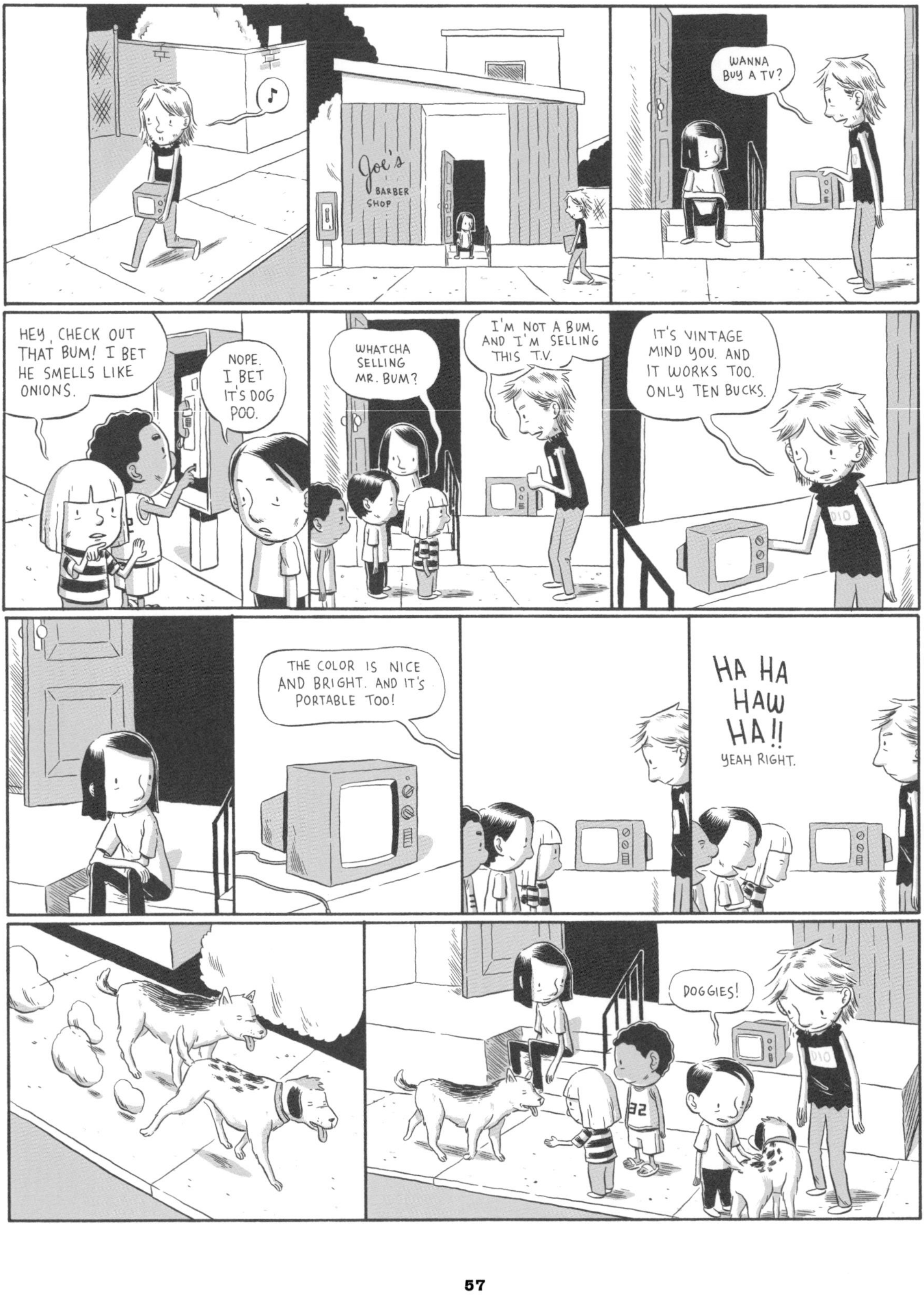
Joe's
BARBER SHOP
WANNA BUY A TV?
HEY, CHECK OUT THAT BUM! I BET HE SMELLS LIKE ONIONS.
NOPE. I BET IT'S DOG POO.
WHATCHA SELLING MR. BUM?
I'M NOT A BUM. AND I'M SELLING THIS T.V.
IT'S VINTAGE MIND YOU. AND IT WORKS TOO. ONLY TEN BUCKS.
DIO
THE COLOR IS NICE AND BRIGHT. AND IT'S PORTABLE TOO!
HA HA HAW HA!!
YEAH RIGHT.
DOGGIES!
32
DIO

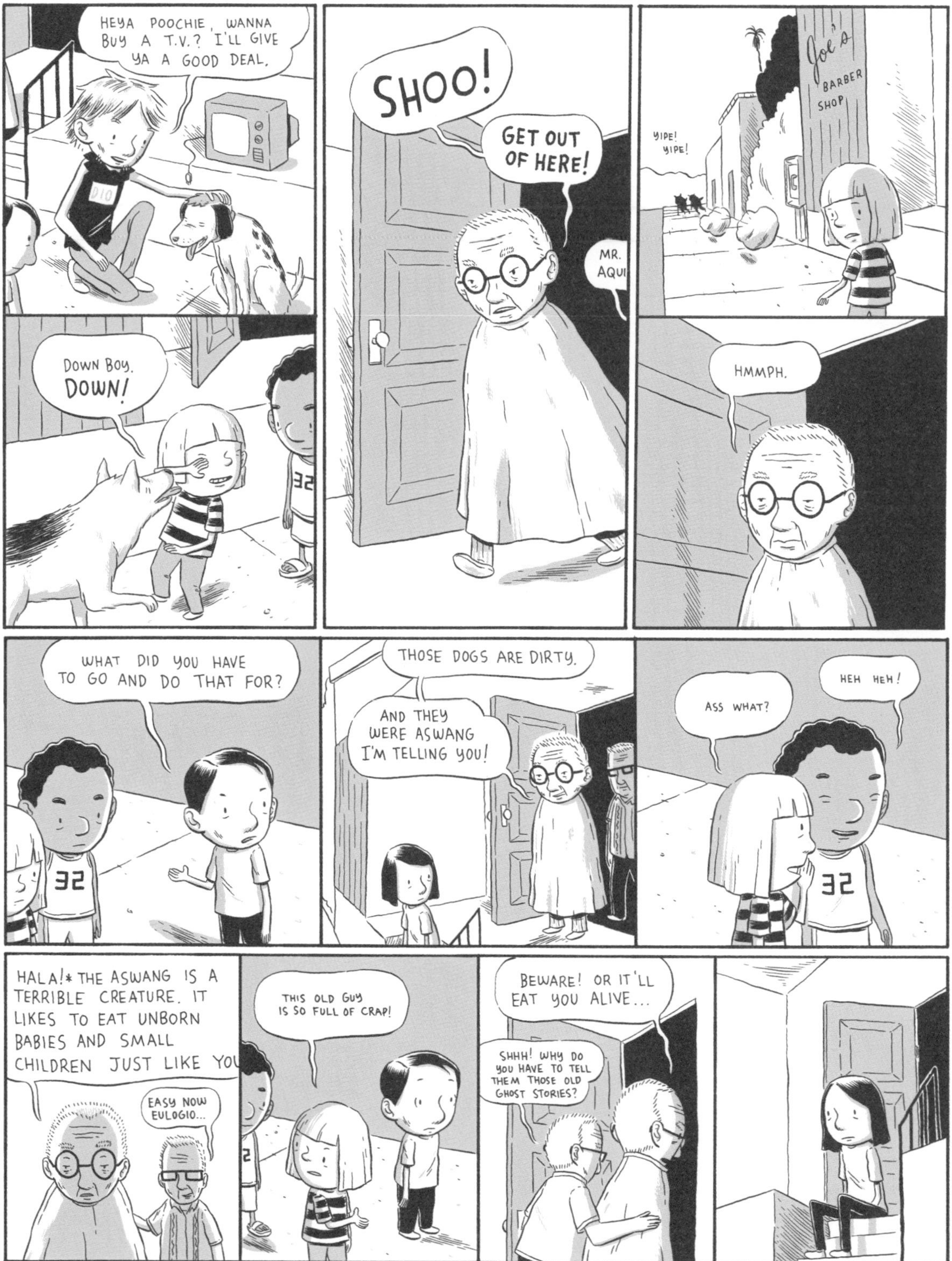
HEYA POOCHIE, WANNA BUY A T.V.? I'LL GIVE YA A GOOD DEAL.
DIO
DOWN BOY. DOWN!
32
SHOO!
GET OUT OF HERE!
MR. AQUI
JOE'S BARBER SHOP
YIPE! YIPE!
HMMPH.
WHAT DID YOU HAVE TO GO AND DO THAT FOR?
32
THOSE DOGS ARE DIRTY.
AND THEY WERE ASWANG I'M TELLING YOU!
ASS WHAT?
HEH HEH!
32
HALA!* THE ASWANG IS A TERRIBLE CREATURE. IT LIKES TO EAT UNBORN BABIES AND SMALL CHILDREN JUST LIKE YOU
EASY NOW EULOGIO...
THIS OLD GUY IS SO FULL OF CRAP!
BEWARE! OR IT'LL EAT YOU ALIVE...
SHHH! WHY DO YOU HAVE TO TELL THEM THOSE OLD GHOST STORIES?

*HAH-LAH: "BEWARE, WATCH OUT"

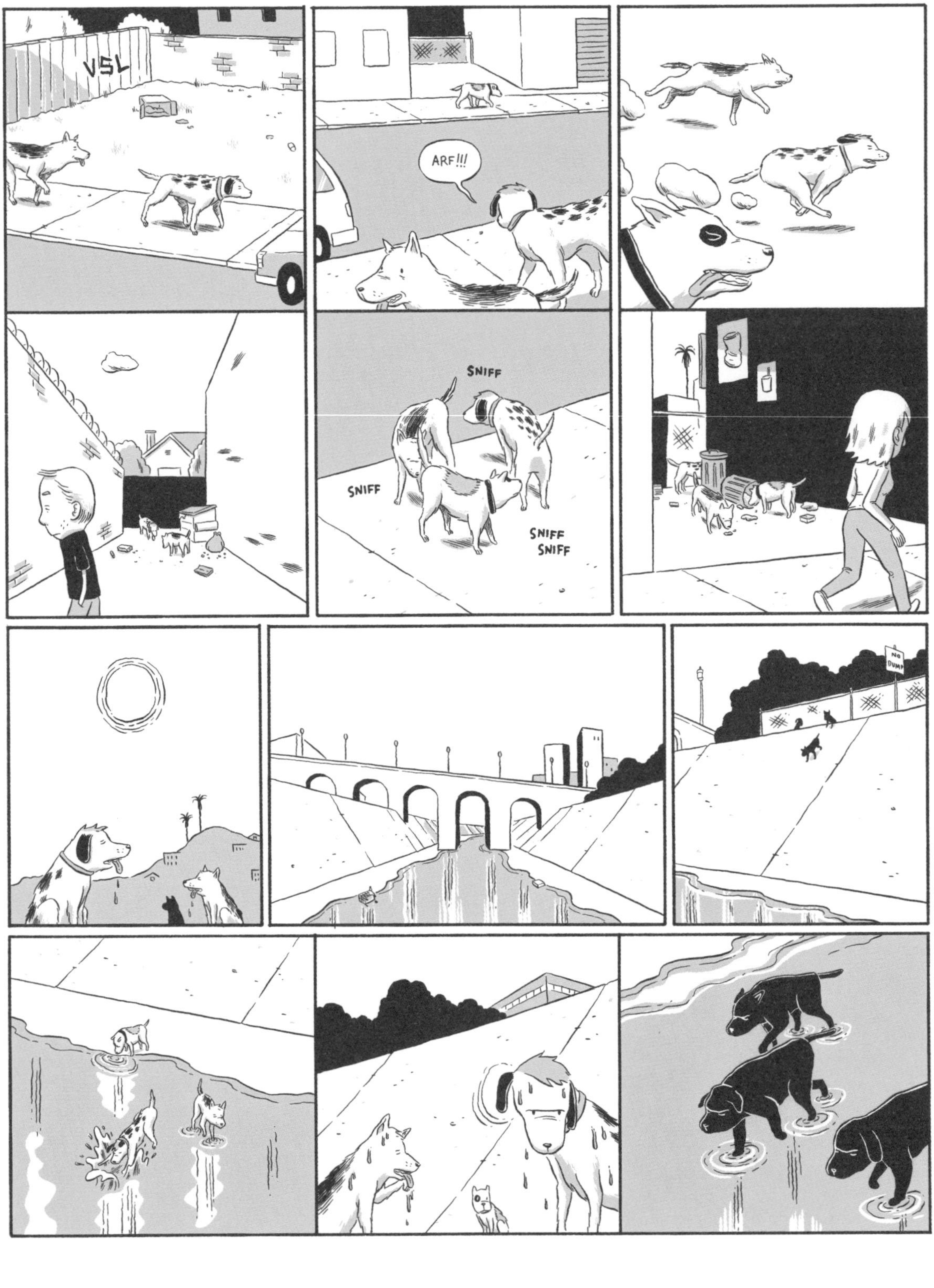
VSL
ARF!!!
SNIFF
SNIFF
SNIFF
SNIFF
NO DUMP

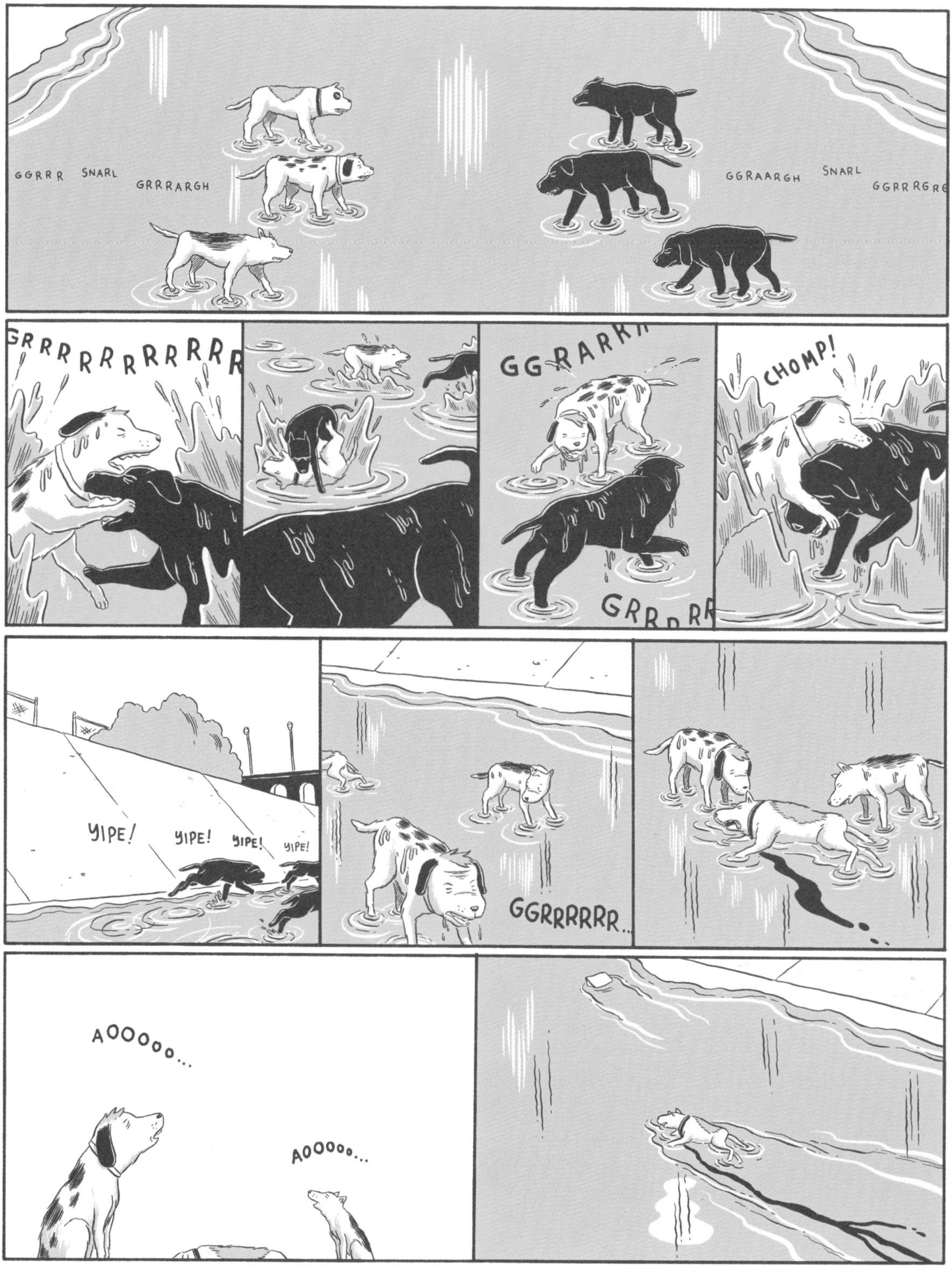
GGRRR
SNARL
GRRRARGH
GGRAARGH
SNARL
GGRRRGRG
GRRRRRRRRRRR
GGRARR
GRRRRR
CHOMP!
YIPE!
YIPE!
YIPE!
YIPE!
GGRRRRRRR...
AOOOOO...
AOOOOO...

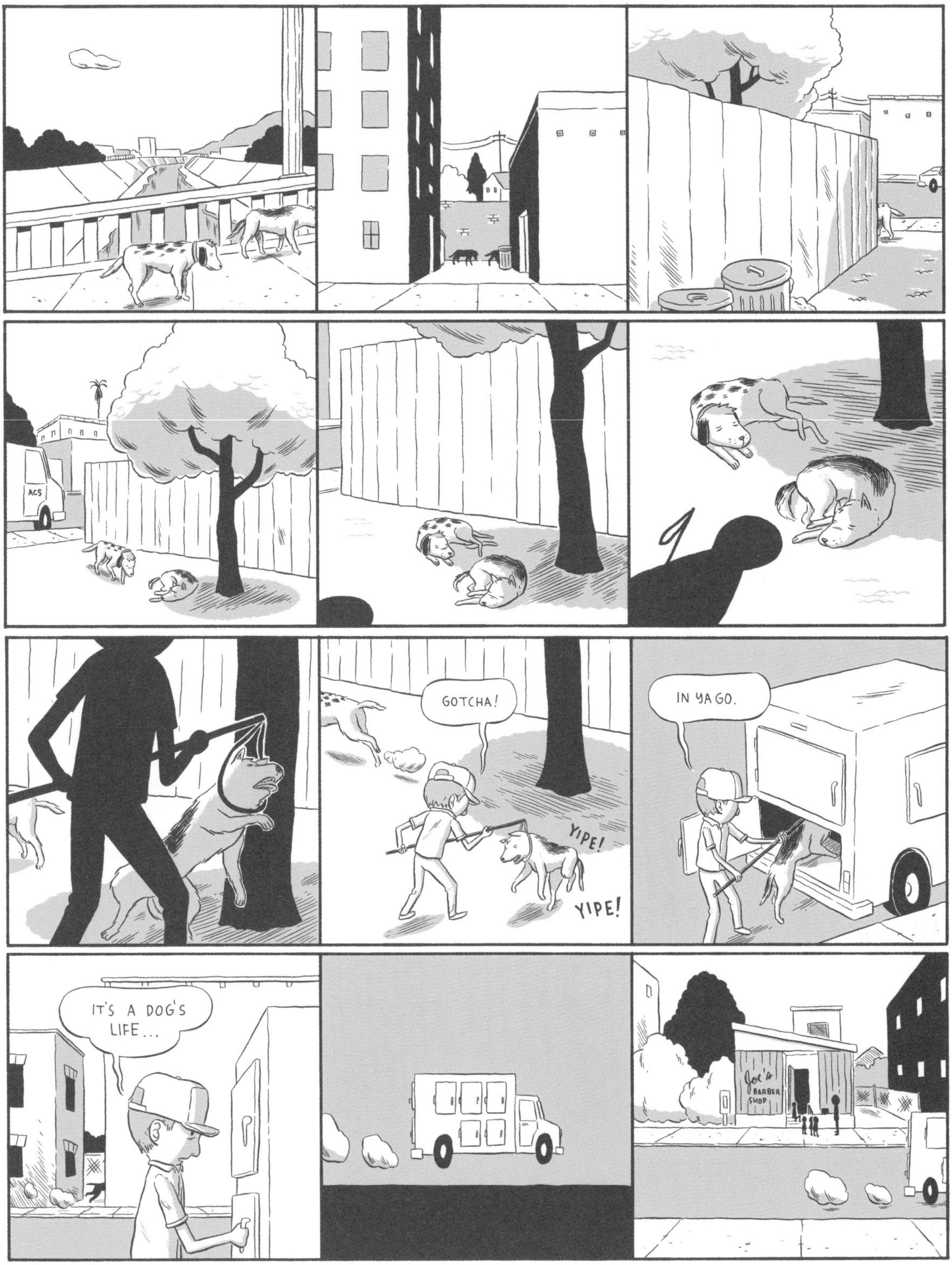
ACS
GOTCHA!
YIPE!
YIPE!
IN YA GO.
IT'S A DOG'S LIFE...
Joe's BARBER SHOP

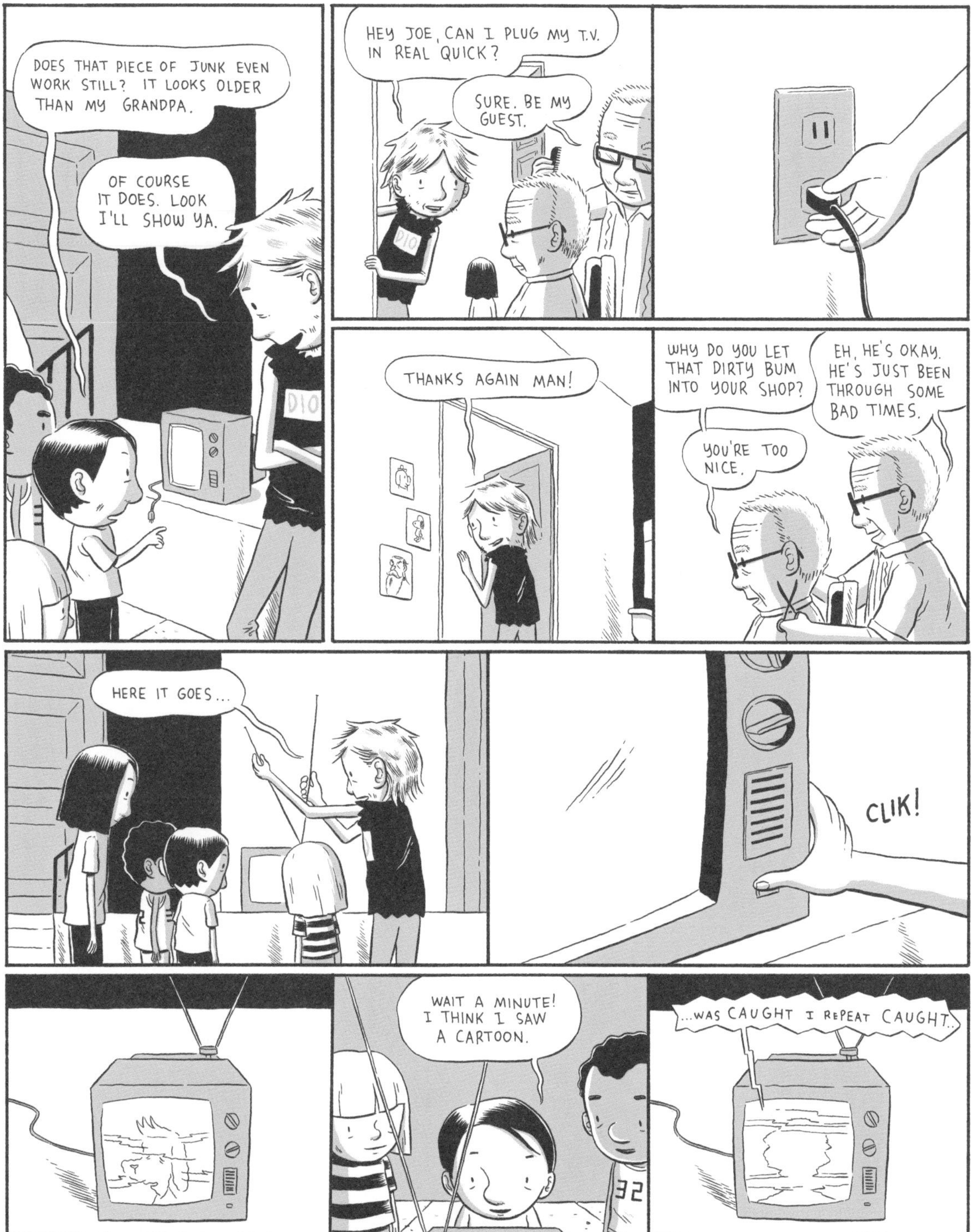
DOES THAT PIECE OF JUNK EVEN WORK STILL? IT LOOKS OLDER THAN MY GRANDPA.
OF COURSE IT DOES. LOOK I'LL SHOW YA.
DIO
HEY JOE, CAN I PLUG MY T.V. IN REAL QUICK?
SURE. BE MY GUEST.
DIO
THANKS AGAIN MAN!
WHY DO YOU LET THAT DIRTY BUM INTO YOUR SHOP?
EH, HE'S OKAY. HE'S JUST BEEN THROUGH SOME BAD TIMES.
YOU'RE TOO NICE.
HERE IT GOES...
CLIK!
WAIT A MINUTE! I THINK I SAW A CARTOON.
32
...WAS CAUGHT I REPEAT CAUGHT...

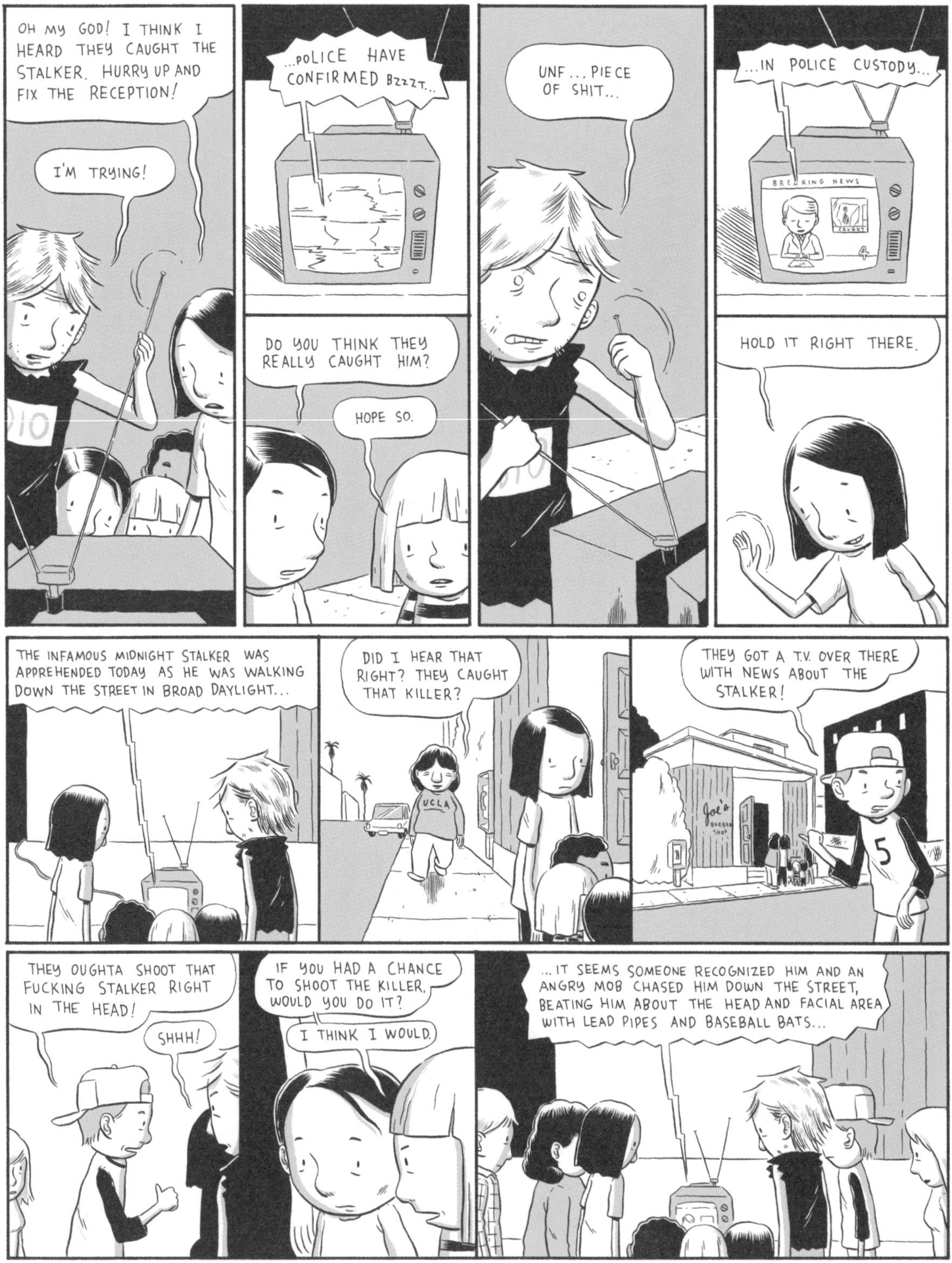
OH MY GOD! I THINK I HEARD THEY CAUGHT THE STALKER. HURRY UP AND FIX THE RECEPTION!
I'M TRYING!
...POLICE HAVE CONFIRMED Bzzzt...
DO YOU THINK THEY REALLY CAUGHT HIM?
HOPE SO.
UNF... PIECE OF SHIT...
...IN POLICE CUSTODY...
BREAKING NEWS
CAUGHT
HOLD IT RIGHT THERE.
THE INFAMOUS MIDNIGHT STALKER WAS APPREHENDED TODAY AS HE WAS WALKING DOWN THE STREET IN BROAD DAYLIGHT...
DID I HEAR THAT RIGHT? THEY CAUGHT THAT KILLER?
UCLA
THEY GOT A T.V. OVER THERE WITH NEWS ABOUT THE STALKER!
Joe's BARBER SHOP
THEY OUGHTA SHOOT THAT FUCKING STALKER RIGHT IN THE HEAD!
SHHH!
IF YOU HAD A CHANCE TO SHOOT THE KILLER, WOULD YOU DO IT?
I THINK I WOULD.
...IT SEEMS SOMEONE RECOGNIZED HIM AND AN ANGRY MOB CHASED HIM DOWN THE STREET, BEATING HIM ABOUT THE HEAD AND FACIAL AREA WITH LEAD PIPES AND BASEBALL BATS...

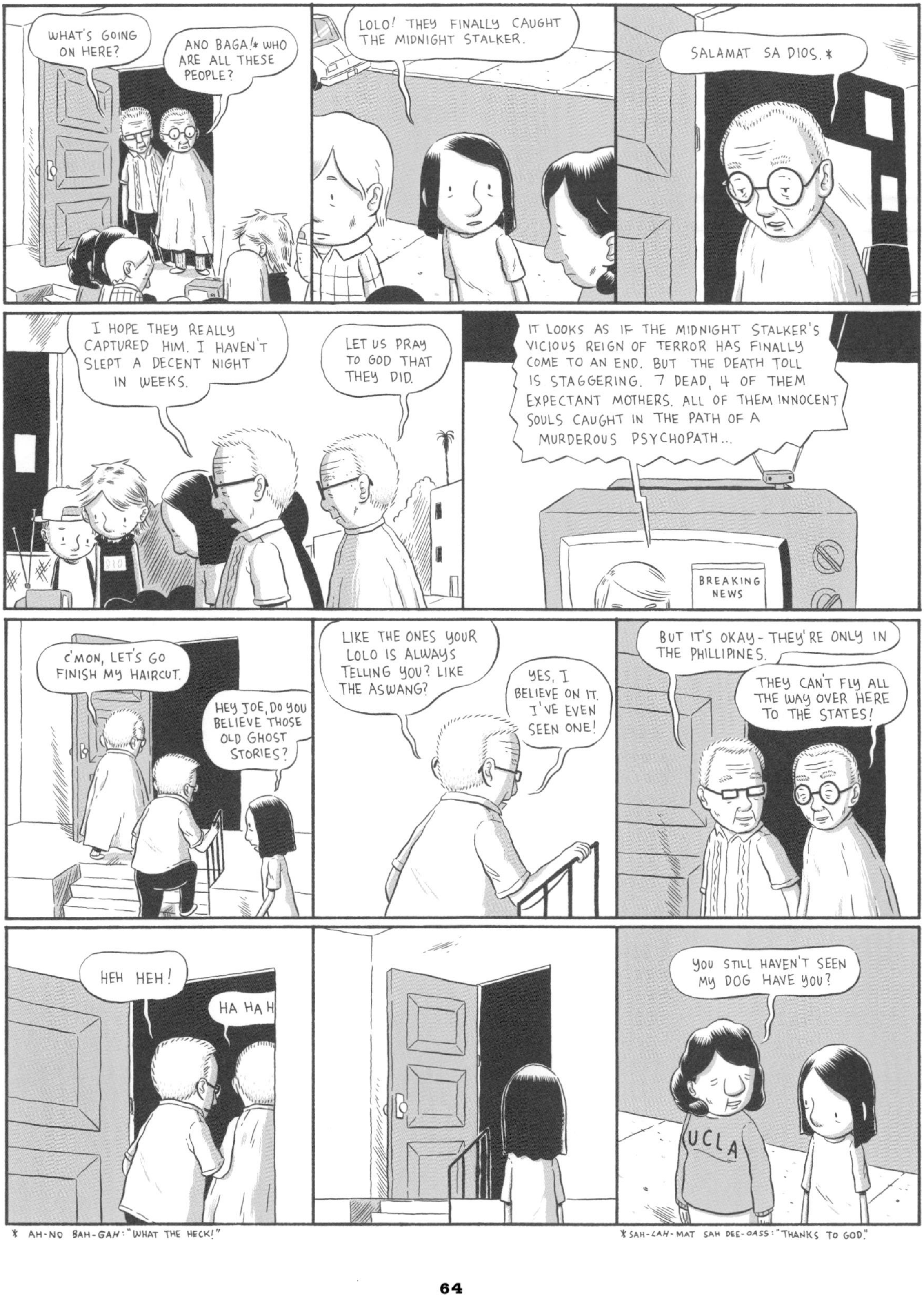
WHAT'S GOING ON HERE?
ANO BAGA!* WHO ARE ALL THESE PEOPLE?
LOLO! THEY FINALLY CAUGHT THE MIDNIGHT STALKER.
SALAMAT SA DIOS.*
I HOPE THEY REALLY CAPTURED HIM. I HAVEN'T SLEPT A DECENT NIGHT IN WEEKS.
LET US PRAY TO GOD THAT THEY DID.
IT LOOKS AS IF THE MIDNIGHT STALKER'S VICIOUS REIGN OF TERROR HAS FINALLY COME TO AN END. BUT THE DEATH TOLL IS STAGGERING. 7 DEAD, 4 OF THEM EXPECTANT MOTHERS. ALL OF THEM INNOCENT SOULS CAUGHT IN THE PATH OF A MURDEROUS PSYCHOPATH...
BREAKING NEWS
C'MON, LET'S GO FINISH MY HAIRCUT.
HEY JOE, DO YOU BELIEVE THOSE OLD GHOST STORIES?
LIKE THE ONES YOUR LOLO IS ALWAYS TELLING YOU? LIKE THE ASWANG?
YES, I BELIEVE ON IT. I'VE EVEN SEEN ONE!
BUT IT'S OKAY- THEY'RE ONLY IN THE PHILLIPINES.
THEY CAN'T FLY ALL THE WAY OVER HERE TO THE STATES!
HEH HEH!
HA HA H
YOU STILL HAVEN'T SEEN MY DOG HAVE YOU?
UCLA

* AH-NO BAH-GAH: "WHAT THE HECK!"

* SAH-LAH-MAT SAH DEE-OASS: "THANKS TO GOD."

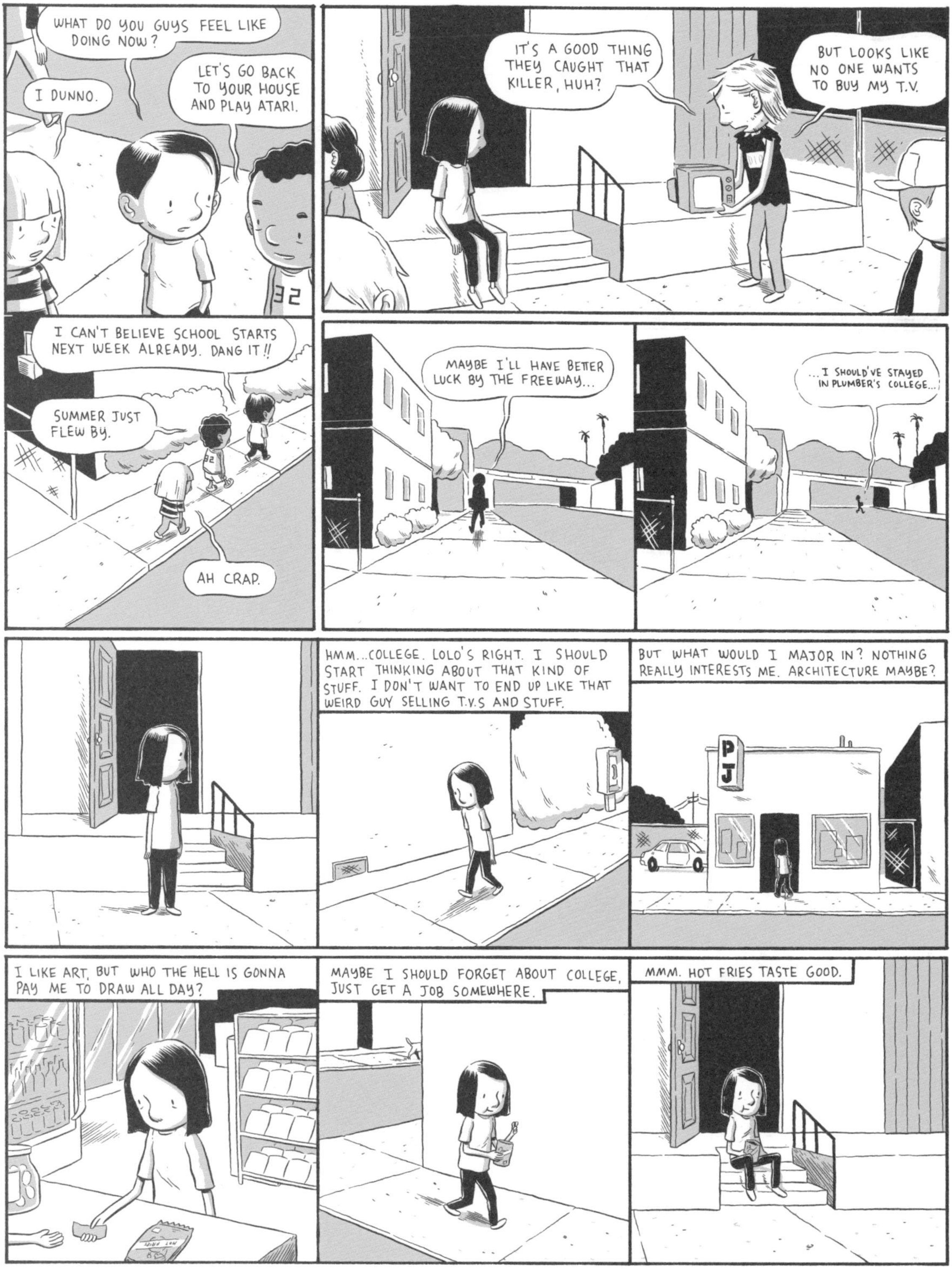
WHAT DO YOU GUYS FEEL LIKE DOING NOW?
I DUNNO.
LET'S GO BACK TO YOUR HOUSE AND PLAY ATARI.
32
IT'S A GOOD THING THEY CAUGHT THAT KILLER, HUH?
BUT LOOKS LIKE NO ONE WANTS TO BUY MY T.V.
I CAN'T BELIEVE SCHOOL STARTS NEXT WEEK ALREADY. DANG IT!!
SUMMER JUST FLEW BY.
AH CRAP.
MAYBE I'LL HAVE BETTER LUCK BY THE FREEWAY...
...I SHOULD'VE STAYED IN PLUMBER'S COLLEGE...
HMM...COLLEGE. LOLO'S RIGHT. I SHOULD START THINKING ABOUT THAT KIND OF STUFF. I DON'T WANT TO END UP LIKE THAT WEIRD GUY SELLING T.V.S AND STUFF.
BUT WHAT WOULD I MAJOR IN? NOTHING REALLY INTERESTS ME. ARCHITECTURE MAYBE?
PJ
I LIKE ART, BUT WHO THE HELL IS GONNA PAY ME TO DRAW ALL DAY?
MAYBE I SHOULD FORGET ABOUT COLLEGE, JUST GET A JOB SOMEWHERE.
MMM. HOT FRIES TASTE GOOD.

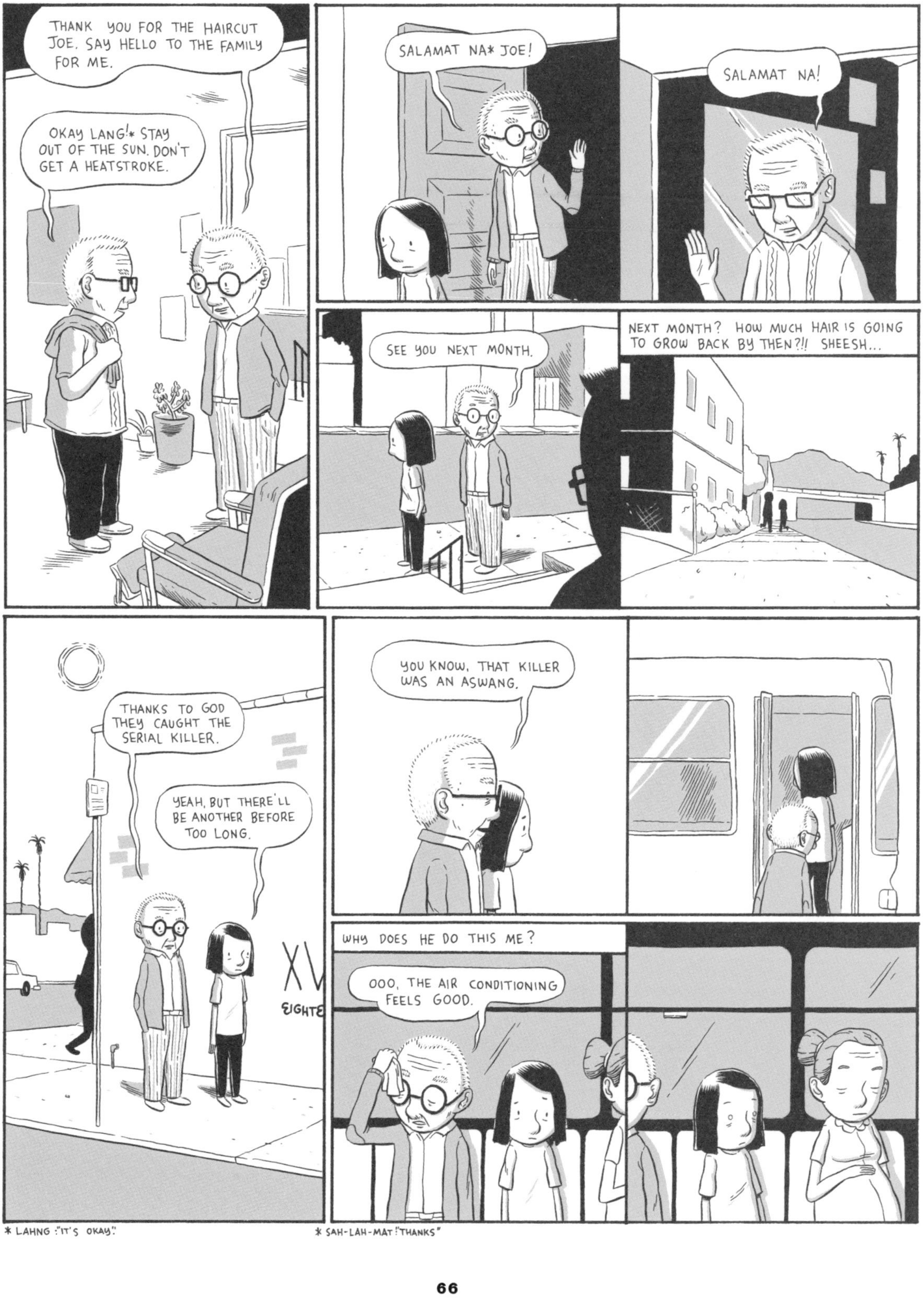

THANK YOU FOR THE HAIRCUT JOE. SAY HELLO TO THE FAMILY FOR ME.
OKAY LANG!* STAY OUT OF THE SUN. DON'T GET A HEATSTROKE.
SALAMAT NA* JOE!
SALAMAT NA!
SEE YOU NEXT MONTH.
NEXT MONTH? HOW MUCH HAIR IS GOING TO GROW BACK BY THEN?!! SHEESH...
THANKS TO GOD THEY CAUGHT THE SERIAL KILLER.
YEAH, BUT THERE'LL BE ANOTHER BEFORE TOO LONG.
YOU KNOW, THAT KILLER WAS AN ASWANG.
WHY DOES HE DO THIS ME?
OOO, THE AIR CONDITIONING FEELS GOOD.

* LAHNG: "IT'S OKAY".

* SAH-LAH-MAT: "THANKS"

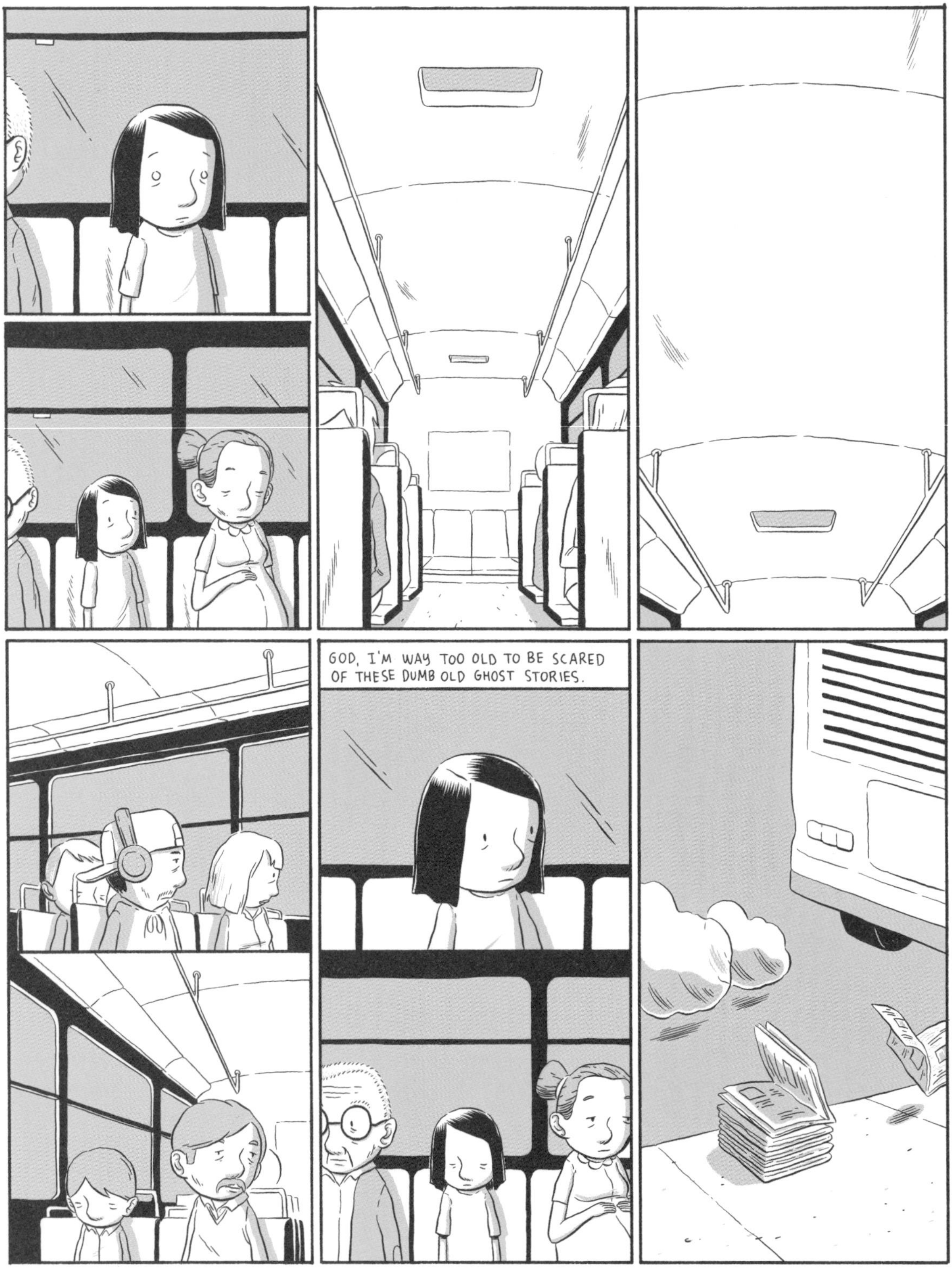
GOD, I'M WAY TOO OLD TO BE SCARED OF THESE DUMB OLD GHOST STORIES.

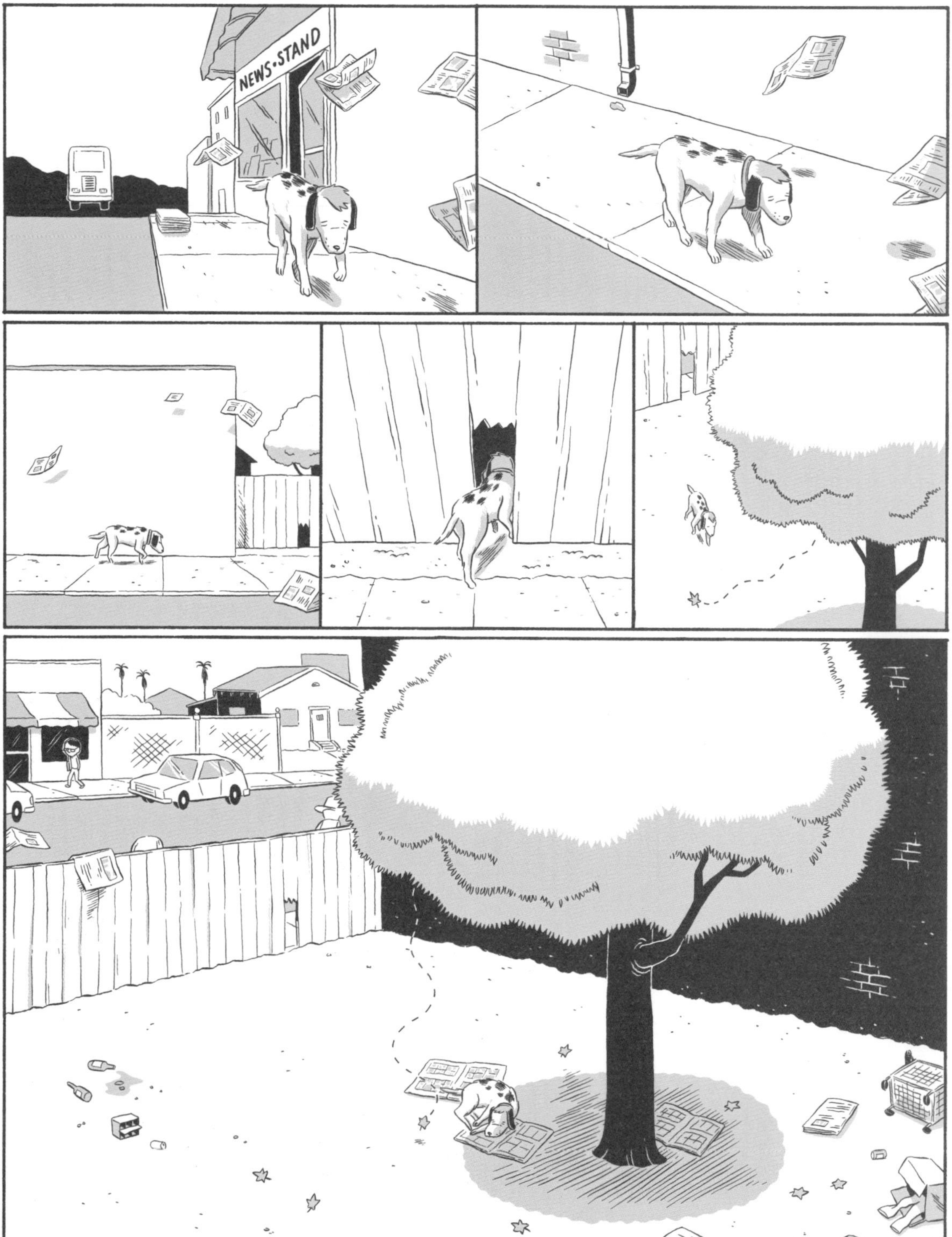
NEWS•STAND

mart

Dan Zettwoch

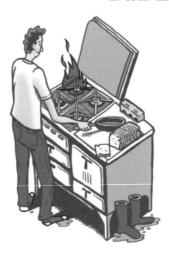

Born in Louisville, Kentucky – the birthplace of Muhammad Ali and the cheeseburger – in 1977, Dan Zettwoch is a third-generation cartoonist. His grandfather drew comics during WWII and in the 1970s and 80s his father did the same while working as a craftsman at American Telephone & Telegraph Company. They never got paid to draw comics and thus gradually transferred their creative efforts to woodworking, painting, and mechanized sculpture.

Meanwhile, as a child, Dan Zettwoch read the comics most plentiful in the nickel boxes at the Jefferson County Flea Market: *Cracked* magazine and *ROM: Spaceknight*. He moved to St. Louis, Missouri in 1995 to attend school at Washington University, where he discovered comics he liked better and he even drew a strip for the campus paper. His first self-published works were not comics however, but fanzines dedicated to hardcore punk music. Eventually he started stapling together booklets full of his comics, which were about things like professional wrestling, slot car racing, and Civil War-era battleships, and he never looked back.

Zettwoch's stories have appeared in publications such as *Kramers Ergot, EXPO 2001, Hi-Horse Omnibus, Arthur, Bogus Dead,* and the *Riverfront Times.* He currently lives in St. Louis, Missouri, where he earns money by making illustrations and diagrams. He also operates The Catastrophe Shop – a distribution outlet for self-published comics – and works hard on his new comic book series, *Redbird*.

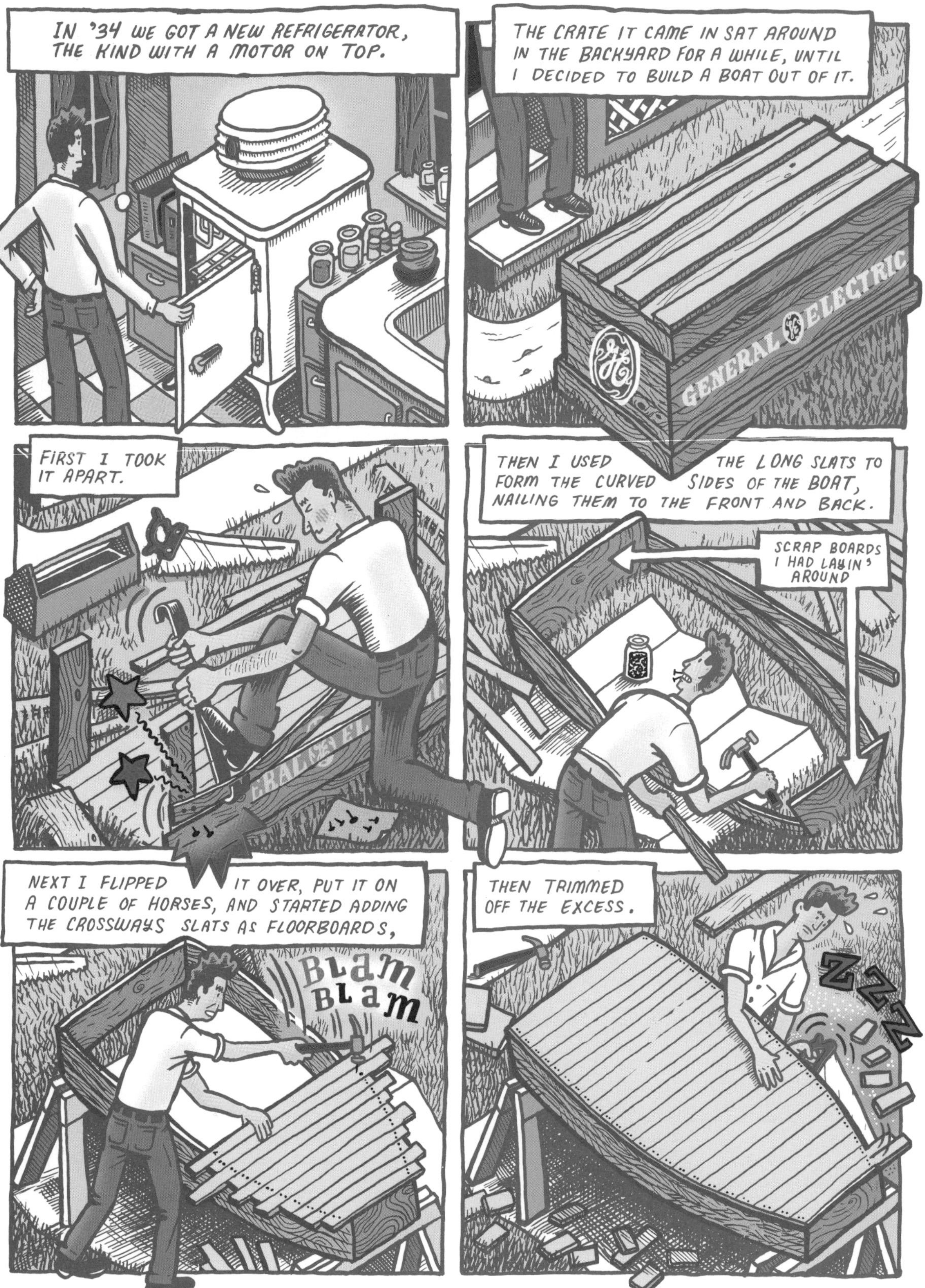
IN '34 WE GOT A NEW REFRIGERATOR, THE KIND WITH A MOTOR ON TOP.
THE CRATE IT CAME IN SAT AROUND IN THE BACKYARD FOR A WHILE, UNTIL I DECIDED TO BUILD A BOAT OUT OF IT.
GENERAL ELECTRIC
FIRST I TOOK IT APART.
THEN I USED THE LONG SLATS TO FORM THE CURVED SIDES OF THE BOAT, NAILING THEM TO THE FRONT AND BACK.
SCRAP BOARDS I HAD LAYIN' AROUND
NEXT I FLIPPED IT OVER, PUT IT ON A COUPLE OF HORSES, AND STARTED ADDING THE CROSSWAYS SLATS AS FLOORBOARDS,
BLAM BLAM
THEN TRIMMED OFF THE EXCESS.
ZZZ

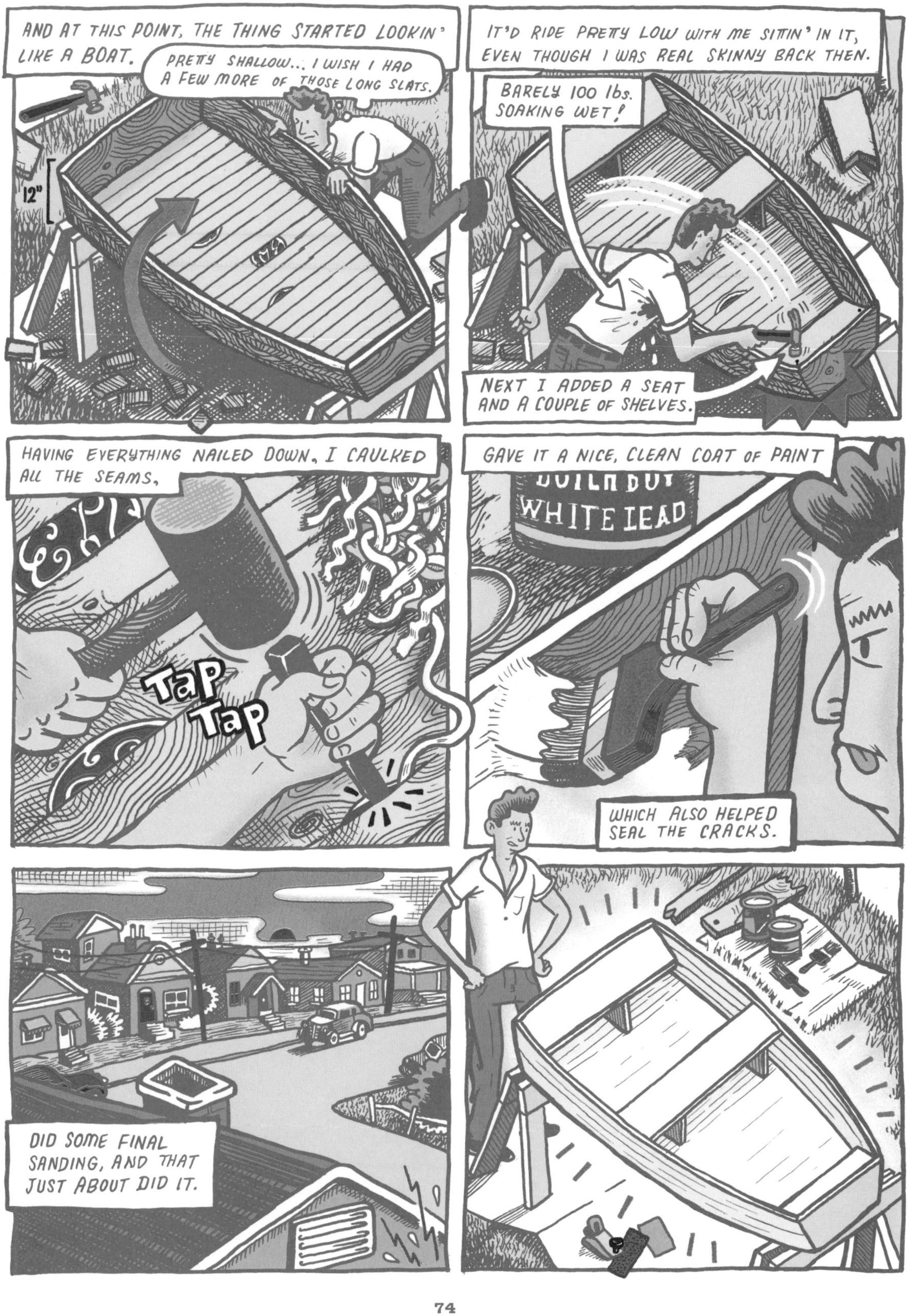
AND AT THIS POINT, THE THING STARTED LOOKIN' LIKE A BOAT.
PRETTY SHALLOW... I WISH I HAD A FEW MORE OF THOSE LONG SLATS.
12"
IT'D RIDE PRETTY LOW WITH ME SITTIN' IN IT, EVEN THOUGH I WAS REAL SKINNY BACK THEN.
BARELY 100 lbs. SOAKING WET!
NEXT I ADDED A SEAT AND A COUPLE OF SHELVES.
HAVING EVERYTHING NAILED DOWN, I CAULKED ALL THE SEAMS,
TAP TAP
GAVE IT A NICE, CLEAN COAT OF PAINT
WHITE LEAD
WHICH ALSO HELPED SEAL THE CRACKS.
DID SOME FINAL SANDING, AND THAT JUST ABOUT DID IT.

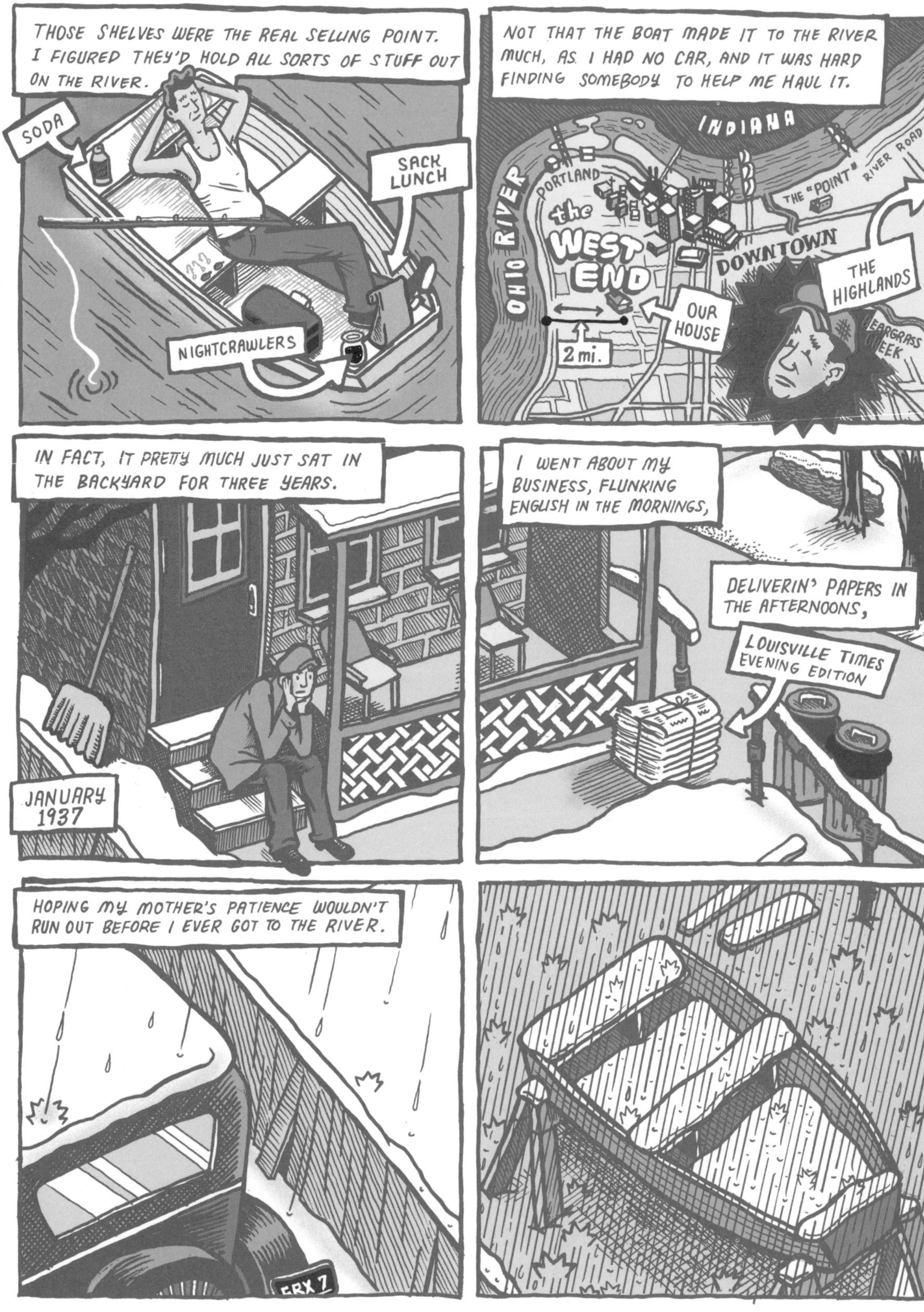
THOSE SHELVES WERE THE REAL SELLING POINT. I FIGURED THEY'D HOLD ALL SORTS OF STUFF OUT ON THE RIVER.
SODA
SACK LUNCH
NIGHTCRAWLERS
NOT THAT THE BOAT MADE IT TO THE RIVER MUCH, AS I HAD NO CAR, AND IT WAS HARD FINDING SOMEBODY TO HELP ME HAUL IT.
INDIANA
OHIO RIVER
PORTLAND
the WEST END
THE "POINT"
RIVER ROAD
DOWNTOWN
THE HIGHLANDS
OUR HOUSE
2 mi.
IN FACT, IT PRETTY MUCH JUST SAT IN THE BACKYARD FOR THREE YEARS.
JANUARY 1937
I WENT ABOUT MY BUSINESS, FLUNKING ENGLISH IN THE MORNINGS,
DELIVERIN' PAPERS IN THE AFTERNOONS,
LOUISVILLE TIMES EVENING EDITION
HOPING MY MOTHER'S PATIENCE WOULDN'T RUN OUT BEFORE I EVER GOT TO THE RIVER.

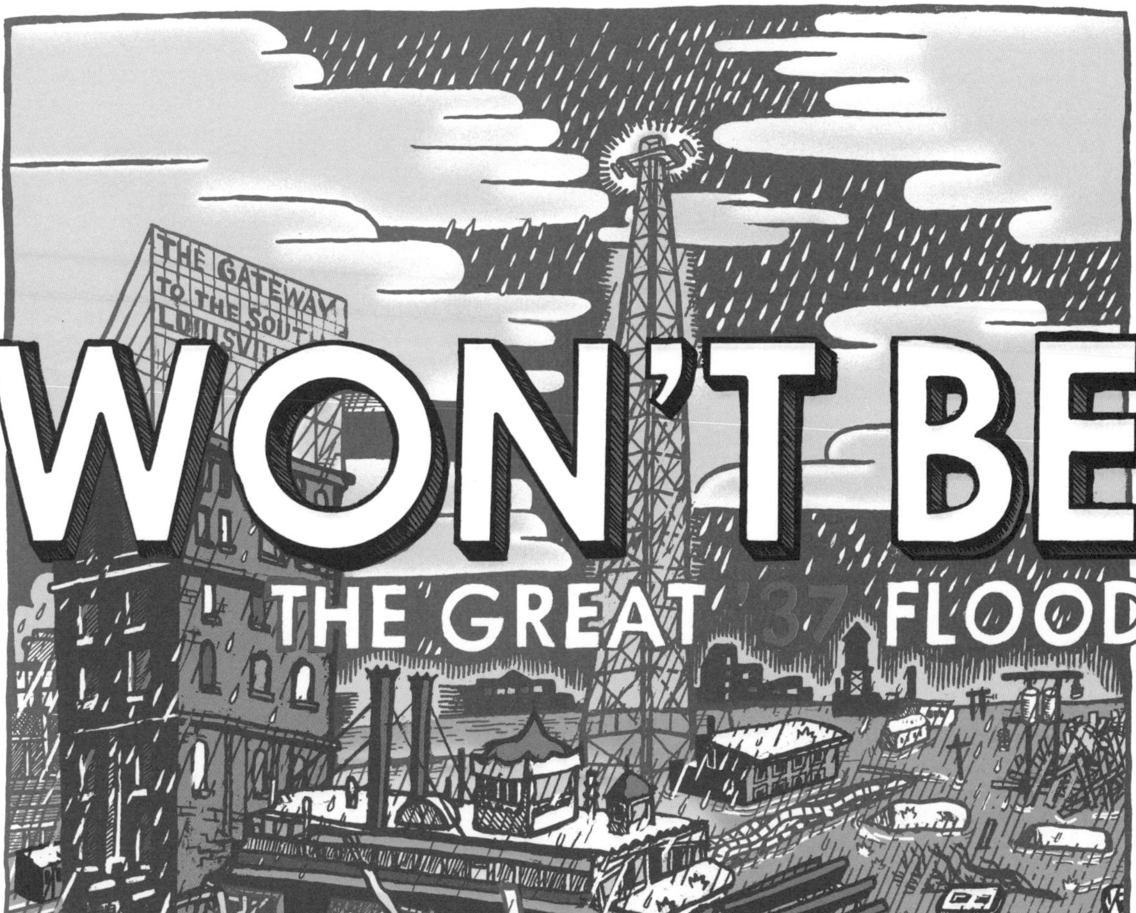
THE GATEWAY TO THE SOU
LOUISVIL
WON'T BE
THE GREAT '37 FLOOD

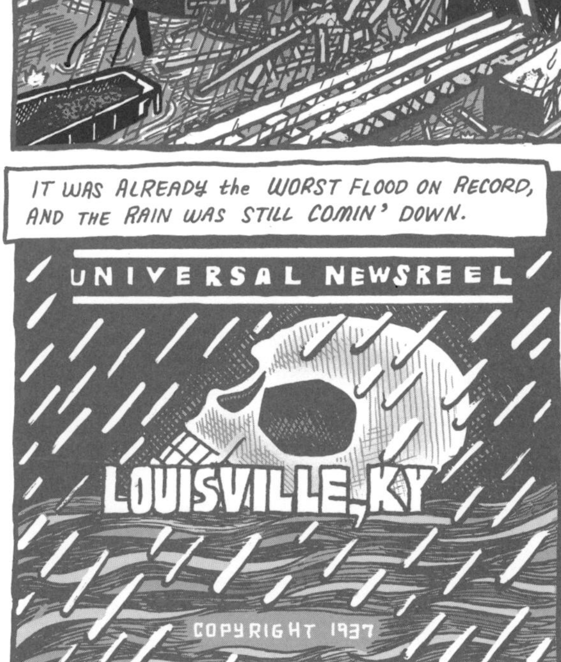
IT WAS ALREADY the WORST FLOOD ON RECORD, AND THE RAIN WAS STILL COMIN' DOWN.
UNIVERSAL NEWSREEL
LOUISVILLE, KY
COPYRIGHT 1937

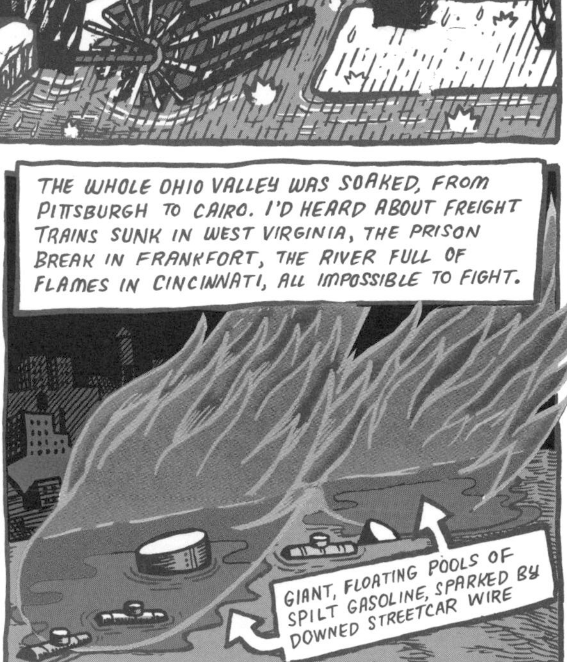
THE WHOLE OHIO VALLEY WAS SOAKED, FROM PITTSBURGH TO CAIRO. I'D HEARD ABOUT FREIGHT TRAINS SUNK IN WEST VIRGINIA, THE PRISON BREAK IN FRANKFORT, THE RIVER FULL OF FLAMES IN CINCINNATI, ALL IMPOSSIBLE TO FIGHT.
GIANT, FLOATING POOLS OF SPILT GASOLINE, SPARKED BY DOWNED STREETCAR WIRE

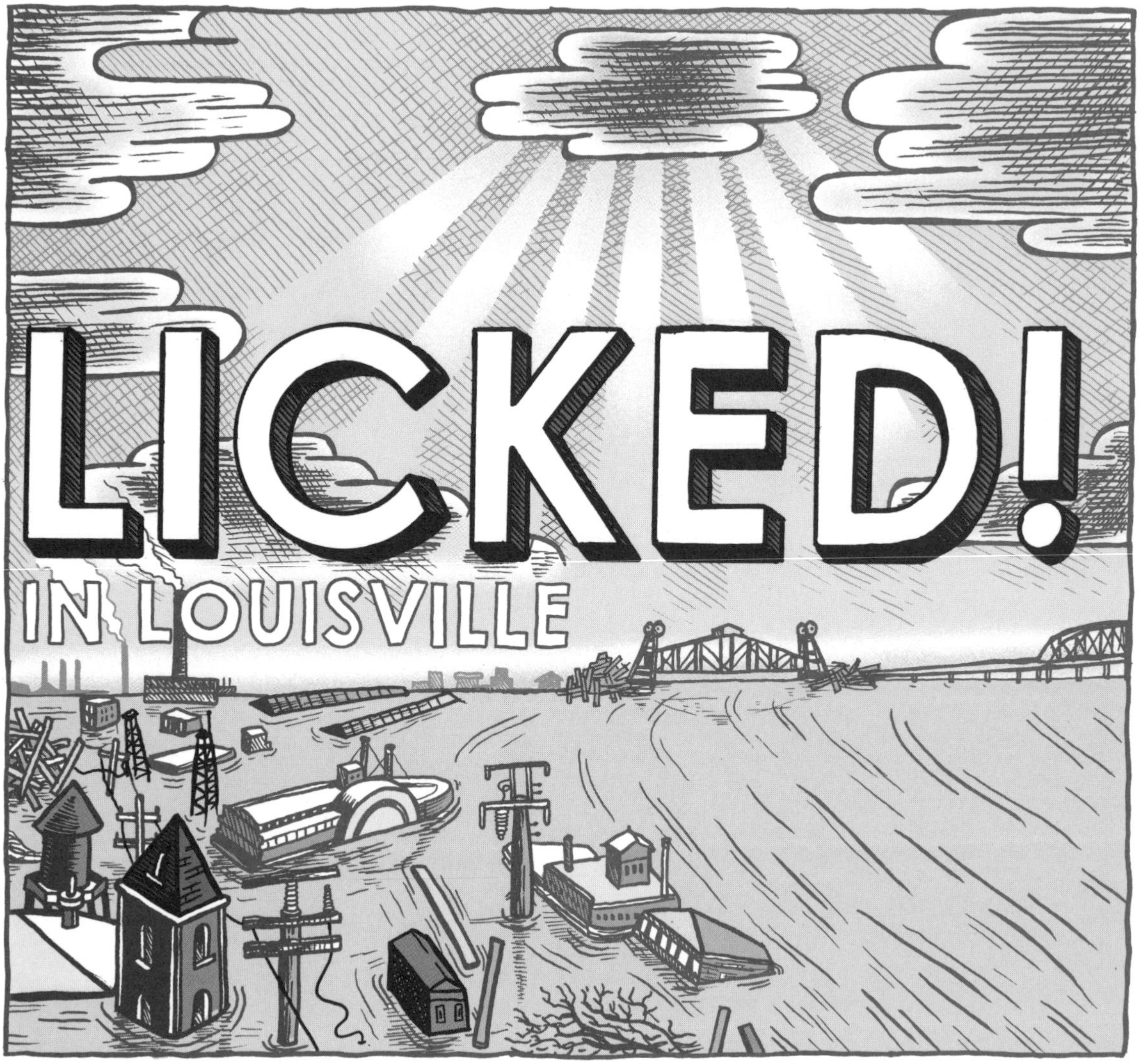
LICKED!
IN LOUISVILLE

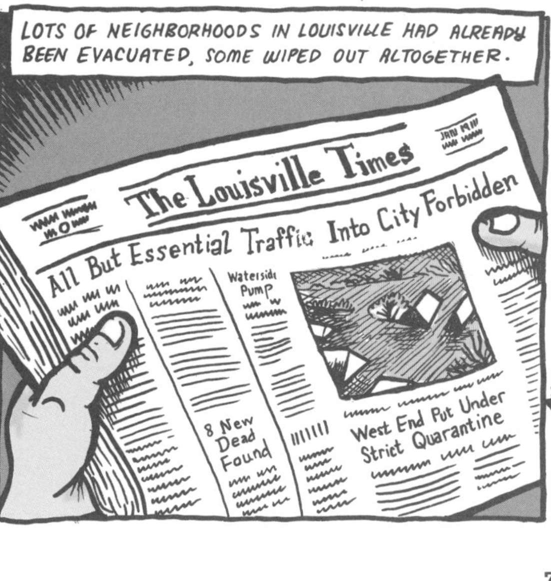
LOTS OF NEIGHBORHOODS IN LOUISVILLE HAD ALREADY BEEN EVACUATED, SOME WIPED OUT ALTOGETHER.
The Louisville Times
All But Essential Traffic Into City Forbidden
Waterside Pump
8 New Dead Found
West End Put Under Strict Quarantine

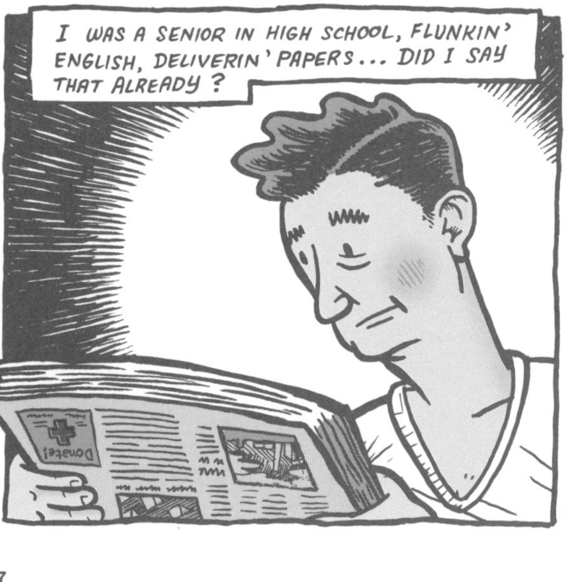
I WAS A SENIOR IN HIGH SCHOOL, FLUNKIN' ENGLISH, DELIVERIN' PAPERS... DID I SAY THAT ALREADY?
Donate!

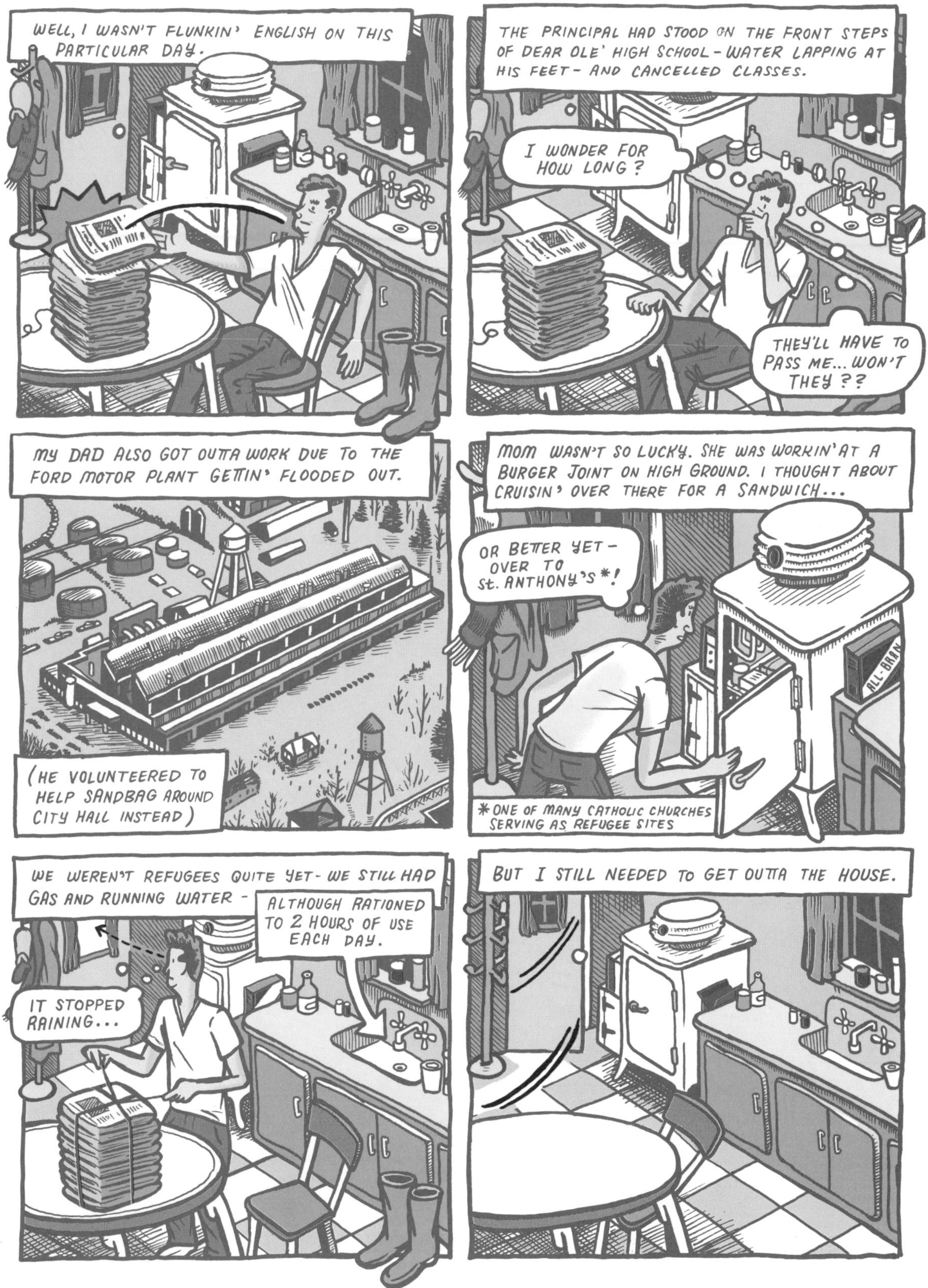
WELL, I WASN'T FLUNKIN' ENGLISH ON THIS PARTICULAR DAY.
THE PRINCIPAL HAD STOOD ON THE FRONT STEPS OF DEAR OLE' HIGH SCHOOL - WATER LAPPING AT HIS FEET - AND CANCELLED CLASSES.
I WONDER FOR HOW LONG?
THEY'LL HAVE TO PASS ME... WON'T THEY??
MY DAD ALSO GOT OUTTA WORK DUE TO THE FORD MOTOR PLANT GETTIN' FLOODED OUT.
(HE VOLUNTEERED TO HELP SANDBAG AROUND CITY HALL INSTEAD)
MOM WASN'T SO LUCKY. SHE WAS WORKIN' AT A BURGER JOINT ON HIGH GROUND. I THOUGHT ABOUT CRUISIN' OVER THERE FOR A SANDWICH...
OR BETTER YET - OVER TO St. ANTHONY'S*!
ALL-BRAN
* ONE OF MANY CATHOLIC CHURCHES SERVING AS REFUGEE SITES
WE WEREN'T REFUGEES QUITE YET - WE STILL HAD GAS AND RUNNING WATER -
ALTHOUGH RATIONED TO 2 HOURS OF USE EACH DAY.
IT STOPPED RAINING...
BUT I STILL NEEDED TO GET OUTTA THE HOUSE.

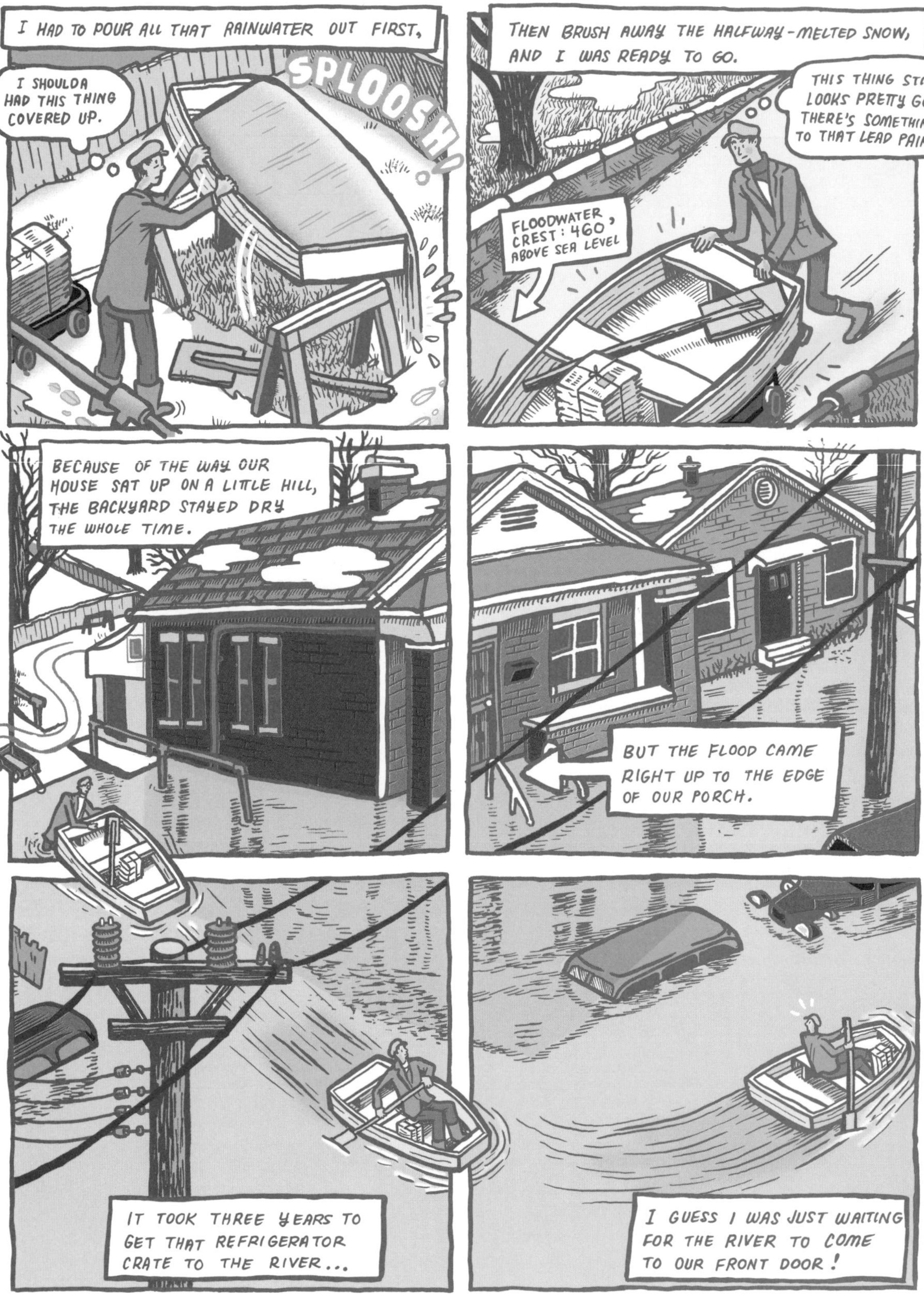
I HAD TO POUR ALL THAT RAINWATER OUT FIRST,
I SHOULDA HAD THIS THING COVERED UP.
SPLOOSH!
THEN BRUSH AWAY THE HALFWAY-MELTED SNOW, AND I WAS READY TO GO.
THIS THING STILL LOOKS PRETTY GOOD. THERE'S SOMETHING TO THAT LEAD PAINT.
FLOODWATER, CREST: 460 ABOVE SEA LEVEL
BECAUSE OF THE WAY OUR HOUSE SAT UP ON A LITTLE HILL, THE BACKYARD STAYED DRY THE WHOLE TIME.
BUT THE FLOOD CAME RIGHT UP TO THE EDGE OF OUR PORCH.
IT TOOK THREE YEARS TO GET THAT REFRIGERATOR CRATE TO THE RIVER...
I GUESS I WAS JUST WAITING FOR THE RIVER TO COME TO OUR FRONT DOOR!

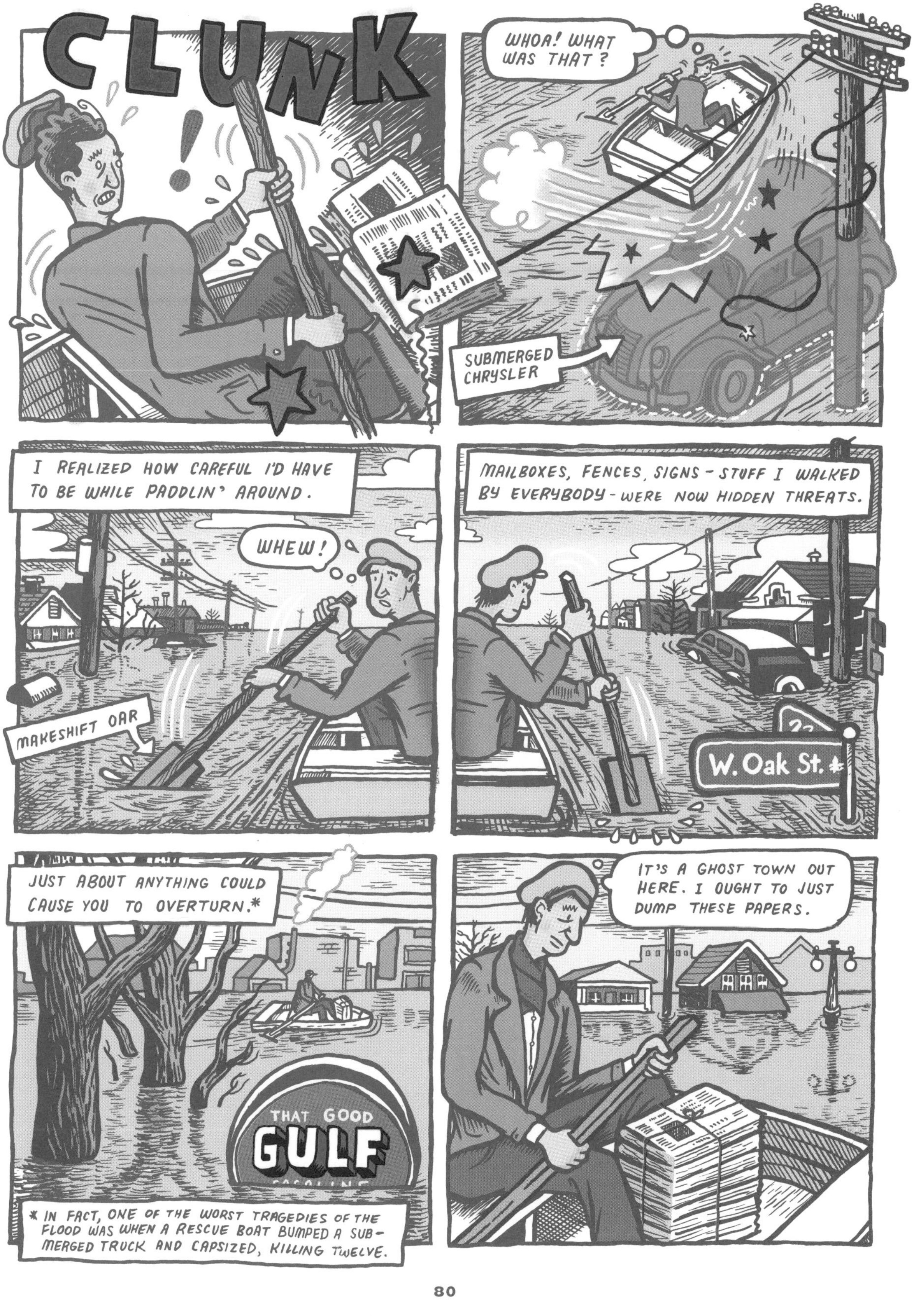
CLUNK
!
WHOA! WHAT WAS THAT?
SUBMERGED CHRYSLER
I REALIZED HOW CAREFUL I'D HAVE TO BE WHILE PADDLIN' AROUND.
WHEW!
MAKESHIFT OAR
MAILBOXES, FENCES, SIGNS - STUFF I WALKED BY EVERYBODY - WERE NOW HIDDEN THREATS.
W. Oak St.
JUST ABOUT ANYTHING COULD CAUSE YOU TO OVERTURN.*
THAT GOOD
GULF
* IN FACT, ONE OF THE WORST TRAGEDIES OF THE FLOOD WAS WHEN A RESCUE BOAT BUMPED A SUBMERGED TRUCK AND CAPSIZED, KILLING TWELVE.
IT'S A GHOST TOWN OUT HERE. I OUGHT TO JUST DUMP THESE PAPERS.

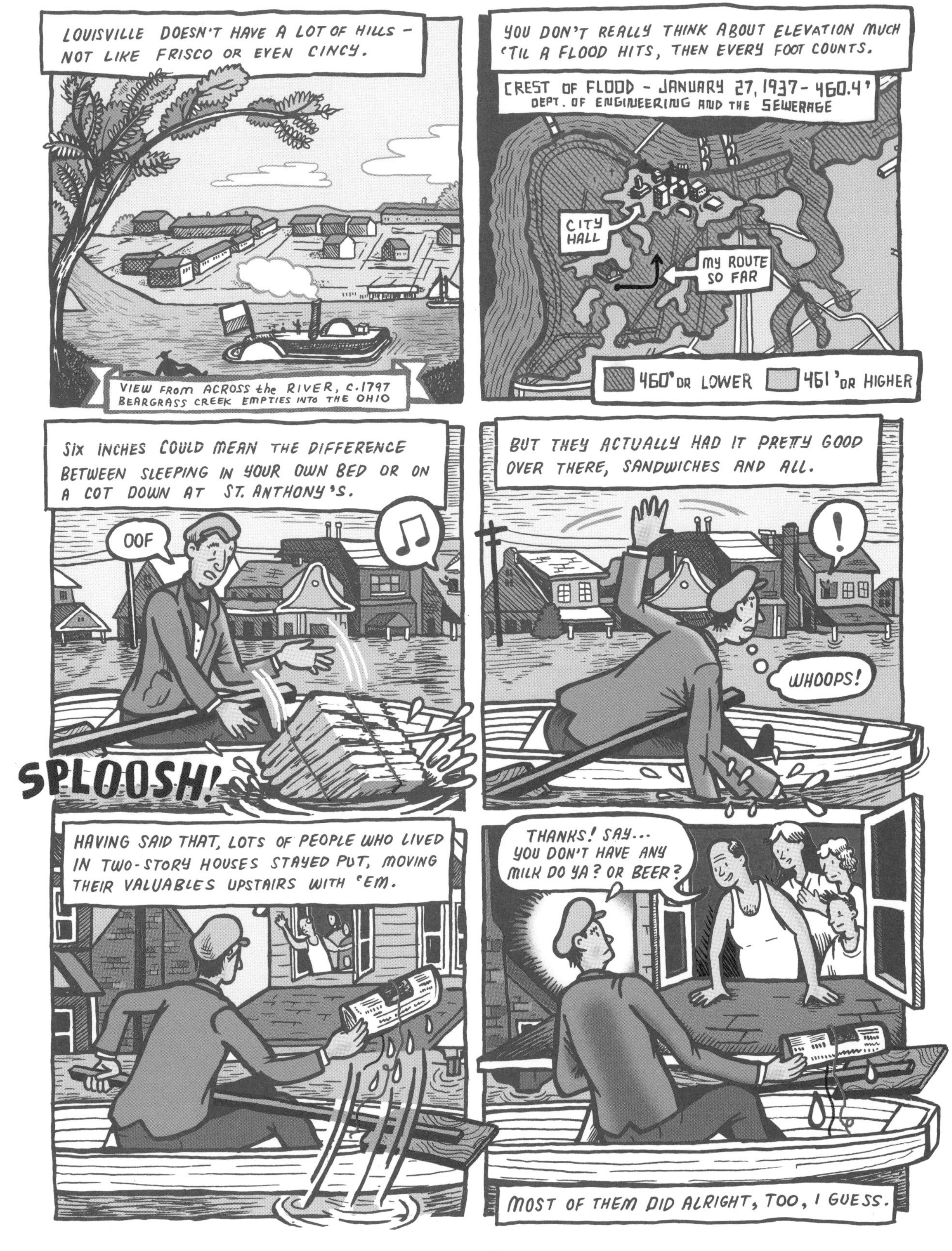
LOUISVILLE DOESN'T HAVE A LOT OF HILLS - NOT LIKE FRISCO OR EVEN CINCY.
VIEW FROM ACROSS the RIVER, c.1797
BEARGRASS CREEK EMPTIES INTO THE OHIO
YOU DON'T REALLY THINK ABOUT ELEVATION MUCH 'TIL A FLOOD HITS, THEN EVERY FOOT COUNTS.
CREST OF FLOOD - JANUARY 27, 1937 - 460.4'
DEPT. OF ENGINEERING AND THE SEWERAGE
CITY HALL
MY ROUTE SO FAR
460' OR LOWER
461' OR HIGHER
SIX INCHES COULD MEAN THE DIFFERENCE BETWEEN SLEEPING IN YOUR OWN BED OR ON A COT DOWN AT ST. ANTHONY'S.
OOF
♫
SPLOOSH!
BUT THEY ACTUALLY HAD IT PRETTY GOOD OVER THERE, SANDWICHES AND ALL.
!
WHOOPS!
HAVING SAID THAT, LOTS OF PEOPLE WHO LIVED IN TWO-STORY HOUSES STAYED PUT, MOVING THEIR VALUABLES UPSTAIRS WITH 'EM.
THANKS! SAY... YOU DON'T HAVE ANY MILK DO YA? OR BEER?
MOST OF THEM DID ALRIGHT, TOO, I GUESS.

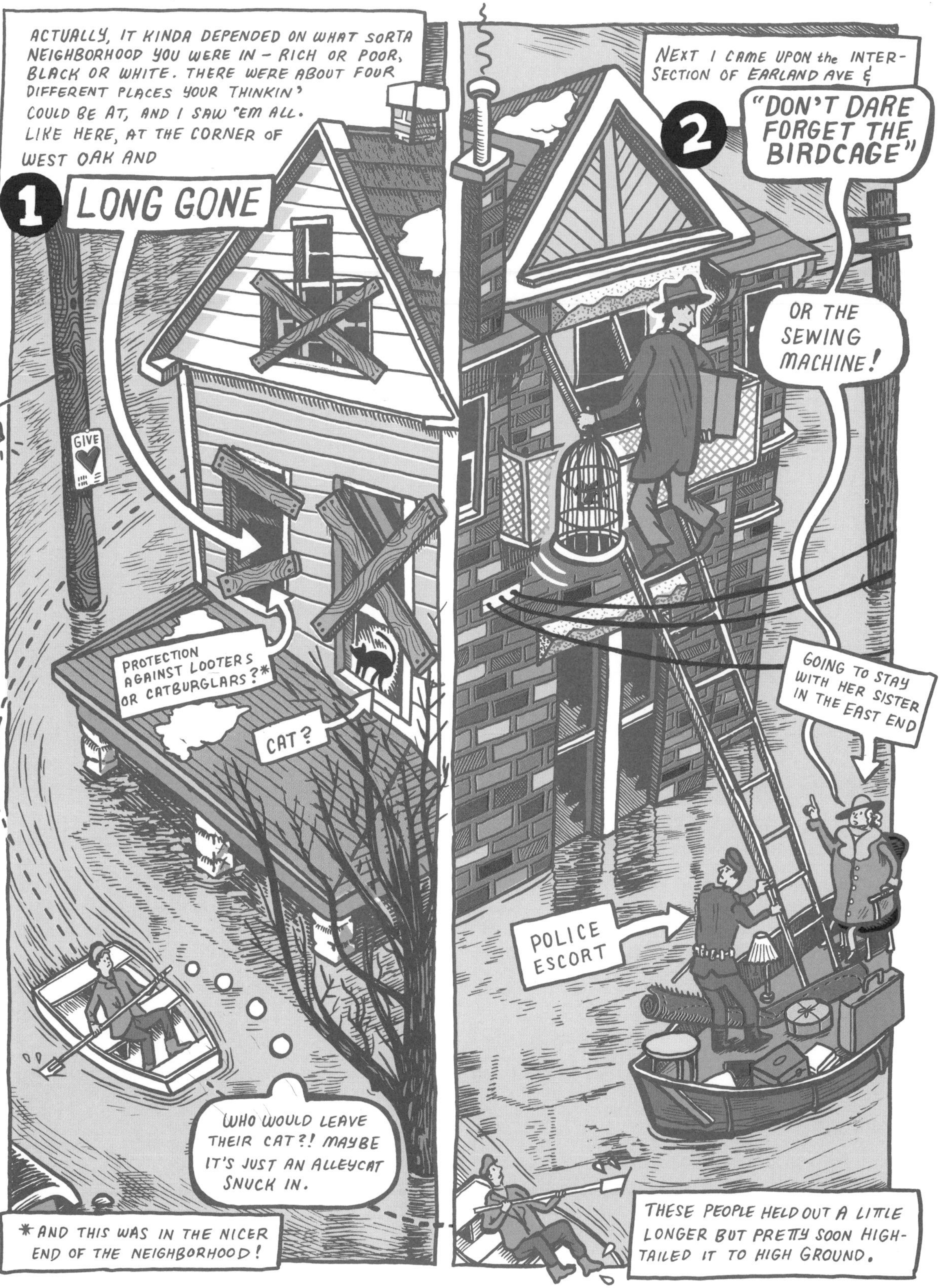
ACTUALLY, IT KINDA DEPENDED ON WHAT SORTA NEIGHBORHOOD YOU WERE IN – RICH OR POOR, BLACK OR WHITE. THERE WERE ABOUT FOUR DIFFERENT PLACES YOUR THINKIN' COULD BE AT, AND I SAW 'EM ALL. LIKE HERE, AT THE CORNER OF WEST OAK AND
1
LONG GONE
GIVE
PROTECTION AGAINST LOOTERS OR CATBURGLARS?*
CAT?
WHO WOULD LEAVE THEIR CAT?! MAYBE IT'S JUST AN ALLEYCAT SNUCK IN.
* AND THIS WAS IN THE NICER END OF THE NEIGHBORHOOD!
NEXT I CAME UPON the INTER-SECTION OF EARLAND AVE &
2
"DON'T DARE FORGET THE BIRDCAGE"
OR THE SEWING MACHINE!
GOING TO STAY WITH HER SISTER IN THE EAST END
POLICE ESCORT
THESE PEOPLE HELD OUT A LITTLE LONGER BUT PRETTY SOON HIGH-TAILED IT TO HIGH GROUND.

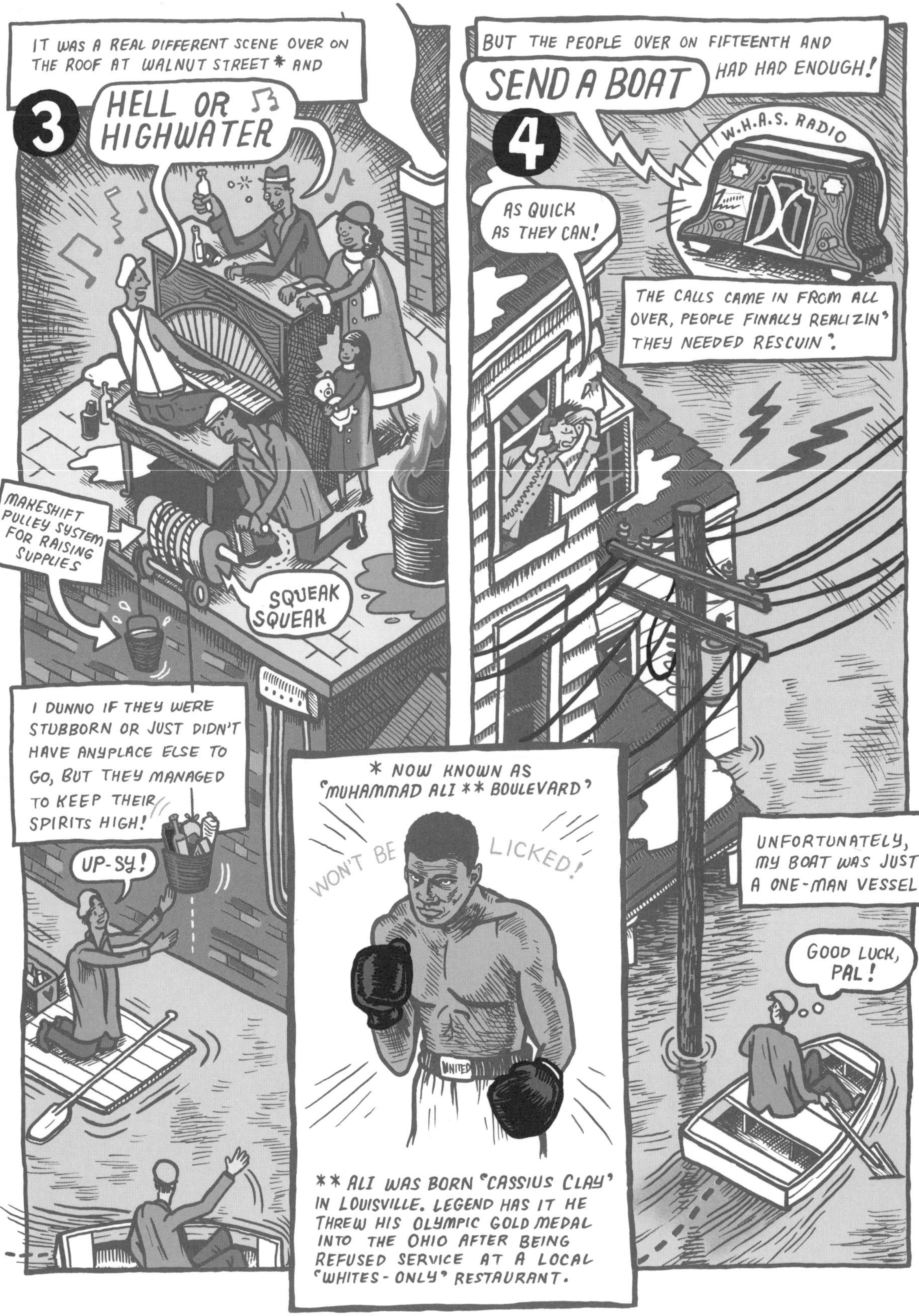

IT WAS A REAL DIFFERENT SCENE OVER ON THE ROOF AT WALNUT STREET * AND
3
HELL OR HIGHWATER
MAKESHIFT PULLEY SYSTEM FOR RAISING SUPPLIES
SQUEAK SQUEAK
I DUNNO IF THEY WERE STUBBORN OR JUST DIDN'T HAVE ANYPLACE ELSE TO GO, BUT THEY MANAGED TO KEEP THEIR SPIRITS HIGH!
UP-SY!
* NOW KNOWN AS 'MUHAMMAD ALI ** BOULEVARD'
WON'T BE LICKED!
UNITED
** ALI WAS BORN 'CASSIUS CLAY' IN LOUISVILLE. LEGEND HAS IT HE THREW HIS OLYMPIC GOLD MEDAL INTO THE OHIO AFTER BEING REFUSED SERVICE AT A LOCAL 'WHITES-ONLY' RESTAURANT.
BUT THE PEOPLE OVER ON FIFTEENTH AND
SEND A BOAT
HAD HAD ENOUGH!
4
W.H.A.S. RADIO
AS QUICK AS THEY CAN!
THE CALLS CAME IN FROM ALL OVER, PEOPLE FINALLY REALIZIN' THEY NEEDED RESCUIN'.
UNFORTUNATELY, MY BOAT WAS JUST A ONE-MAN VESSEL.
GOOD LUCK, PAL!

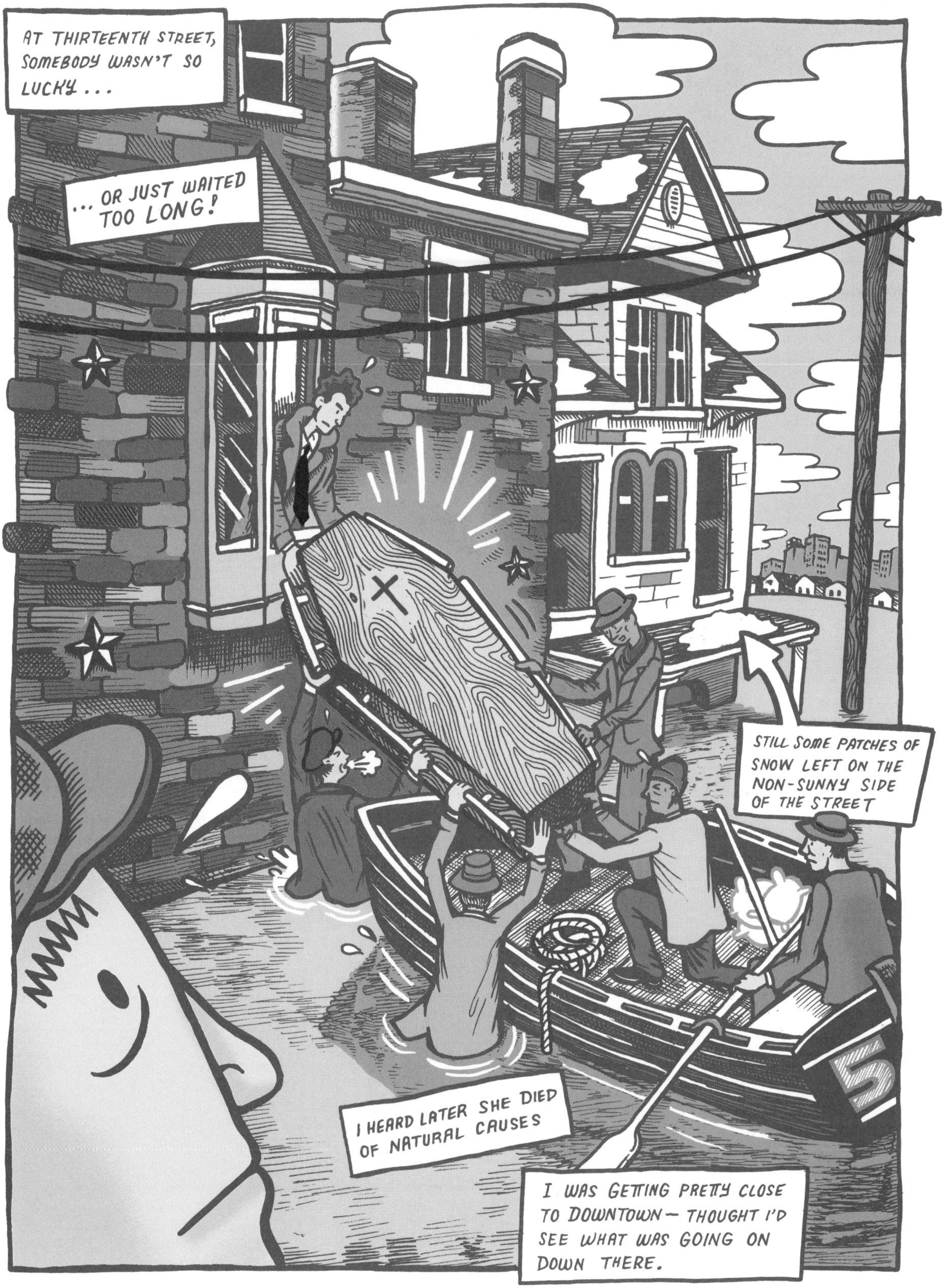
AT THIRTEENTH STREET, SOMEBODY WASN'T SO LUCKY...
... OR JUST WAITED TOO LONG!
STILL SOME PATCHES OF SNOW LEFT ON THE NON-SUNNY SIDE OF THE STREET
5
I HEARD LATER SHE DIED OF NATURAL CAUSES
I WAS GETTING PRETTY CLOSE TO DOWNTOWN — THOUGHT I'D SEE WHAT WAS GOING ON DOWN THERE.

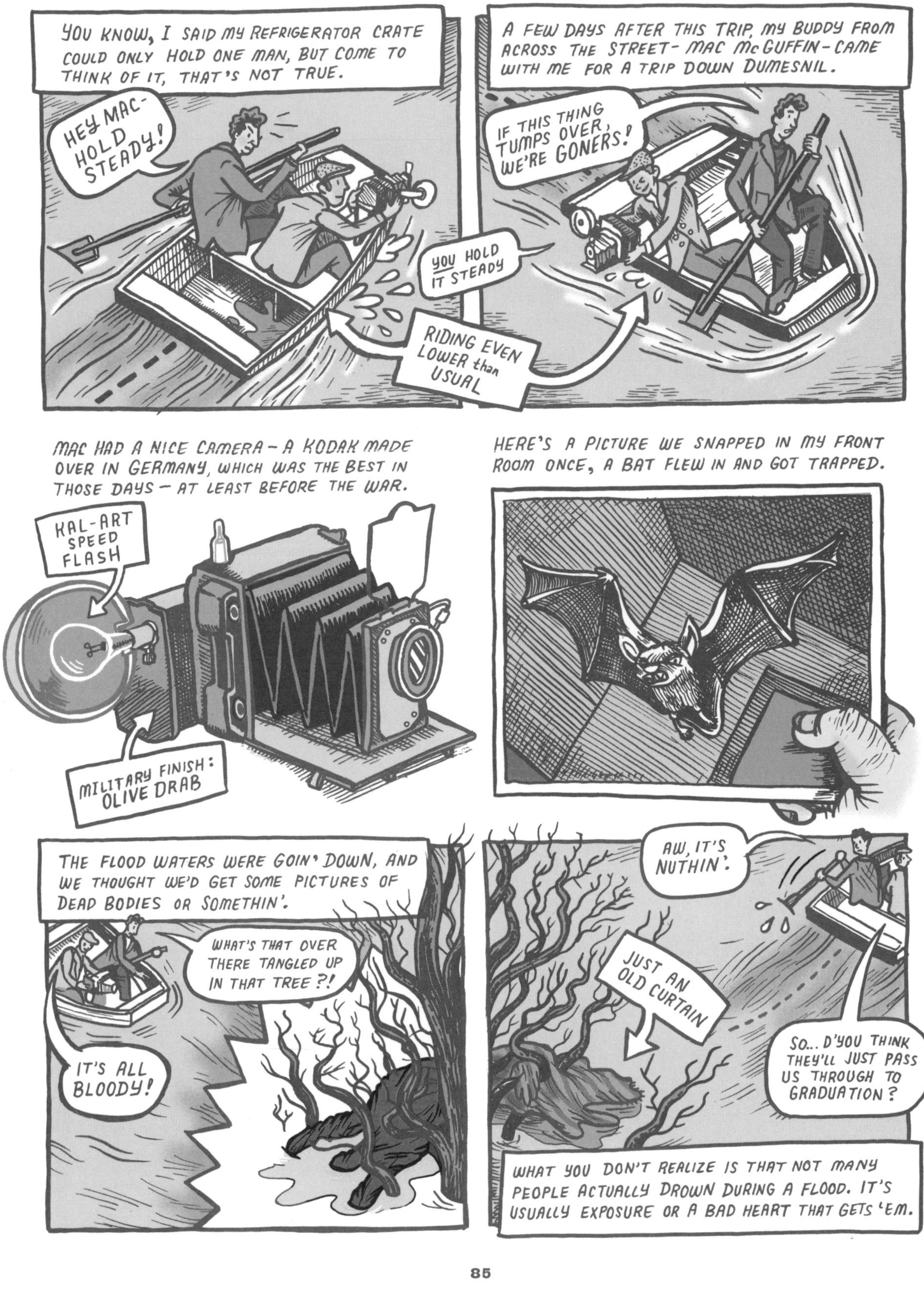
YOU KNOW, I SAID MY REFRIGERATOR CRATE COULD ONLY HOLD ONE MAN, BUT COME TO THINK OF IT, THAT'S NOT TRUE.
HEY MAC- HOLD STEADY!
YOU HOLD IT STEADY
A FEW DAYS AFTER THIS TRIP, MY BUDDY FROM ACROSS THE STREET- MAC McGUFFIN-CAME WITH ME FOR A TRIP DOWN DUMESNIL.
IF THIS THING TUMPS OVER, WE'RE GONERS!
RIDING EVEN LOWER than USUAL
MAC HAD A NICE CAMERA – A KODAK MADE OVER IN GERMANY, WHICH WAS THE BEST IN THOSE DAYS – AT LEAST BEFORE THE WAR.
KAL-ART SPEED FLASH
MILITARY FINISH: OLIVE DRAB
HERE'S A PICTURE WE SNAPPED IN MY FRONT ROOM ONCE, A BAT FLEW IN AND GOT TRAPPED.
THE FLOOD WATERS WERE GOIN' DOWN, AND WE THOUGHT WE'D GET SOME PICTURES OF DEAD BODIES OR SOMETHIN'.
WHAT'S THAT OVER THERE TANGLED UP IN THAT TREE?!
IT'S ALL BLOODY!
AW, IT'S NUTHIN'.
JUST AN OLD CURTAIN
SO... D'YOU THINK THEY'LL JUST PASS US THROUGH TO GRADUATION?
WHAT YOU DON'T REALIZE IS THAT NOT MANY PEOPLE ACTUALLY DROWN DURING A FLOOD. IT'S USUALLY EXPOSURE OR A BAD HEART THAT GETS 'EM.

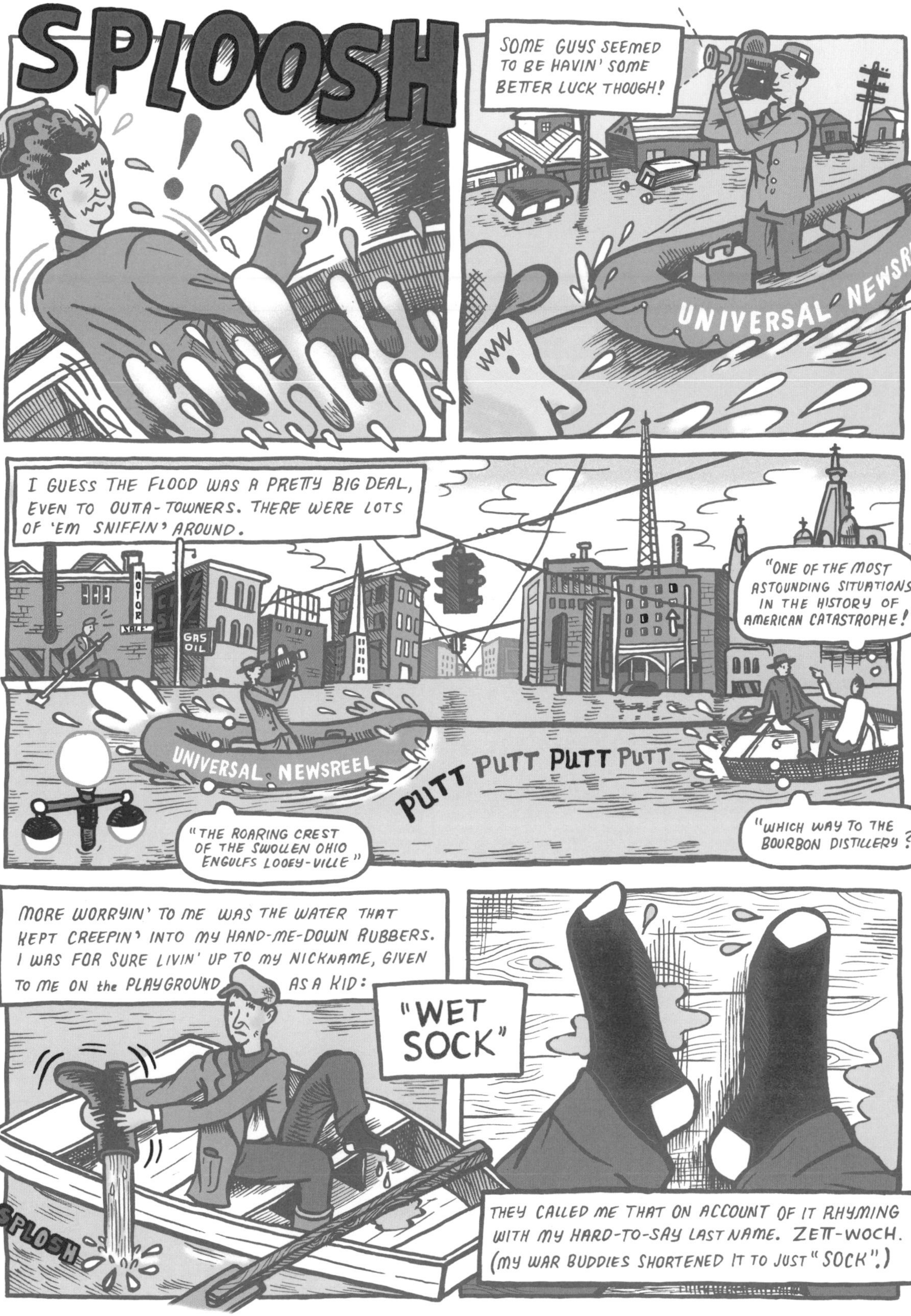
SPLOOSH
SOME GUYS SEEMED TO BE HAVIN' SOME BETTER LUCK THOUGH!
UNIVERSAL NEWSREEL
I GUESS THE FLOOD WAS A PRETTY BIG DEAL, EVEN TO OUTTA-TOWNERS. THERE WERE LOTS OF 'EM SNIFFIN' AROUND.
MOTOR
SALES
GAS
OIL
UNIVERSAL NEWSREEL
"THE ROARING CREST OF THE SWOLLEN OHIO ENGULFS LOOEY-VILLE"
PUTT PUTT PUTT PUTT PUTT
"ONE OF THE MOST ASTOUNDING SITUATIONS IN THE HISTORY OF AMERICAN CATASTROPHE!"
"WHICH WAY TO THE BOURBON DISTILLERY?"
MORE WORRYIN' TO ME WAS THE WATER THAT KEPT CREEPIN' INTO MY HAND-ME-DOWN RUBBERS. I WAS FOR SURE LIVIN' UP TO MY NICKNAME, GIVEN TO ME ON THE PLAYGROUND AS A KID:
"WET SOCK"
SPLOSH
THEY CALLED ME THAT ON ACCOUNT OF IT RHYMING WITH MY HARD-TO-SAY LAST NAME. ZETT-WOCH. (MY WAR BUDDIES SHORTENED IT TO JUST "SOCK".)

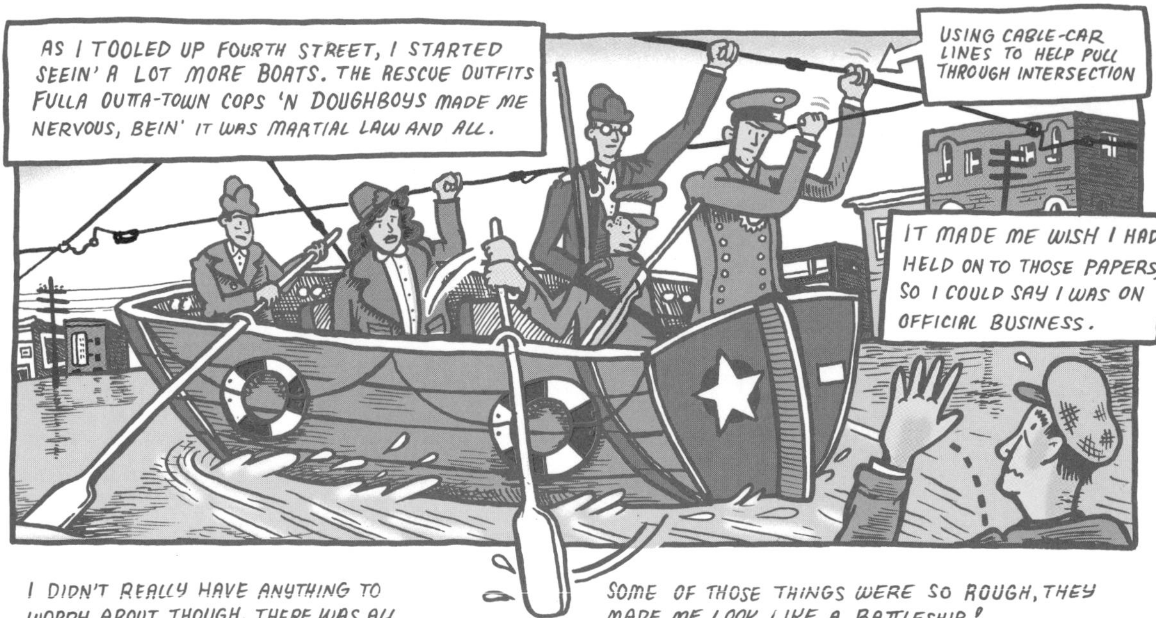
AS I TOOLED UP FOURTH STREET, I STARTED SEEIN' A LOT MORE BOATS. THE RESCUE OUTFITS FULLA OUTTA-TOWN COPS 'N DOUGHBOYS MADE ME NERVOUS, BEIN' IT WAS MARTIAL LAW AND ALL.
USING CABLE-CAR LINES TO HELP PULL THROUGH INTERSECTION
IT MADE ME WISH I HAD HELD ON TO THOSE PAPERS, SO I COULD SAY I WAS ON OFFICIAL BUSINESS.

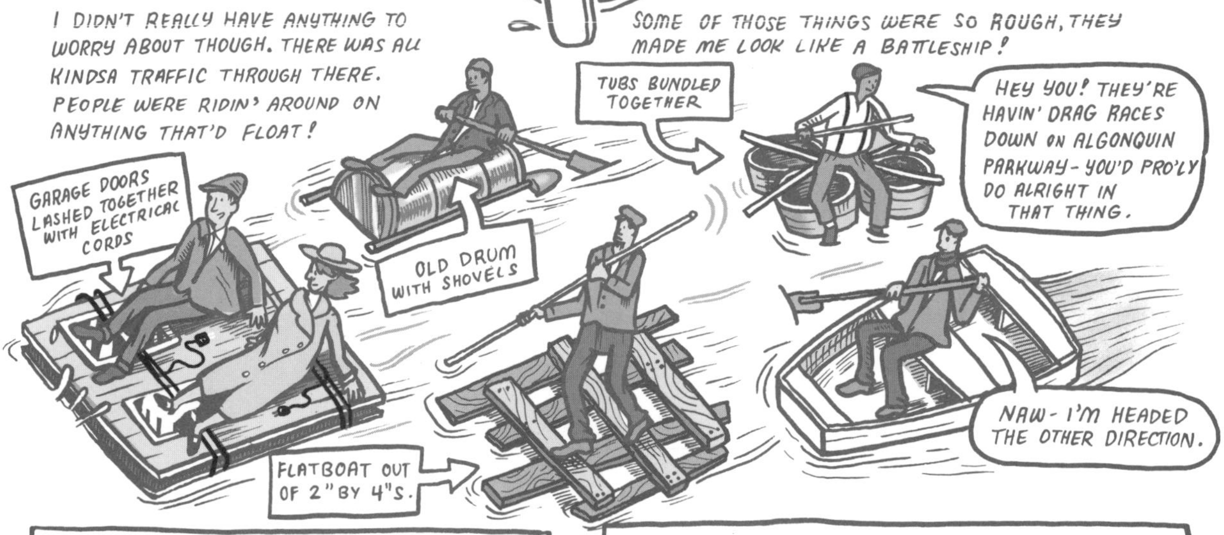
I DIDN'T REALLY HAVE ANYTHING TO WORRY ABOUT THOUGH. THERE WAS ALL KINDSA TRAFFIC THROUGH THERE. PEOPLE WERE RIDIN' AROUND ON ANYTHING THAT'D FLOAT!
GARAGE DOORS LASHED TOGETHER WITH ELECTRICAL CORDS
OLD DRUM WITH SHOVELS
FLATBOAT OUT OF 2" BY 4"S.
SOME OF THOSE THINGS WERE SO ROUGH, THEY MADE ME LOOK LIKE A BATTLESHIP!
TUBS BUNDLED TOGETHER
HEY YOU! THEY'RE HAVIN' DRAG RACES DOWN ON ALGONQUIN PARKWAY - YOU'D PRO'LY DO ALRIGHT IN THAT THING.
NAW - I'M HEADED THE OTHER DIRECTION.

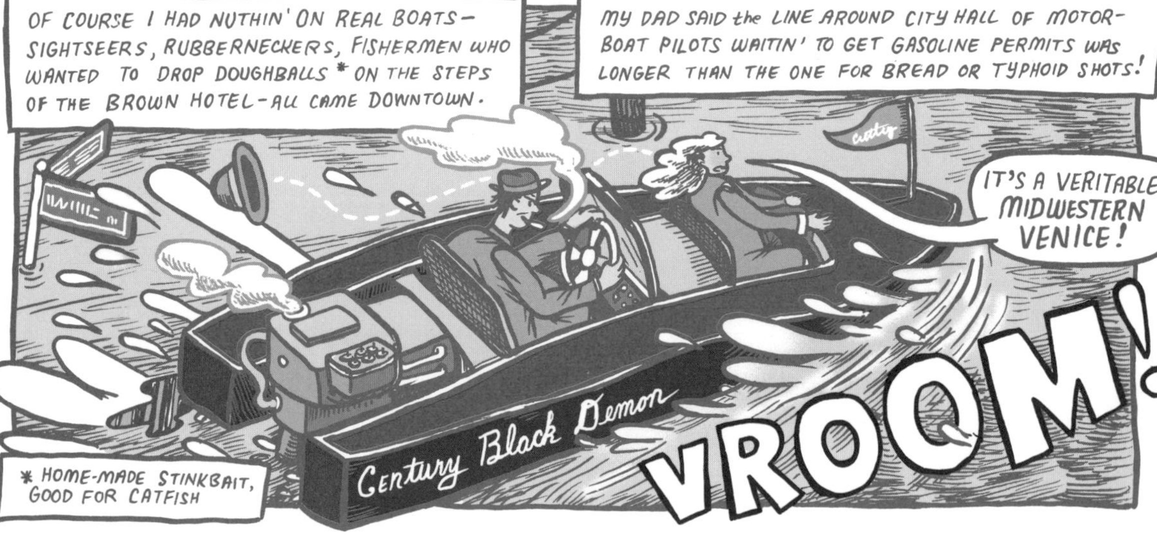
OF COURSE I HAD NUTHIN' ON REAL BOATS - SIGHTSEERS, RUBBERNECKERS, FISHERMEN WHO WANTED TO DROP DOUGHBALLS * ON THE STEPS OF THE BROWN HOTEL - ALL CAME DOWNTOWN.
MY DAD SAID the LINE AROUND CITY HALL OF MOTOR-BOAT PILOTS WAITIN' TO GET GASOLINE PERMITS WAS LONGER THAN THE ONE FOR BREAD OR TYPHOID SHOTS!
IT'S A VERITABLE MIDWESTERN VENICE!
Century Black Demon
VROOM!
* HOME-MADE STINKBAIT, GOOD FOR CATFISH

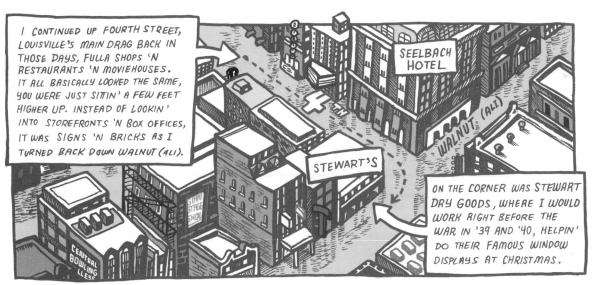

I CONTINUED UP FOURTH STREET, LOUISVILLE'S MAIN DRAG BACK IN THOSE DAYS, FULLA SHOPS 'N RESTAURANTS 'N MOVIEHOUSES. IT ALL BASICALLY LOOKED THE SAME, YOU WERE JUST SITTIN' A FEW FEET HIGHER UP. INSTEAD OF LOOKIN' INTO STOREFRONTS 'N BOX OFFICES, IT WAS. SIGNS 'N BRICKS AS I TURNED BACK DOWN WALNUT (ALI).

SEELBACH HOTEL

WALNUT (ALI)

STEWART'S

ON THE CORNER WAS STEWART DRY GOODS, WHERE I WOULD WORK RIGHT BEFORE THE WAR IN '39 AND '40, HELPIN' DO THEIR FAMOUS WINDOW DISPLAYS AT CHRISTMAS.

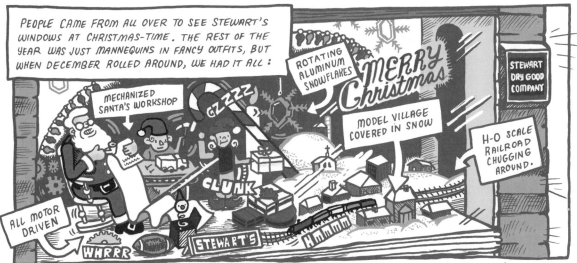

PEOPLE CAME FROM ALL OVER TO SEE STEWART'S WINDOWS AT CHRISTMAS-TIME. THE REST OF THE YEAR WAS JUST MANNEQUINS IN FANCY OUTFITS, BUT WHEN DECEMBER ROLLED AROUND, WE HAD IT ALL:

ROTATING ALUMINUM SNOWFLAKES

MERRY Christmas

STEWART DRY GOOD COMPANY

MECHANIZED SANTA'S WORKSHOP

GZZZZ

MODEL VILLAGE COVERED IN SNOW

H-O SCALE RAILROAD CHUGGING AROUND.

CLUNK

ALL MOTOR DRIVEN

WHRRR

STEWART'S

HMMMM

YEAH, THOSE WINDOWS WERE REALLY SOMETHING. WE HAD A WHOLE TEAM OF GUYS TO WORK ON 'EM... INCLUDING A GAY FELLA! I SPECIALIZED IN SIGN PAINTING (I HAD TAKEN A CLASS AT DEAR OL' HIGH).

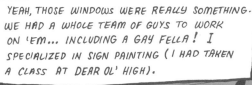

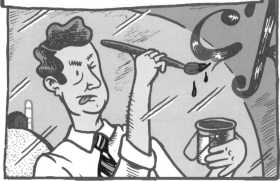

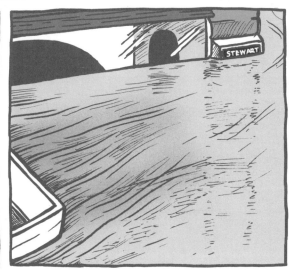

STEWART

88

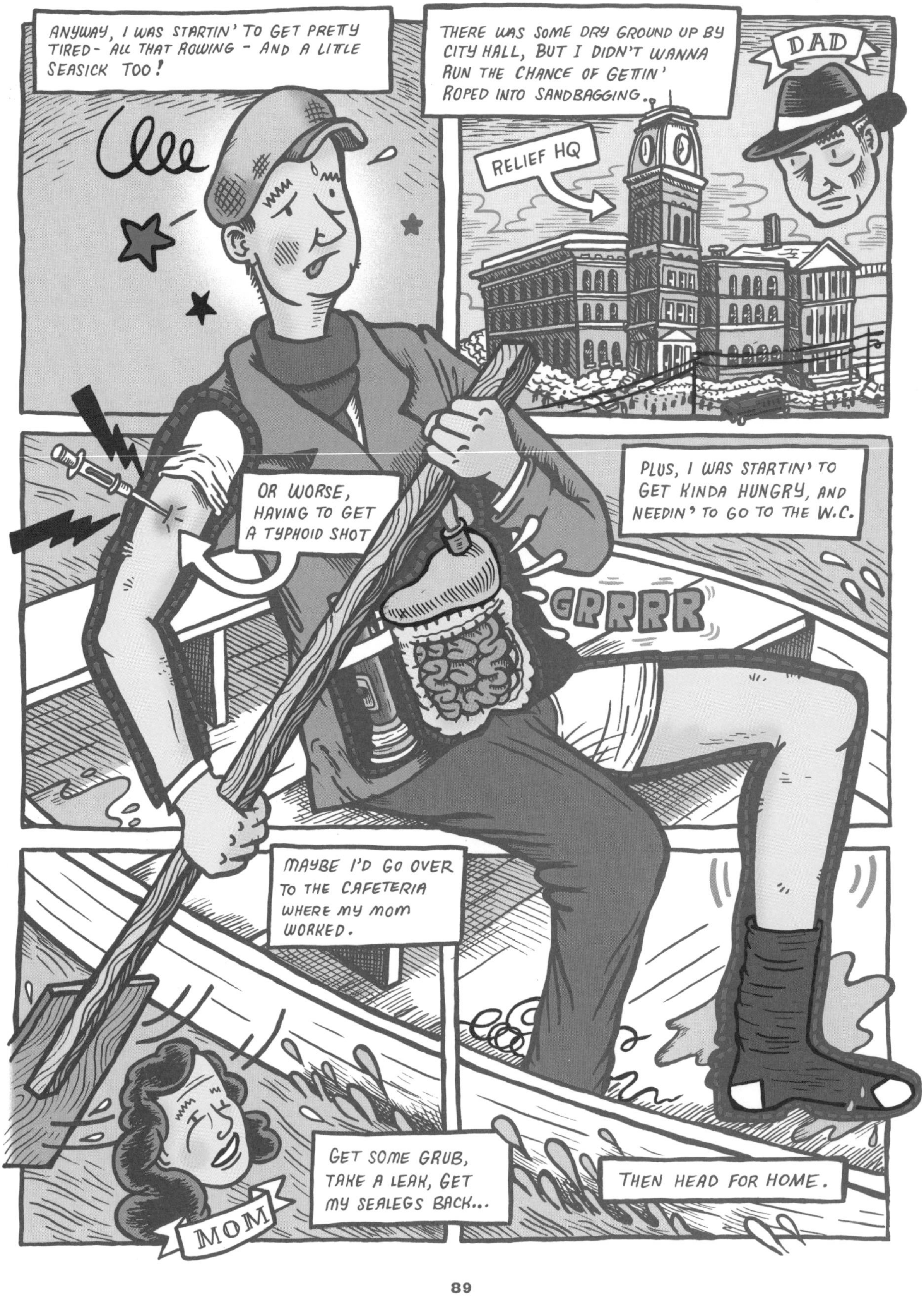
ANYWAY, I WAS STARTIN' TO GET PRETTY TIRED- ALL THAT ROWING - AND A LITTLE SEASICK TOO!
THERE WAS SOME DRY GROUND UP BY CITY HALL, BUT I DIDN'T WANNA RUN THE CHANCE OF GETTIN' ROPED INTO SANDBAGGING...
DAD
RELIEF HQ
OR WORSE, HAVING TO GET A TYPHOID SHOT
PLUS, I WAS STARTIN' TO GET KINDA HUNGRY, AND NEEDIN' TO GO TO THE W.C.
GRRRR
MAYBE I'D GO OVER TO THE CAFETERIA WHERE MY MOM WORKED.
GET SOME GRUB, TAKE A LEAK, GET MY SEALEGS BACK...
THEN HEAD FOR HOME.
MOM

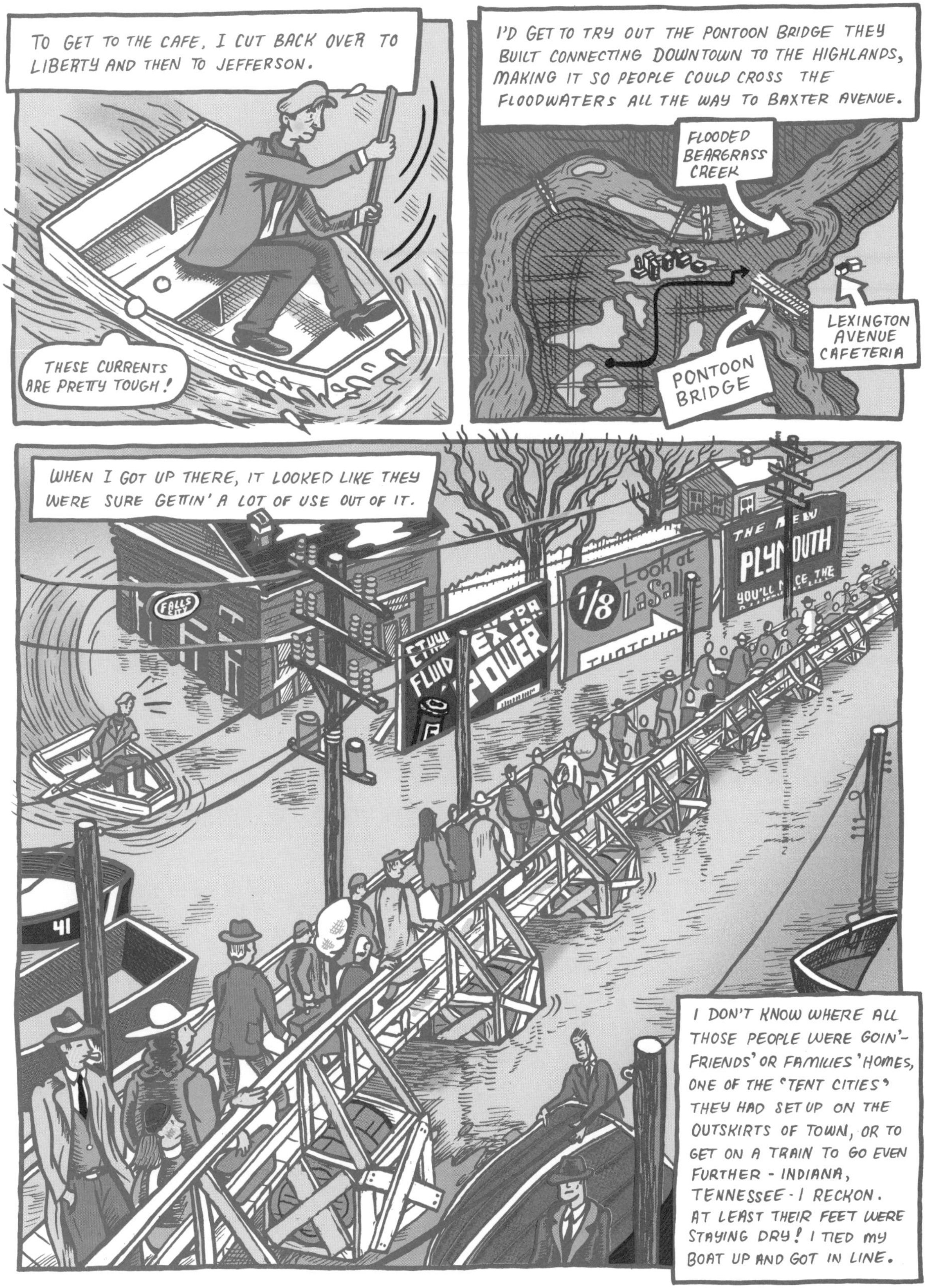
TO GET TO THE CAFE, I CUT BACK OVER TO LIBERTY AND THEN TO JEFFERSON.
THESE CURRENTS ARE PRETTY TOUGH!
I'D GET TO TRY OUT THE PONTOON BRIDGE THEY BUILT CONNECTING DOWNTOWN TO THE HIGHLANDS, MAKING IT SO PEOPLE COULD CROSS THE FLOODWATERS ALL THE WAY TO BAXTER AVENUE.
FLOODED BEARGRASS CREEK
LEXINGTON AVENUE CAFETERIA
PONTOON BRIDGE
WHEN I GOT UP THERE, IT LOOKED LIKE THEY WERE SURE GETTIN' A LOT OF USE OUT OF IT.
FALLS CITY
FLUID
EXTRA POWER
1/8
Look at LaSalle
PLYMOUTH
41
I DON'T KNOW WHERE ALL THOSE PEOPLE WERE GOIN'- FRIENDS' OR FAMILIES' HOMES, ONE OF THE "TENT CITIES" THEY HAD SET UP ON THE OUTSKIRTS OF TOWN, OR TO GET ON A TRAIN TO GO EVEN FURTHER - INDIANA, TENNESSEE - I RECKON. AT LEAST THEIR FEET WERE STAYING DRY! I TIED MY BOAT UP AND GOT IN LINE.

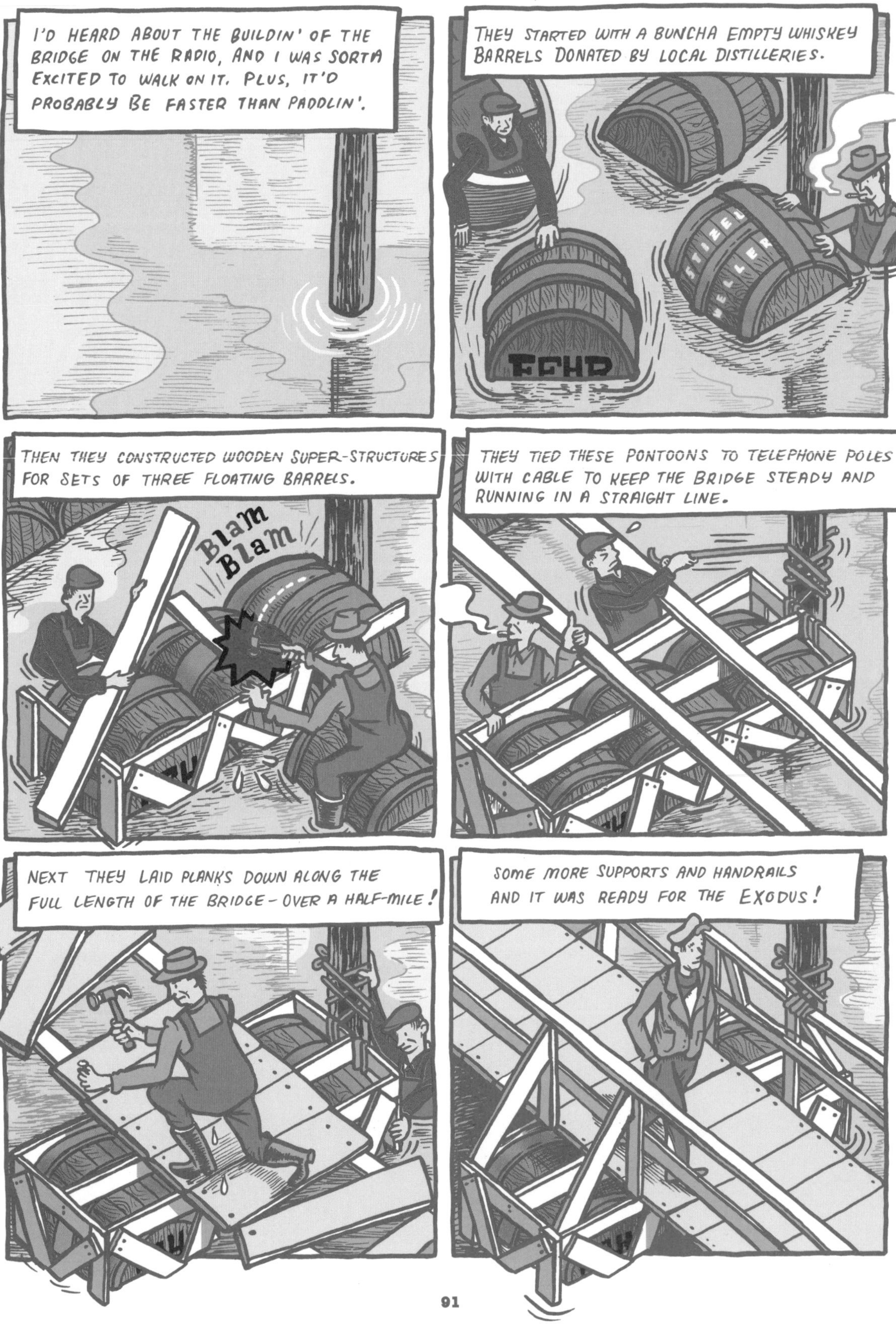
I'D HEARD ABOUT THE BUILDIN' OF THE BRIDGE ON THE RADIO, AND I WAS SORTA EXCITED TO WALK ON IT. PLUS, IT'D PROBABLY BE FASTER THAN PADDLIN'.
THEY STARTED WITH A BUNCHA EMPTY WHISKEY BARRELS DONATED BY LOCAL DISTILLERIES.
THEN THEY CONSTRUCTED WOODEN SUPER-STRUCTURES FOR SETS OF THREE FLOATING BARRELS.
Blam Blam
THEY TIED THESE PONTOONS TO TELEPHONE POLES WITH CABLE TO KEEP THE BRIDGE STEADY AND RUNNING IN A STRAIGHT LINE.
NEXT THEY LAID PLANKS DOWN ALONG THE FULL LENGTH OF THE BRIDGE - OVER A HALF-MILE!
SOME MORE SUPPORTS AND HANDRAILS AND IT WAS READY FOR THE EXODUS!

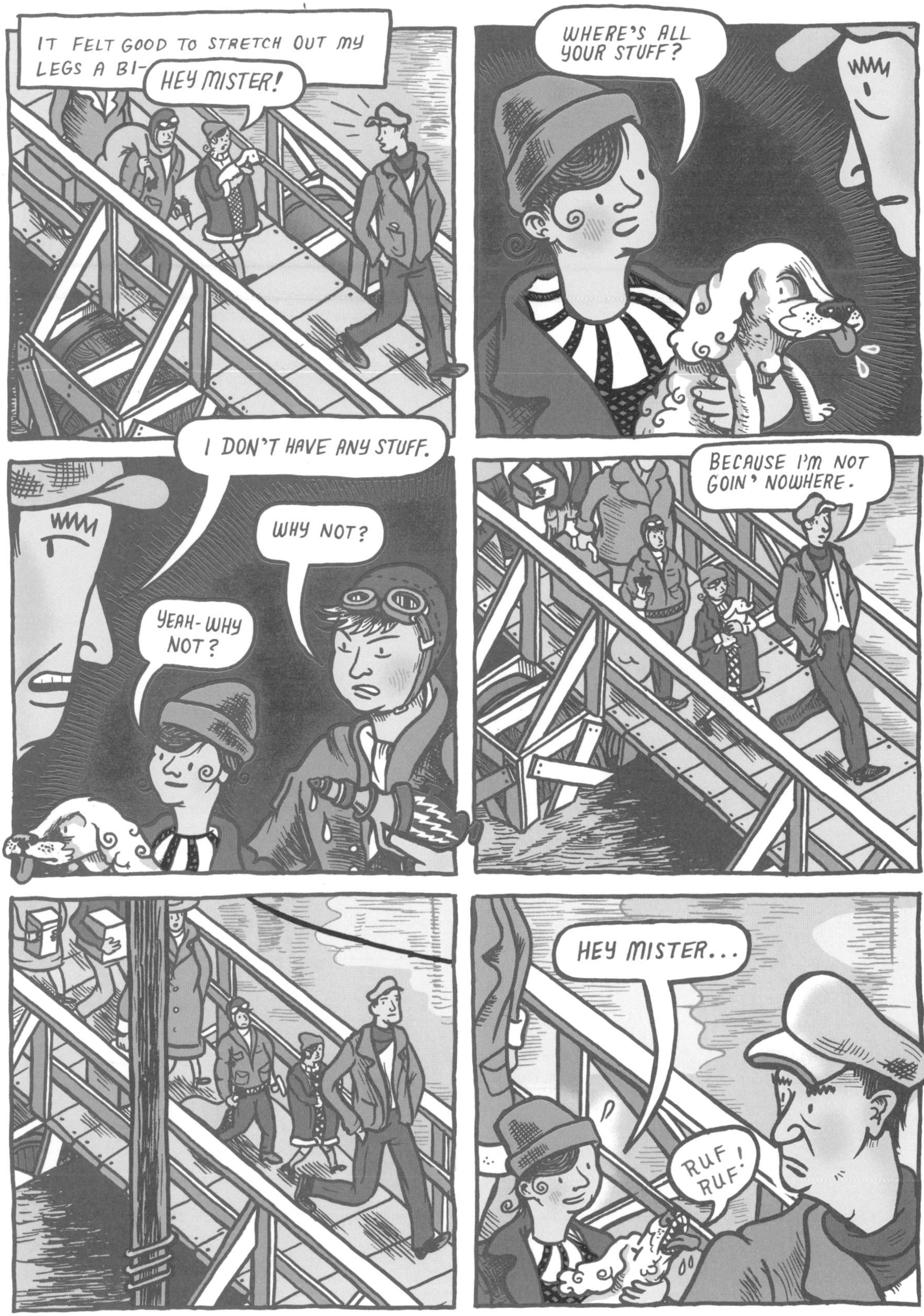
IT FELT GOOD TO STRETCH OUT MY LEGS A BI-
HEY MISTER!
WHERE'S ALL YOUR STUFF?
I DON'T HAVE ANY STUFF.
WHY NOT?
YEAH- WHY NOT?
BECAUSE I'M NOT GOIN' NOWHERE.
HEY MISTER...
RUF RUF!

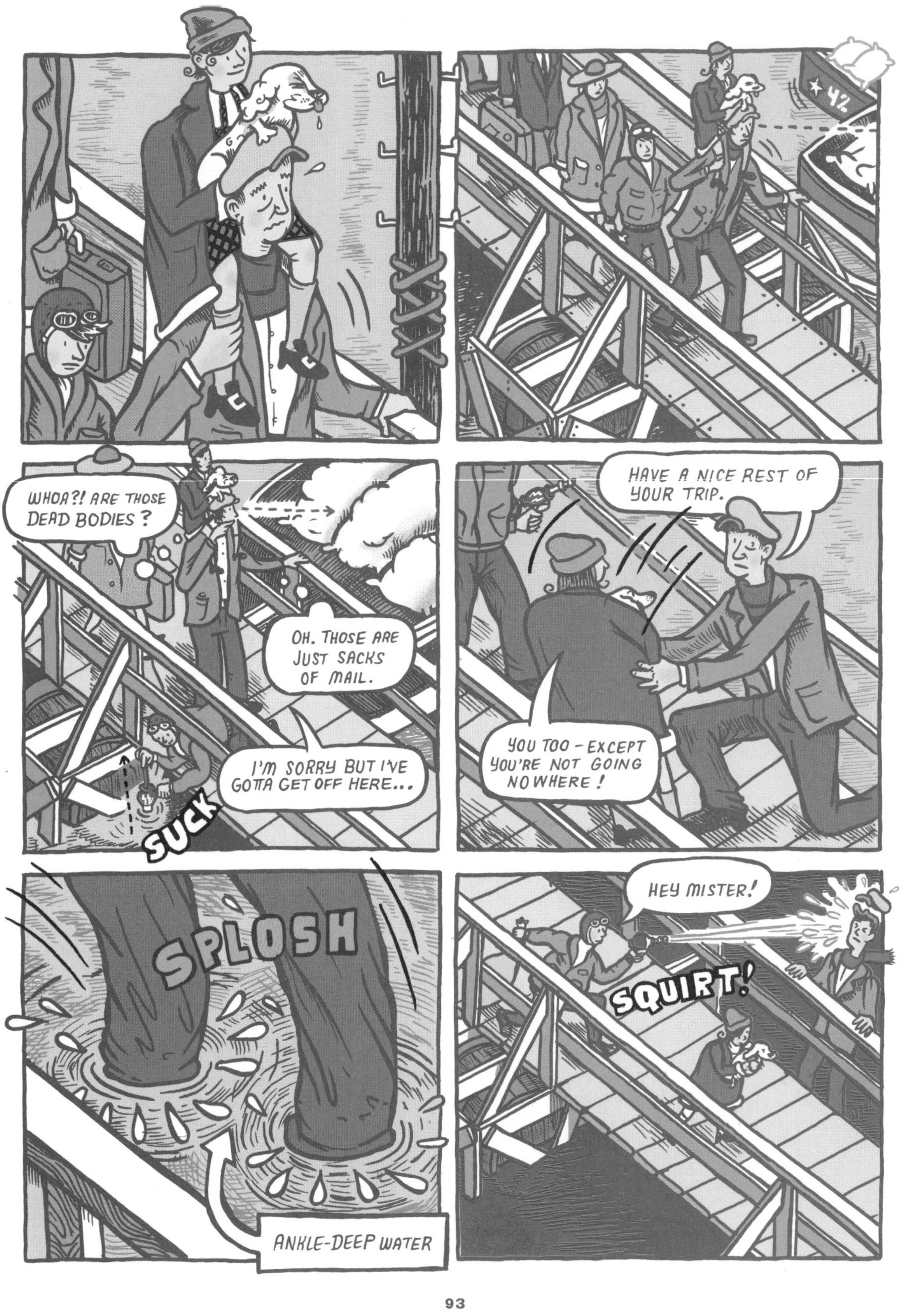
42
WHOA?! ARE THOSE DEAD BODIES?
OH. THOSE ARE JUST SACKS OF MAIL.
I'M SORRY BUT I'VE GOTTA GET OFF HERE...
SUCK
HAVE A NICE REST OF YOUR TRIP.
YOU TOO - EXCEPT YOU'RE NOT GOING NOWHERE!
SPLOSH
ANKLE-DEEP WATER
HEY MISTER!
SQUIRT!

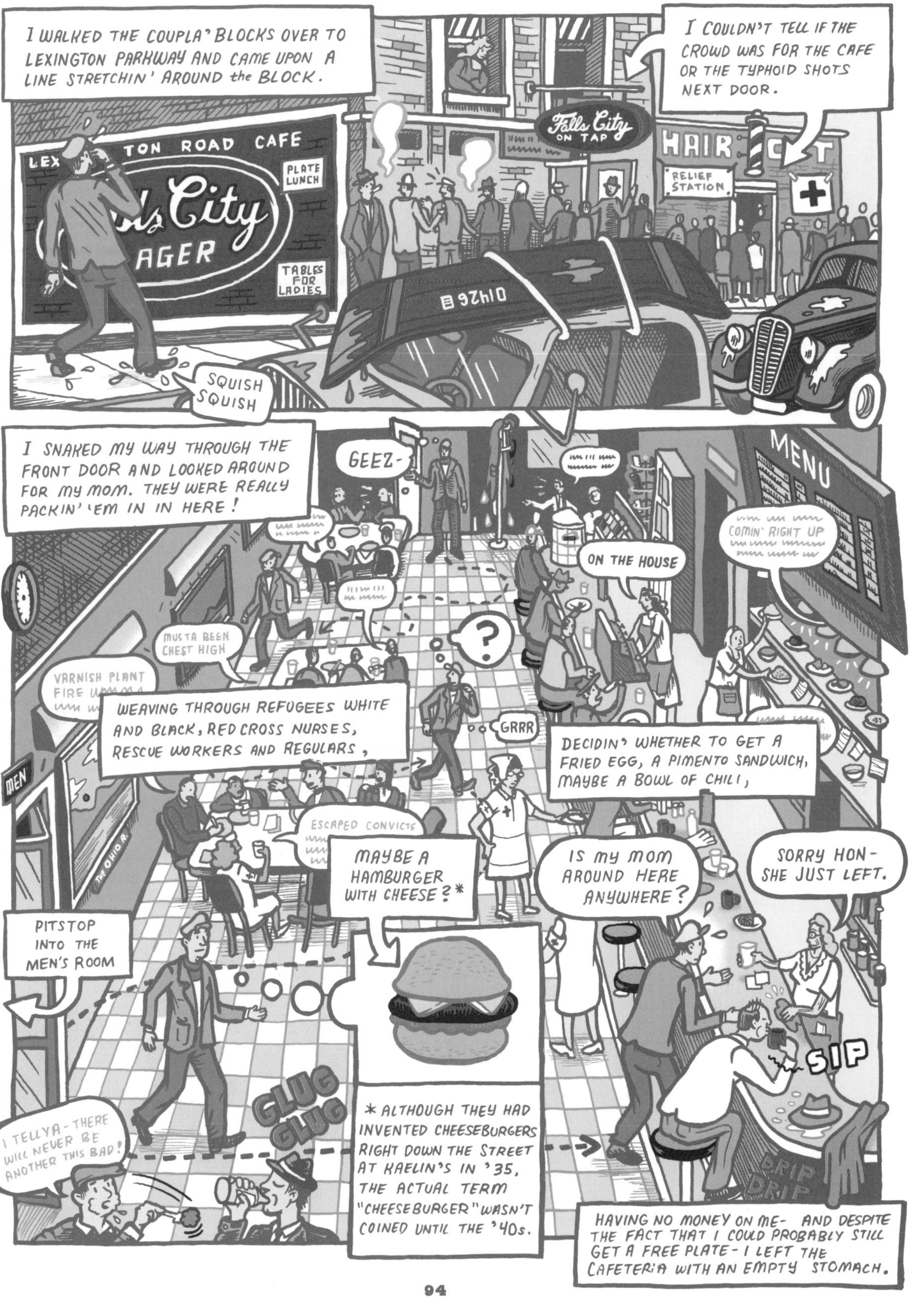
I WALKED THE COUPLA' BLOCKS OVER TO LEXINGTON PARKWAY AND CAME UPON A LINE STRETCHIN' AROUND the BLOCK.
I COULDN'T TELL IF THE CROWD WAS FOR THE CAFE OR THE TYPHOID SHOTS NEXT DOOR.
LEX TON ROAD CAFE
PLATE LUNCH
TABLES FOR LADIES
Falls City ON TAP
HAIR CUT
RELIEF STATION
SQUISH SQUISH
I SNAKED MY WAY THROUGH THE FRONT DOOR AND LOOKED AROUND FOR MY MOM. THEY WERE REALLY PACKIN' 'EM IN IN HERE!
GEEZ-
MENU
COMIN' RIGHT UP
ON THE HOUSE
MUSTA BEEN CHEST HIGH
?
VARNISH PLANT FIRE
WEAVING THROUGH REFUGEES WHITE AND BLACK, RED CROSS NURSES, RESCUE WORKERS AND REGULARS,
GRRR
DECIDIN' WHETHER TO GET A FRIED EGG, A PIMENTO SANDWICH, MAYBE A BOWL OF CHILI,
MEN
ESCAPED CONVICTS
THE OHIO R.
MAYBE A HAMBURGER WITH CHEESE?*
IS MY MOM AROUND HERE ANYWHERE?
SORRY HON- SHE JUST LEFT.
PITSTOP INTO THE MEN'S ROOM
SIP
GLUG GLUG
I TELLYA- THERE WILL NEVER BE ANOTHER THIS BAD!
*ALTHOUGH THEY HAD INVENTED CHEESEBURGERS RIGHT DOWN THE STREET AT KAELIN'S IN '35, THE ACTUAL TERM "CHEESEBURGER" WASN'T COINED UNTIL THE '40s.
DRIP DRIP
HAVING NO MONEY ON ME- AND DESPITE THE FACT THAT I COULD PROBABLY STILL GET A FREE PLATE- I LEFT THE CAFETERIA WITH AN EMPTY STOMACH.

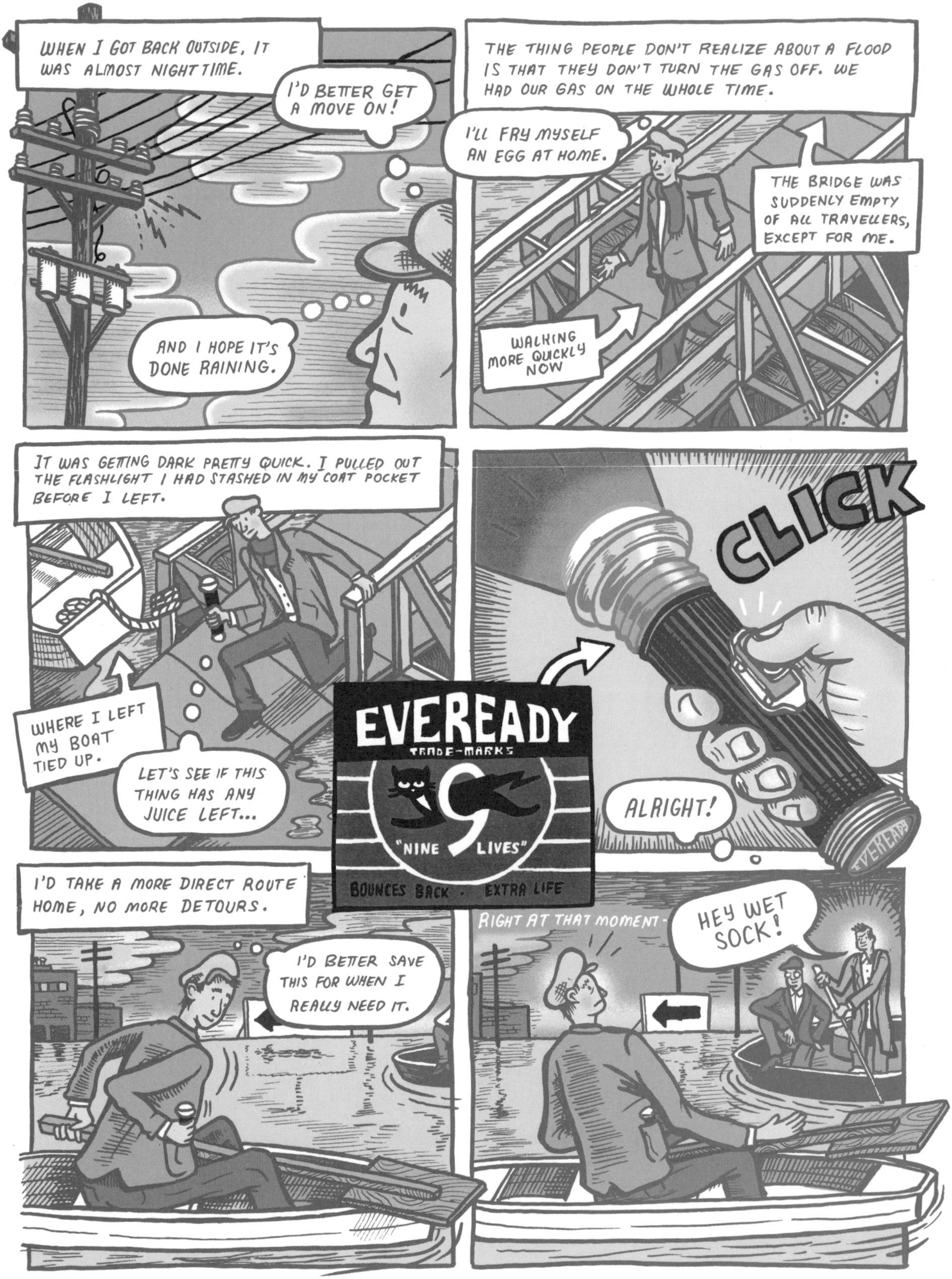

WHEN I GOT BACK OUTSIDE, IT WAS ALMOST NIGHT TIME.
I'D BETTER GET A MOVE ON!
AND I HOPE IT'S DONE RAINING.
THE THING PEOPLE DON'T REALIZE ABOUT A FLOOD IS THAT THEY DON'T TURN THE GAS OFF. WE HAD OUR GAS ON THE WHOLE TIME.
I'LL FRY MYSELF AN EGG AT HOME.
THE BRIDGE WAS SUDDENLY EMPTY OF ALL TRAVELLERS, EXCEPT FOR ME.
WALKING MORE QUICKLY NOW
IT WAS GETTING DARK PRETTY QUICK. I PULLED OUT THE FLASHLIGHT I HAD STASHED IN MY COAT POCKET BEFORE I LEFT.
WHERE I LEFT MY BOAT TIED UP.
LET'S SEE IF THIS THING HAS ANY JUICE LEFT...
CLICK
EVEREADY
TRADE-MARKS
"NINE 9 LIVES"
BOUNCES BACK · EXTRA LIFE
ALRIGHT!
EVEREADY
I'D TAKE A MORE DIRECT ROUTE HOME, NO MORE DETOURS.
I'D BETTER SAVE THIS FOR WHEN I REALLY NEED IT.
RIGHT AT THAT MOMENT-
HEY WET SOCK!

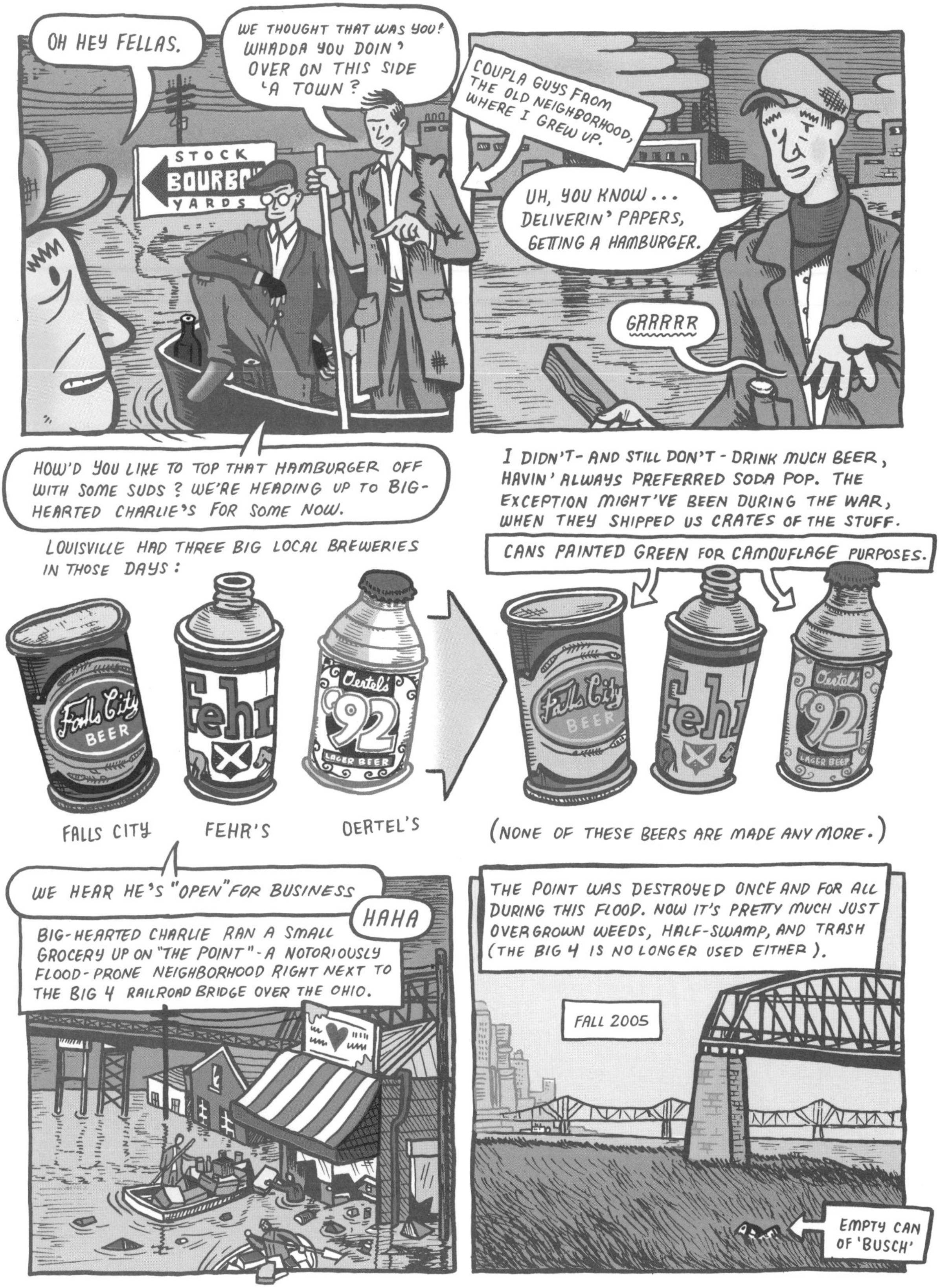

OH HEY FELLAS.
WE THOUGHT THAT WAS YOU! WHADDA YOU DOIN' OVER ON THIS SIDE 'A TOWN?
STOCK
YARDS
COUPLA GUYS FROM THE OLD NEIGHBORHOOD, WHERE I GREW UP.
UH, YOU KNOW... DELIVERIN' PAPERS, GETTING A HAMBURGER.
GRRRRR
HOW'D YOU LIKE TO TOP THAT HAMBURGER OFF WITH SOME SUDS? WE'RE HEADING UP TO BIG-HEARTED CHARLIE'S FOR SOME NOW.
I DIDN'T - AND STILL DON'T - DRINK MUCH BEER, HAVIN' ALWAYS PREFERRED SODA POP. THE EXCEPTION MIGHT'VE BEEN DURING THE WAR, WHEN THEY SHIPPED US CRATES OF THE STUFF.
LOUISVILLE HAD THREE BIG LOCAL BREWERIES IN THOSE DAYS:
Falls City BEER
Fehr
Oertel's '92 LAGER BEER
FALLS CITY
FEHR'S
OERTEL'S
CANS PAINTED GREEN FOR CAMOUFLAGE PURPOSES.
(NONE OF THESE BEERS ARE MADE ANY MORE.)
WE HEAR HE'S "OPEN" FOR BUSINESS
HAHA
BIG-HEARTED CHARLIE RAN A SMALL GROCERY UP ON "THE POINT" - A NOTORIOUSLY FLOOD-PRONE NEIGHBORHOOD RIGHT NEXT TO THE BIG 4 RAILROAD BRIDGE OVER THE OHIO.
THE POINT WAS DESTROYED ONCE AND FOR ALL DURING THIS FLOOD. NOW IT'S PRETTY MUCH JUST OVERGROWN WEEDS, HALF-SWAMP, AND TRASH (THE BIG 4 IS NO LONGER USED EITHER).
FALL 2005
EMPTY CAN OF 'BUSCH'

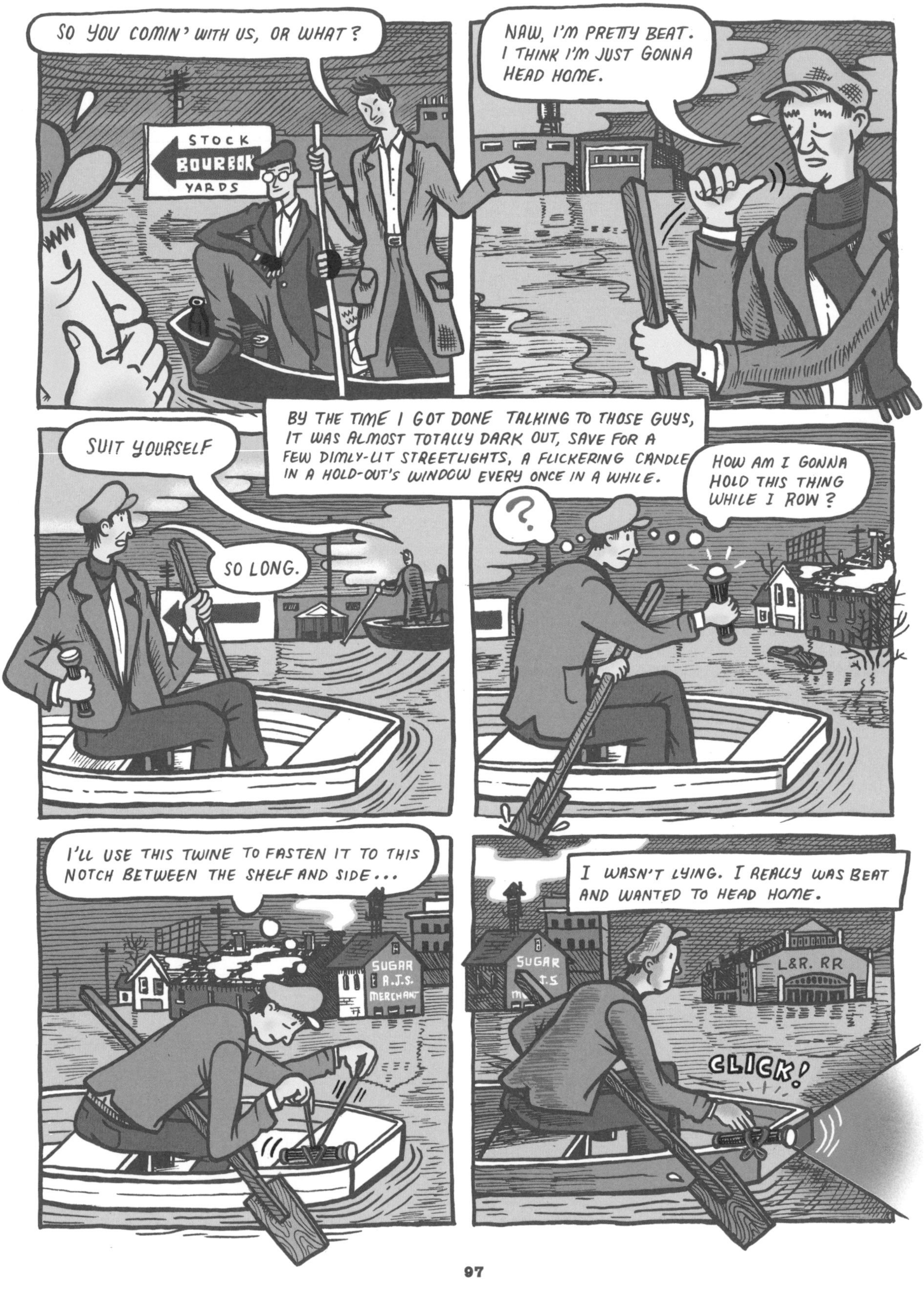
SO YOU COMIN' WITH US, OR WHAT?
STOCK
BOURBON
YARDS
NAW, I'M PRETTY BEAT. I THINK I'M JUST GONNA HEAD HOME.
SUIT YOURSELF
BY THE TIME I GOT DONE TALKING TO THOSE GUYS, IT WAS ALMOST TOTALLY DARK OUT, SAVE FOR A FEW DIMLY-LIT STREETLIGHTS, A FLICKERING CANDLE IN A HOLD-OUT'S WINDOW EVERY ONCE IN A WHILE.
SO LONG.
?
HOW AM I GONNA HOLD THIS THING WHILE I ROW?
I'LL USE THIS TWINE TO FASTEN IT TO THIS NOTCH BETWEEN THE SHELF AND SIDE...
SUGAR
A.J.S.
MERCHANT
I WASN'T LYING. I REALLY WAS BEAT AND WANTED TO HEAD HOME.
SUGAR
L&R. RR
CLICK!

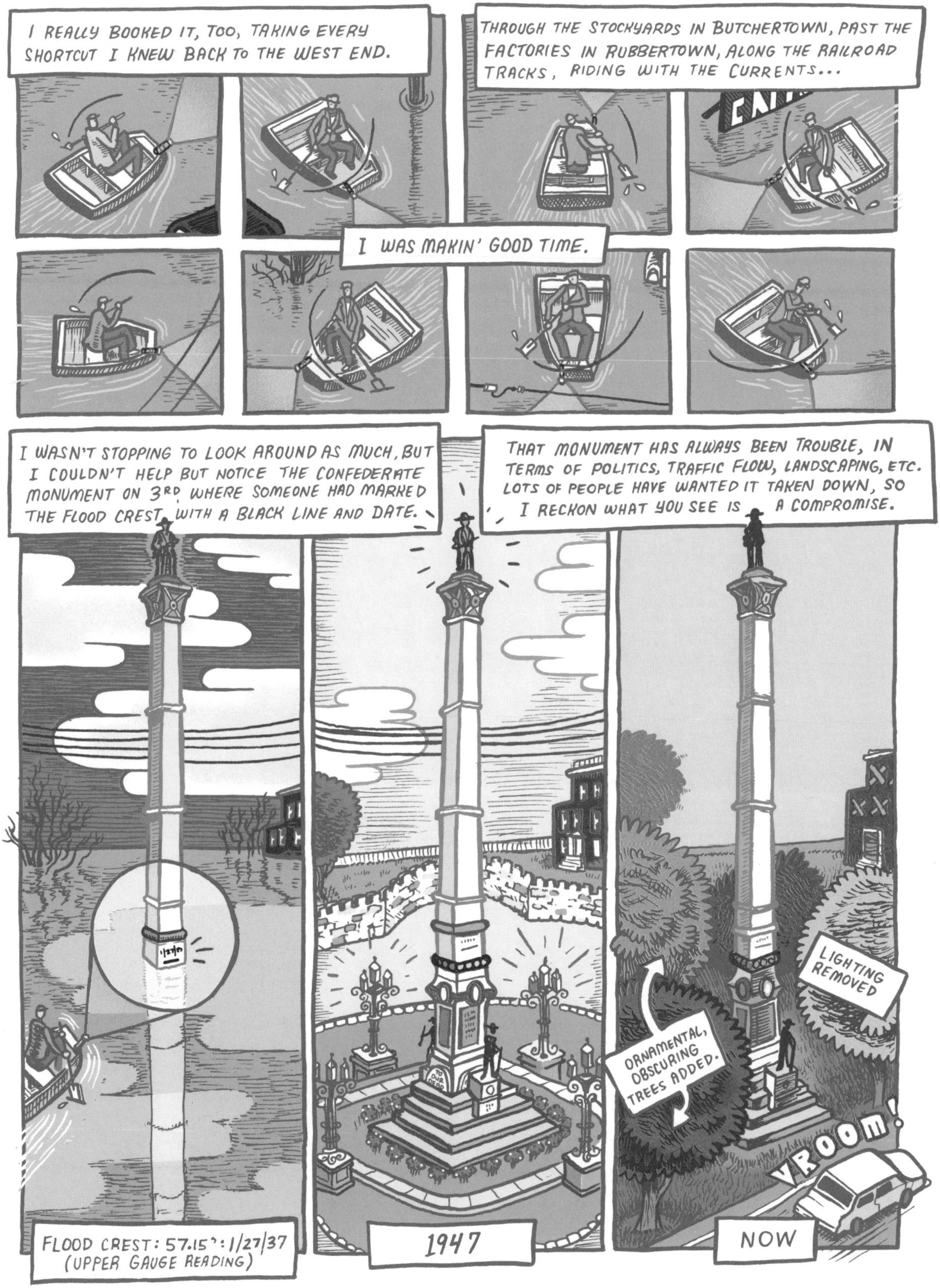
I REALLY BOOKED IT, TOO, TAKING EVERY SHORTCUT I KNEW BACK TO THE WEST END.
THROUGH THE STOCKYARDS IN BUTCHERTOWN, PAST THE FACTORIES IN RUBBERTOWN, ALONG THE RAILROAD TRACKS, RIDING WITH THE CURRENTS...
I WAS MAKIN' GOOD TIME.
I WASN'T STOPPING TO LOOK AROUND AS MUCH, BUT I COULDN'T HELP BUT NOTICE THE CONFEDERATE MONUMENT ON 3RD WHERE SOMEONE HAD MARKED THE FLOOD CREST WITH A BLACK LINE AND DATE.
THAT MONUMENT HAS ALWAYS BEEN TROUBLE, IN TERMS OF POLITICS, TRAFFIC FLOW, LANDSCAPING, ETC. LOTS OF PEOPLE HAVE WANTED IT TAKEN DOWN, SO I RECKON WHAT YOU SEE IS A COMPROMISE.
FLOOD CREST: 57.15": 1/27/37 (UPPER GAUGE READING)
1947
LIGHTING REMOVED
ORNAMENTAL, OBSCURING TREES ADDED.
VROOM!
NOW

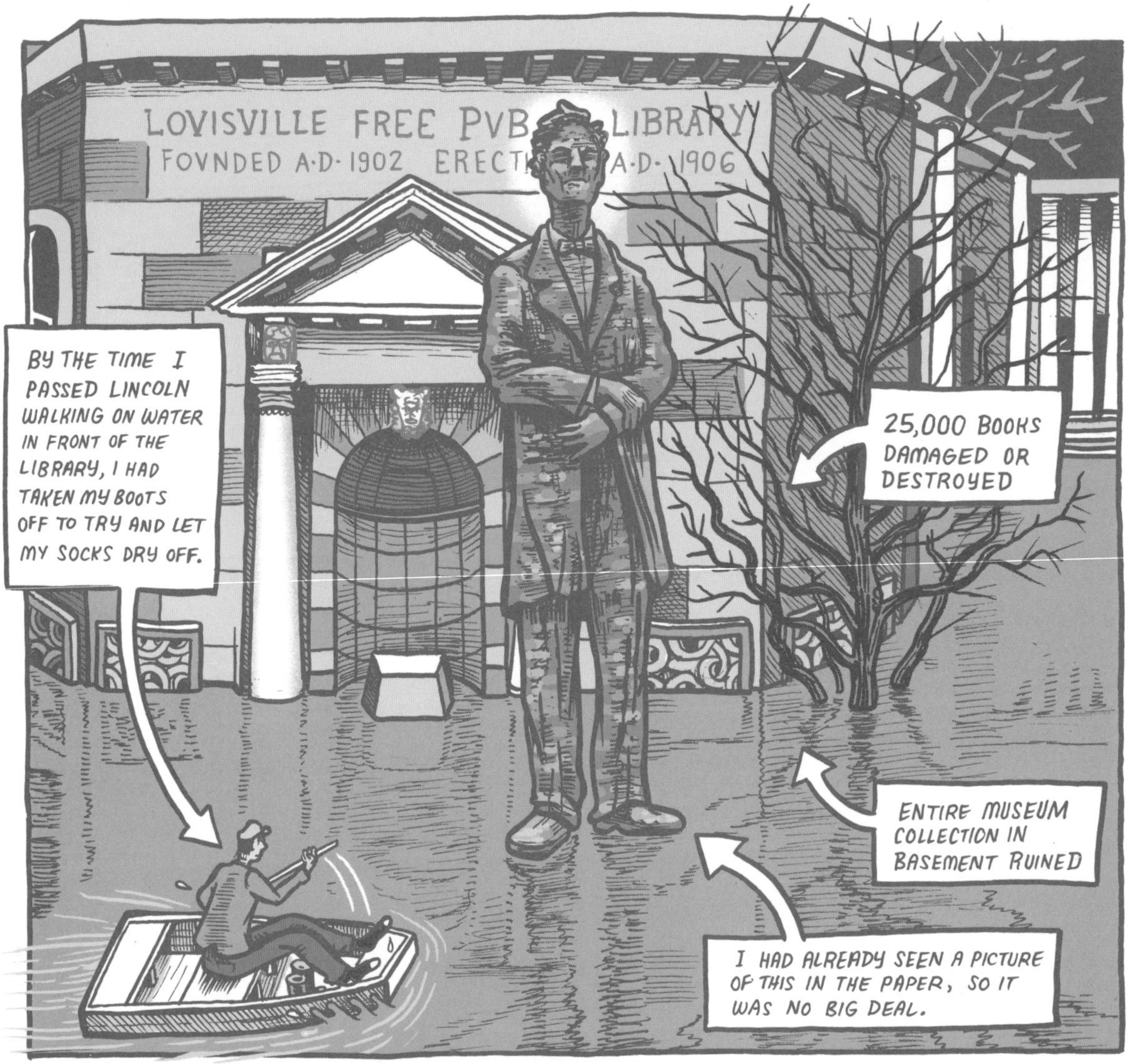
LOUISVILLE FREE PUB LIBRARY
FOUNDED A·D· 1902 ERECT A·D· 1906
BY THE TIME I PASSED LINCOLN WALKING ON WATER IN FRONT OF THE LIBRARY, I HAD TAKEN MY BOOTS OFF TO TRY AND LET MY SOCKS DRY OFF.
25,000 BOOKS DAMAGED OR DESTROYED
ENTIRE MUSEUM COLLECTION IN BASEMENT RUINED
I HAD ALREADY SEEN A PICTURE OF THIS IN THE PAPER, SO IT WAS NO BIG DEAL.
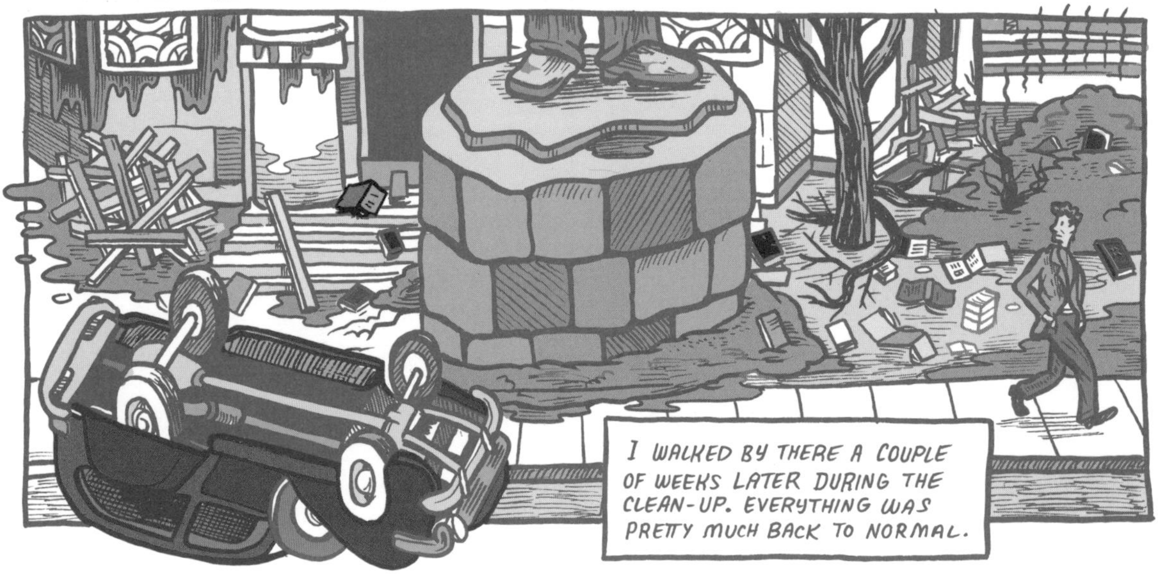
I WALKED BY THERE A COUPLE OF WEEKS LATER DURING THE CLEAN-UP. EVERYTHING WAS PRETTY MUCH BACK TO NORMAL.

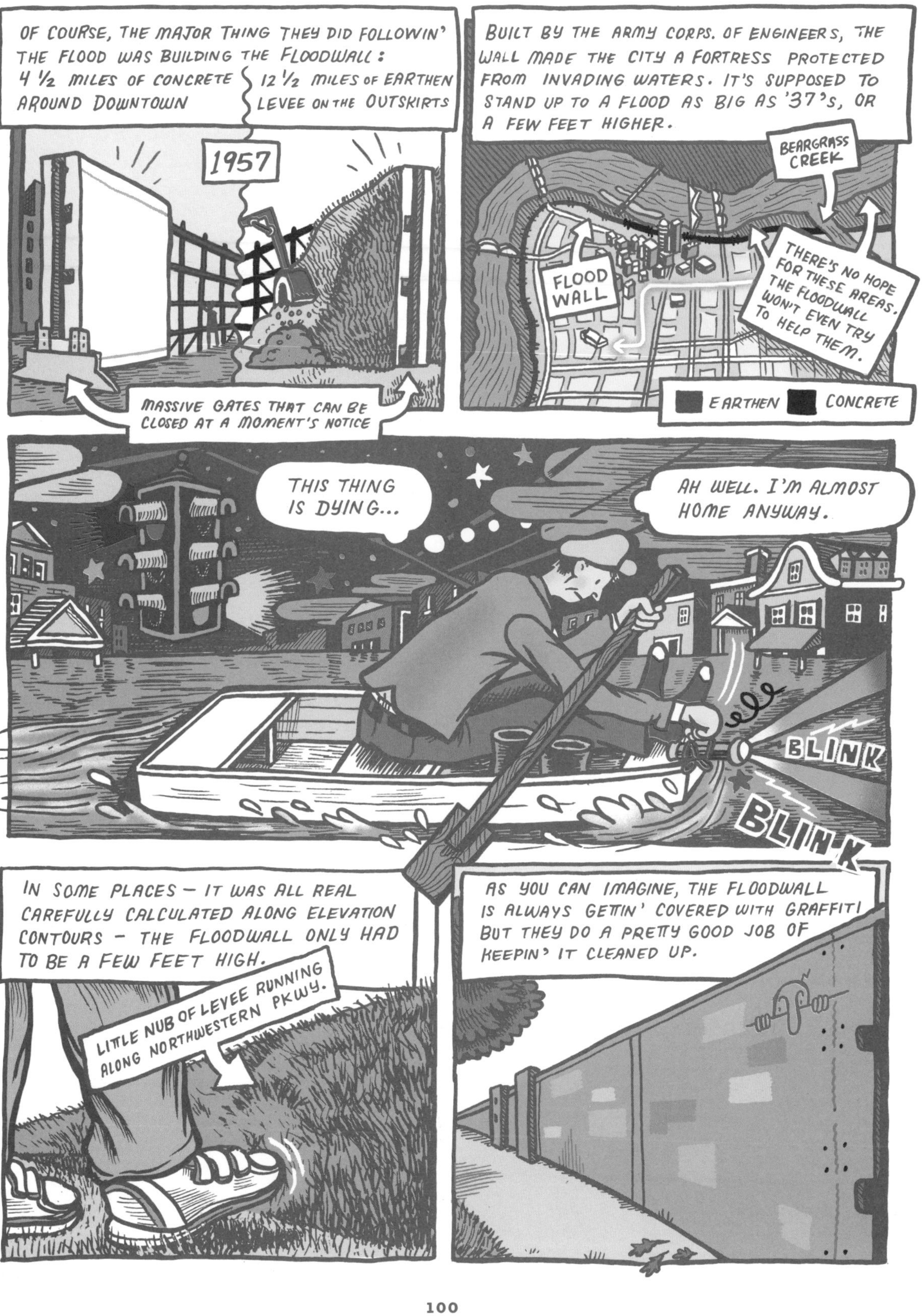
OF COURSE, THE MAJOR THING THEY DID FOLLOWIN' THE FLOOD WAS BUILDING THE FLOODWALL:
4 1/2 MILES OF CONCRETE AROUND DOWNTOWN
12 1/2 MILES OF EARTHEN LEVEE ON THE OUTSKIRTS
1957
MASSIVE GATES THAT CAN BE CLOSED AT A MOMENT'S NOTICE
BUILT BY THE ARMY CORPS. OF ENGINEERS, THE WALL MADE THE CITY A FORTRESS PROTECTED FROM INVADING WATERS. IT'S SUPPOSED TO STAND UP TO A FLOOD AS BIG AS '37'S, OR A FEW FEET HIGHER.
BEARGRASS CREEK
FLOOD WALL
THERE'S NO HOPE FOR THESE AREAS. THE FLOODWALL WON'T EVEN TRY TO HELP THEM.
EARTHEN
CONCRETE
THIS THING IS DYING...
AH WELL. I'M ALMOST HOME ANYWAY.
BLINK
BLINK
IN SOME PLACES — IT WAS ALL REAL CAREFULLY CALCULATED ALONG ELEVATION CONTOURS — THE FLOODWALL ONLY HAD TO BE A FEW FEET HIGH.
LITTLE NUB OF LEVEE RUNNING ALONG NORTHWESTERN PKWY.
AS YOU CAN IMAGINE, THE FLOODWALL IS ALWAYS GETTIN' COVERED WITH GRAFFITI BUT THEY DO A PRETTY GOOD JOB OF KEEPIN' IT CLEANED UP.

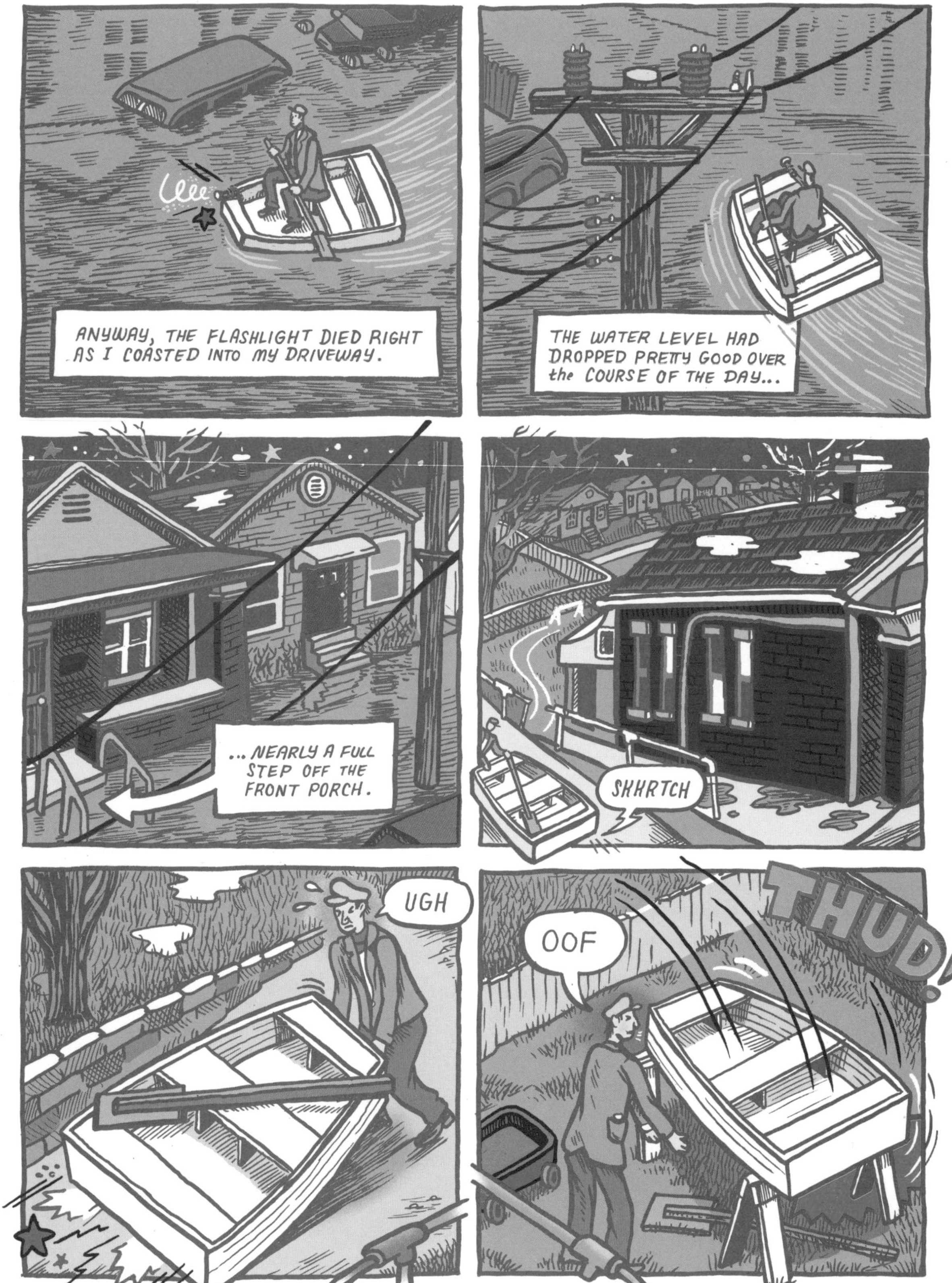
ANYWAY, THE FLASHLIGHT DIED RIGHT AS I COASTED INTO MY DRIVEWAY.
THE WATER LEVEL HAD DROPPED PRETTY GOOD OVER the COURSE OF THE DAY...
...NEARLY A FULL STEP OFF THE FRONT PORCH.
SHHRTCH
UGH
OOF
THUD!

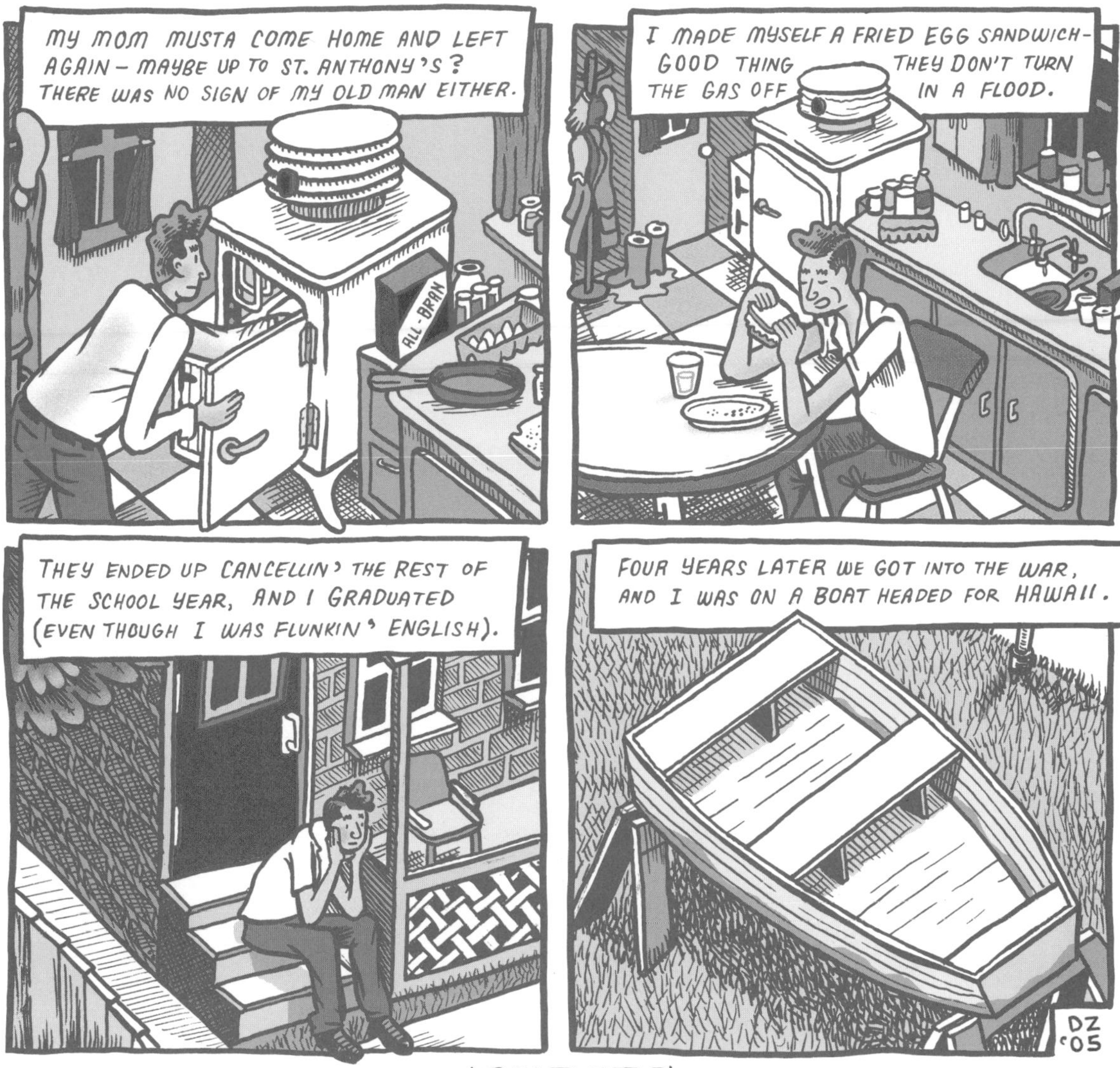
MY MOM MUSTA COME HOME AND LEFT AGAIN – MAYBE UP TO ST. ANTHONY'S? THERE WAS NO SIGN OF MY OLD MAN EITHER.
ALL-BRAN
I MADE MYSELF A FRIED EGG SANDWICH – GOOD THING THEY DON'T TURN THE GAS OFF IN A FLOOD.
THEY ENDED UP CANCELLIN' THE REST OF THE SCHOOL YEAR, AND I GRADUATED (EVEN THOUGH I WAS FLUNKIN' ENGLISH).
FOUR YEARS LATER WE GOT INTO THE WAR, AND I WAS ON A BOAT HEADED FOR HAWAII.
DZ '05

SOURCES

- 1937 THE FLOOD: THE WORST NATURAL DISASTER IN AMERICAN HISTORY. WRITTEN, DIR, & PROD, TIM YOUNG. VIDEOCASSETTE, TIM YOUNG PRODUCTIONS, INC., 1993.
- AMERICAN NATIONAL RED CROSS. THE OHIO-MISSISSIPPI VALLEY FLOOD DISASTER OF 1937 REPORT OF RELIEF OPERATIONS, WASHINGTON D.C.: AMERICAN RED CROSS, 1938.
- "FLOOD NUMBER," KENTUCKY MEDICAL JOURNAL - PART II, WOMEN'S AUXILIARY SECTION, APRIL 1937: 41+.
- KLEBER, JOHN E., ed. THE ENCYCLOPEDIA OF LOUISVILLE. LEXINGTON: UNIVERSITY PRESS OF KENTUCKY, 2001.
- LESY, MICHAEL. REAL LIFE: LOUISVILLE IN THE TWENTIES. NEW YORK: PANTHEON, 1976.
- OERTEL BREWING CO., PICTURE STORY OF THE 1937 FLOOD. LOUISVILLE: OERTEL BREWING CO INC., 1940.
- PUCKETT, RON, ed., MARY-HELEN BUTLER CLARK, ed., AND ELAINE RHODE, ed. MEMORIES OF LOUISVILLE'S 1937 FLOOD LOUISVILLE: PCR PUBLICATIONS, DATE UNKNOWN.
- SOUVENIR: LOUISVILLE'S GREATEST FLOOD! JEFFERSONVILLE & NEW ALBANY. CINCINNATI: JOHNSON & HARDIN CO.
- THOMAS, LOWELL. HUNGRY WATERS, THE STORY OF THE GREAT FLOOD TOGETHER WITH AN ACCOUNT OF FAMOUS FLOODS OF HISTORY AND PLANS FOR FLOOD CONTROL AND PREVENTION. CHICAGO: JOHN C. WINSTON, 1937.
- THOMAS, SAMUEL W, ed. VIEWS OF LOUISVILLE SINCE 1766, 4TH ed. LOUISVILLE: C THOMAS HARDIN, 1993.
- ZETTWOCH, DALTON. ASSORTED SKETCHES, DIAGRAMS, & BAT PHOTOGRAPH. UNPUBLISHED, 1938-2005.
- ZETTWOCH, DALTON. PERSONAL INTERVIEWS. SUMMER 2005.
- ZETTWOCH, DOUGLAS. PERSONAL INTERVIEW & GUIDED TOUR OF LOUISVILLE'S FLOODWALL AND PUMPING STATIONS, AUGUST 2005.
- ZETTWOCH, DONALD. ASSORTED PHOTOGRAPHS OF LOUISVILLE'S WEST END AND THE OLD HOUSE. UNPUBLISHED, 2005.

WON'T BE LICKED!

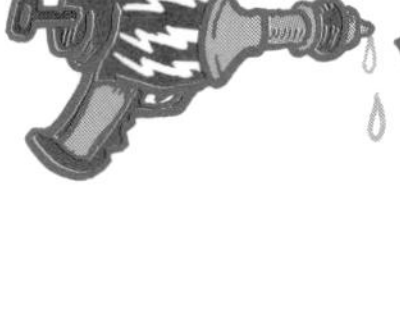

BUCK ROGERS LIQUID HELIUM TOY SQUIRT GUN, 1935